Education in a Federal UK

Britain's two recent referenda – on Brexit (2016) and on Scottish independence (2014) – have raised in the public mind fundamental questions about the future of the UK. It seems that for the first time, the public, the media and the political elite have woken up to the fact that in different parts of the UK, there are different histories, different aspirations and different imagined futures in relation to a whole range of vitally important political issues. But what the public debate often fails to recognise is that in many areas of public life – perhaps especially education – the UK is already a federal state and in key respects has been so for many years.

The aim of this volume is therefore to take stock: to try and capture what the current state of educational policy and practice is across the whole of the UK. This has been achieved by commissioning two different papers from each of the four countries – Wales, Scotland, Northern Ireland and England. The first is an overview, exploring the distinctive history, principles and current policies of each country. The second paper has been specifically chosen as a case study of a key policy that highlights the distinctiveness of each country – the Foundation Phase for Wales, assessment policy in Scotland, 'shared education' initiatives in Northern Ireland and higher education policy in England. Taken together these eight papers give an important insight into the complexities of educational policy and practice across the whole of the UK today.

This book was originally published as a special issue of the *Oxford Review of Education*.

John Furlong is Emeritus Professor of Education at the University of Oxford and an Emeritus Fellow of Green Templeton College, Oxford, UK. His research interests centre on both teacher education and educational research policy and the links between them. In 2015, his book *Education: an anatomy of the discipline* (Routledge) was awarded first prize by the British Society for Educational Studies for the best educational research book of the year.

Ingrid Lunt is Emeritus Professor of Education at the University of Oxford and an Emeritus Fellow of Green Templeton College, Oxford, UK. A psychologist by background she has served as President of the British Psychological Society and of the European Federation of Psychologists Associations. Her research interests include higher education, in particular doctoral education, and professional qualification systems internationally.

Education in a Federal UK

Edited by
John Furlong and Ingrid Lunt

Routledge
Taylor & Francis Group

LONDON AND NEW YORK

First published 2018 by Routledge

2 Park Square, Milton Park, Abingdon, Oxfordshire OX14 4RN
52 Vanderbilt Avenue, New York, NY 10017

Routledge is an imprint of the Taylor & Francis Group, an informa business

First issued in paperback 2020

Introduction, Chapters 1–5 & 7–8© 2018 Taylor & Francis
Chapter 6 © 2018 Nicholas Hillman. Originally published as Open Access.

British Library Cataloguing in Publication Data
A catalogue record for this book is available from the British Library

ISBN 13: 978-0-8153-7314-8 (hbk)
ISBN 13: 978-0-367-59278-3 (pbk)

Typeset in Myriad Pro
by RefineCatch Limited, Bungay, Suffolk

Publisher's Note
The publisher accepts responsibility for any inconsistencies that may have
arisen during the conversion of this book from journal articles to book chapters,
namely the possible inclusion of journal terminology.

Disclaimer
Every effort has been made to contact copyright holders for their permission to
reprint material in this book. The publishers would be grateful to hear from any
copyright holder who is not here acknowledged and will undertake to rectify
any errors or omissions in future editions of this book.

Contents

Citation Information

The chapters in this book were originally published in the *Oxford Review of Education*, volume 42, issue 3 (June 2016). When citing this material, please use the original page numbering for each article, as follows:

Editorial
Education in a Federal UK
John Furlong and Ingrid Lunt
Oxford Review of Education, volume 42, issue 3 (June 2016), pp. 249–252

Chapter 1
Education and nationalism in Scotland: governing a 'learning nation'
Margaret Arnott and Jenny Ozga
Oxford Review of Education, volume 42, issue 3 (June 2016), pp. 253–265

Chapter 2
The meaning of curriculum-related examination standards in Scotland and England: a home–international comparison
Jo-Anne Baird and Lena Gray
Oxford Review of Education, volume 42, issue 3 (June 2016), pp. 266–284

Chapter 3
The politics of education and the misrecognition of Wales
Sally Power
Oxford Review of Education, volume 42, issue 3 (June 2016), pp. 285–298

Chapter 4
Implementing curriculum reform in Wales: the case of the Foundation Phase
Chris Taylor, Mirain Rhys and Sam Waldron
Oxford Review of Education, volume 42, issue 3 (June 2016), pp. 299–315

Chapter 5
Education in England – a testbed for network governance?
Geoff Whitty and Emma Wisby
Oxford Review of Education, volume 42, issue 3 (June 2016), pp. 316–329

Chapter 6

The Coalition's higher education reforms in England
Nicholas Hillman
Oxford Review of Education, volume 42, issue 3 (June 2016), pp. 330–345

Chapter 7

Education in Northern Ireland since the Good Friday Agreement: Kabuki theatre meets danse macabre
John Gardner
Oxford Review of Education, volume 42, issue 3 (June 2016), pp. 346–361

Chapter 8

Shared education in Northern Ireland: school collaboration in divided societies
Tony Gallagher
Oxford Review of Education, volume 42, issue 3 (June 2016), pp. 362 375

For any permission-related enquiries please visit:
http://www.tandfonline.com/page/help/permissions

Notes on Contributors

Margaret Arnott is Professor of Public Policy at the University of the West of Scotland, UK.

Jo-Anne Baird is the Pearson Professor of Educational Assessment and Director of the Oxford University Centre for Educational Assessment, UK.

John Furlong is Emeritus Professor of Education at the University of Oxford and an Emeritus Fellow of Green Templeton College, Oxford, UK.

Tony Gallagher is Professor of Education at Queen's University, Northern Ireland.

John Gardner is Senior Deputy Principal/Vice-Chancellor and Professor of Education at the University of Stirling, UK.

Lena Gray is Head of Research in the Centre for Educational Research and Practice at the Assessment and Qualifications Alliance, UK.

Nicholas Hillman has been the Director of HEPI (Higher Education Policy Institute, UK) since January 2014.

Ingrid Lunt is Emeritus Professor of Education at the University of Oxford and an Emeritus Fellow of Green Templeton College, Oxford, UK.

Jenny Ozga is Professor Emeritus in the Department of Education at the University of Oxford, UK, and Honorary Professorial Fellow, School of Social and Political Science at the University of Edinburgh, UK.

Sally Power is a Professor in the School of Social Sciences, Cardiff University, UK. She is also the Co-Director of the Wales Institute of Social and Economic Research, Data and Methods (WISERD).

Mirain Rhys is a Research Associate in the Wales Institute of Social and Economic Research, Data and Methods (WISERD).

Chris Taylor is Professor of Education in Cardiff University. UK. He is also the Cardiff Co-Director of the Wales Institute of Social and Economic Research, Data and Methods (WISERD).

Sam Waldron was a Research Associate in the Wales Institute of Social and Economic Research, Data and Methods (WISERD), having previously worked in the ONS and at the University of Exeter, UK. He is currently working towards qualifying as a Child Psychologist.

Geoff Whitty holds a part-time Research Professorship in Education at Bath Spa University, UK and a Global Innovation Chair in Equity in Higher Education at the University of Newcastle, Australia.

Emma Wisby is Head of Policy and Public Affairs at the UCL Institute of Education, UK.

Education in a Federal UK

The Scottish independence referendum in September 2014 was of fundamental significance in the UK. It raised in the public mind questions not only about the future of Scotland but about the future of the UK as well. Could Scotland survive alone? Could the UK survive without Scotland? Could it survive *with* Scotland but in a much looser federation, a genuine 'federal state' with significantly greater autonomy for all of the 'home nations' (Scotland, Northern Ireland, Wales and England)? Looking back on the fevered debates of the summer of 2014, it seems that for the first time, the public, the media and the political elite were waking up to the fact that in different parts of the UK, there are different histories, different aspirations and different imagined futures in relation to a whole range of vitally important political issues. It was particularly a shock for comfortable middle England.

But what the public debate at that time failed to recognise was that in many areas of public life—including education—the UK was already a federal state and in key respects had been for many years. While the formal devolution that was established from 1999 onwards pushed national differences further, educational policy has a long history of being different in different parts of the UK. In Scotland for example, as Arnott and Ozga argue in their paper in this special issue, the absence of a Scottish state has meant that key Scottish institutions (the law, the church and education) have long been a central element in the assertion of continued distinctiveness from England. In comparison with England, there has been a relative uniformity of school provision (through a comprehensive school system), greater social mobility regardless of social class, a broad curriculum uniting sciences, arts and humanities and public support for teachers and for education more generally.

In Northern Ireland, as Gallagher documents in his paper, since its inception in the early 19th century, public schooling has been fundamentally shaped by the denominational concerns of the Catholic and Protestant communities. As Gallagher argues, at two key moments in the history of schools on the island—the 1830s when a national school system was established for the first time, and in 1923 when the first Northern Irish government came to power—at these two key points there was an official preference that all schools should be open to children from all denominations. At both moments, however, those official aspirations were thwarted by the combined efforts of the Churches, all of which preferred to run their own schools, for their own communities. They still do.

And even in Wales (despite the universal aphorism of 'For Wales see England') the Welsh linguistic, political and cultural context has always given Welsh education a distinctive complexion. Since devolution, that distinctiveness has become ever more apparent, as Power outlines in her paper. Those differences centre on a number of key issues: the commitment to 'progressivism', to 'universalism', to the idea that 'cooperation is better than competition' and above all to the principle that 'good government is good for you'—something that she argues would be an oxymoron in contemporary England.

Of course England has had its own distinctive story too. As Whitty and Wisby argue in their paper, during the 1970s there had been growing antipathy in England towards the 'swollen state' of the immediate post-war years. But under the 1979 Thatcher government this became coupled with a market choice critique of public sector management. In the case of education this focused increasingly on the role of the so-called 'educational establishment' who seemed to favour what the Conservatives saw as highly questionable 'progressive' or 'child-centred' approaches to teaching. Conservatives argued that 'progressive' teaching methods and state allocation of places had brought a dull uniformity to the system and a levelling down of standards. Accordingly, throughout their time in office, the Conservative governments of Margaret Thatcher and John Major acted to increase the power of the 'consumer' and reduce that of the 'producers'. And as Whitty and Wisby argue, it is these fundamental principles that continue to shape educational policy in England today; they also mark a key difference from policies pursued in the rest of the UK.

But if educational polices have been so different across the UK for so long, how is it that public discourse has not recognised these differences? This is an issue that is explicitly addressed by Power in her paper in relation to Wales, though the arguments she advances may well have wider significance. First there has been 'non-recognition', where (through ignorance or laziness) English educational policy is simply assumed to be UK educational policy. As Power argues, this is an approach not only taken by the London based media, it is also not uncommon amongst education academics. A more politically motivated misreading is what she terms 'derision', where selective differences are recognised but where they are interpreted for political reasons from an English perspective. This, Power argues, is particularly pertinent in relation to Wales, where in the run up to both the 2015 and 2016 elections, the English government repeatedly referred to the 'failings' of education in Wales as evidence of the failings of the Labour Party in general.

It was against this background—the reality of growing differences between the four nations of the UK, but the persistent lack of recognition of this fact—that the Editorial Board of the *Oxford Review of Education* chose to commission this special issue. In the wake of the vote on Scottish independence and the open discussion of possible 'federal futures' for the UK, the Board took the view that it was time to take stock; to set down what the current state of educational policy and practice actually is across the UK. Within the confines of a single issue this is a challenging task. As editors we therefore chose to commission two papers from each of the four countries. The first paper was to be an overview, exploring the distinctive history, principles and current policies of each country. These papers are by Arnott and Ozga on Scotland, Power on Wales, Whitty and Wisby on England and Gardner on Northern Ireland. The second paper was specifically chosen as a case study of a key policy that highlighted the distinctiveness of each country. So for Scotland, Baird and Gray address issues of the assessment of educational standards in the light of that country's fundamental curriculum reform; for Wales, Taylor, Rhys and Waldron discuss the Foundation Phase – the flagship educational policy for that country since devolution; for England, Hillman considers Higher Education, a policy that is emblematic of neo-liberal reform more generally; and for Northern Ireland, Gallagher considers policies on shared education—a key post-conflict educational policy. These different case studies cannot of course purport to provide a complete overview of educational differences in the four nations. Nevertheless, taken as a whole, and in combination with the four overview papers, they do go some way to giving an insight into the complexities of educational policy and practice within the UK today.

The special issue begins with Scotland. In their overview of developments in Scotland, Arnott and Ozga describe some of the recent policy activity of the Scottish National Party (SNP) government in the context of the changing and unstable political and constitutional developments in the UK. In questioning the claims made in the run-up to the referendum to the creation of a 'federal state', they highlight the tensions about whether political devolution was to be understood as a 'settlement' (the UK understanding) or a 'process' (the SNP interpretation). Their analysis of key SNP policy texts highlights discourse as a significant resource for the SNP in government; they suggest two 'master discourses', the first economy-driven and emphasising global competitiveness and referencing 'outwards', the second community-driven and emphasising fairness and the idea of a flourishing Scotland and referencing 'inwards'. The SNP government has the challenge of managing the tensions between pressures for modernisation and competitiveness and the maintenance of national integrity and traditions. Initiatives such as the 'Curriculum for Excellence' (discussed in greater detail by Baird and Gray in this issue), the provision of integrated children's services and of higher education serve to illustrate the use of inward and outward referencing which emphasises the growing distinctiveness of the Scottish ambition.

For the case study from Scotland, Baird and Gray present a comparison of the Scottish and English systems for curriculum related examinations standard setting. They set this comparison within the context of reforms of the Scottish Higher examinations in light of the Government's 3–18 curriculum and assessment initiative, *A Curriculum for Excellence*, and the recent decision to reform A-level examinations in response to a fear that A-level standards in England are in decline. Drawing on an analysis of the definitions and therefore conceptualisation of examination standards in the two countries, they consider the different policy positions which reflect, in Scotland, the wider cultural desire for inclusiveness and attainment for all in the education system, and, in England, the concern for common and fair differentiation of standards across different Boards and different subjects.

Power, in her overview of recent educational policy in Wales, begins by outlining some of the ways in which education policy and provision in Wales differs from that of its neighbour, England, and then goes on to critique how these differences have been represented in both the media and by members of the educational research community. Indeed, the paper argues that these representations constitute a form of misrecognition. As Power makes clear, more careful analysis of the evidence on educational performance in Wales suggests that pronouncements of a 'crisis' in Welsh education appear to be as much politically-driven as evidence-based. In many areas, Wales does as well and sometimes better than its neighbours.

However, as Power also persuasively argues, it is important not to underplay the very real challenges that face Wales—challenges which are both like and unlike those facing England, Scotland and Northern Ireland. The paper concludes that we need a serious engagement with national divergences across the four nations of the UK—as well as elsewhere. The case of Wales she suggests highlights the need to undertake not only comparative analysis but also relational analysis if we are to enhance our understanding of the changing politics of education.

The case study from Wales by Taylor, Rhys and Waldron presents evidence on the Foundation Phase—a Welsh Government flagship policy of early years education (for 3 to 7 year-old children). The Foundation Phase was first announced shortly after devolution in a 'paving document' entitled 'The Learning Country' (NAfW, 2001) in which Wales' intention to take its own policy direction in education was firmly announced. The aspiration was to 'get the best for Wales' and the reform of early years education was to be the first step in that process. Marking a radical departure from the more formal, competency-based approach associated with the previous Key Stage 1 National Curriculum, the Foundation Phase advocates a developmental, experiential, play-based approach to teaching and learning. As such, it draws more on experience of early years education in Scandinavia, New Zealand (Te Whāriki) and Reggio Emilia in Northern Italy than that of England. In this paper, Taylor et al. report findings from a three-year mixed methods independent evaluation of the Foundation Phase. It considers the aims and objectives, the theory, assumptions and evidence underlying its rationale, and its content and key inputs. This is then contrasted with how the Foundation Phase was received by practitioners and parents, how it has been implemented and what discernible impact it has had on young children's educational outcomes. The authors conclude by suggesting that a number of contextual issues, arising from the fact that the policy landscape in Wales was still in its infancy, may have constrained the policy's development and subsequent impact.

In their overview of recent educational policy in England, Whitty and Wisby trace the roots of current policy in England back to the 1970s, and the growing antipathy towards the 'swollen' state which led to the reforms of the Thatcher government. In particular, they reference the Education Reform Act of 1988, which set a new direction for education policy, embracing a market-driven approach, greater competitiveness, and 'choice and diversity' among schools. Although the direction has continued under subsequent governments, the marginalisation of local authorities and the increase in direct government control lead Whitty and Wisby to invoke the concept of 'network governance' and to characterise the current position. With the use of this concept they are able to emphasise how different the English approach has become from the other nations in minimising the role of democratically elected local government. In their conclusion they speculate on the future under the conservative government and whether England 'remains an outlier or sets a precedent for the rest of the UK and perhaps the world beyond'.

The English case study has been written by Nick Hillman who draws on his substantial experience working from 2007 to 2013 as Chief of Staff for David Willetts, Minister for Universities and Science and Special Adviser in the Department for Business, Innovation and Skills. He has used this unique insight to discuss the Coalition government's higher education reforms, in particular the introduction of higher tuition fees, and what he refers to as the errors of judgment and the political mistakes which contributed to the reform process. In his conclusion Hillman suggests that the decision to remove the student numbers cap may turn out to be a more dramatic policy change than the decision to raise student fees to a maximum of £9000, and suggests that the Conservative Government's continuation of the reforms show that the Coalition government's policies were more evolutionary than revolutionary.

In his overview paper on Northern Ireland, Gardner argues that the Good Friday Agreement was of fundamental importance in education as in other areas of domestic policy in that it was a significant step forward in securing peace and stability for this troubled region of the British Isles. From the new-found stability, the previous fits and starts of education reform were replaced by a determination for modernisation and innovation, infused with a new energy and momentum. This sense of purpose, Gardner suggests, embraced a complex weave of ideas and ideals; all designed variously to smooth, celebrate and harness community differences for the collective good. Gardner argues that much progress has been made in the intervening years since 1998, particularly in political structures and relationships. However, he suggests that the euphoria of the new dawn of the Agreement had barely begun to shape the future before entrenched 'tribal' tensions reproduced the same political and legislative impasses of former years and visited their all-too-familiar blight on the economic, cultural and educational landscapes. Gardner's paper focuses on two key long-standing dimensions of education that have been sustained by this partisanship: segregation by religion and segregation by academic selection.

The theme of segregation by religion is one that is taken up explicitly in our final case study paper from Northern Ireland by Gallagher. As he argues, during the years of political violence in Northern Ireland, many looked to schools to contribute to reconciliation. A variety of interventions were attempted throughout those years, but there was little evidence that any had produced systemic change. The peace process provided an opportunity for renewed efforts. Gallagher's paper outlines the experience of a series of projects on 'shared education', or the establishment of collaborative networks of Protestant, Catholic and integrated schools in which teachers and pupils move between schools to take classes and share experiences. The paper outlines the genesis of the idea and the research which helped inform the shape of the shared education project. The paper also outlines the corpus of research which has examined various aspects of shared education practice and lays out the emergent model which is helping to inform current government practice in Northern Ireland, and is being adopted in other jurisdictions. The paper concludes by looking at the prospects for real transformation of education in Northern Ireland.

John Furlong and Ingrid Lunt

Education and nationalism in Scotland: governing a 'learning nation'

Margaret Arnott and Jenny Ozga

ABSTRACT

Nationalism is a key resource for the political work of governing Scotland, and education offers the Scottish National Party (SNP) government a policy space in which political nationalism (self determination) along with social and cultural forms of civic nationalism can be formed and propagated, through referencing 'inwards' to established myths and traditions that stress the 'public' nature of schooling/education/universities and their role in construction of 'community'; and referencing 'outwards', especially to selected Nordic comparators, but also to major transnational actors such as OECD, to education's role in economic recovery and progress. The SNP government has been very active in the education policy field, and a significant element of its activity lies in promoting a discourse of collective learning in which a 'learning government' is enabled to lead a 'learning nation' towards the goal of independence. This paper draws on recent research to explore recent and current developments in SNP government education policy, drawing on discourse analysis to highlight the political work that such policy developments seek to do, against the backdrop of continuing constitutional tensions across the UK.

Introduction

In this paper, we locate education policy within the framework of recent and current debates about the future governance of Scotland, and, indeed, of the UK. We first summarise developments in the governing relationship of Scotland to the UK, which set a complex and contested context for this discussion, before reviewing aspects of the Scottish National Party's education policy since 2007, with an emphasis on the ways in which that policy mobilises some of the resources of nationalist sentiment, while also pursuing modernising, economy-focused goals. The SNP government seeks to combine often-competing agendas in education through discursive framing of its policy as combining supposedly national characteristics with intelligent responses to current economic challenges: this is a demanding strategy, and we highlight the significance of discursive resources in sustaining it. It is not our purpose to assess the merit or otherwise of the SNP policy, rather we wish to illustrate the ways in which SNP policy in education works to mobilise a narrative of a 'journey to independence' drawing on historically-embedded themes and myths about fairness, while also referencing particular societies (i.e. the Nordic states). In so doing, we are emphasising the importance of education to the work of governing, against the backdrop of continuing uncertainty about Scotland's place in the UK.

Federalism?

Throughout the 20th century the governance of the UK and the relationship between Scotland and the UK were recurring subjects of political and constitutional debate (Mitchell, 2014; UK Government, 2014a, 2015). These debates intensified following the Scottish Independence Referendum in 2014 and the election of a Conservative UK government in May 2015. The September 2014 referendum on Scottish independence and subsequent events signally failed to settle the issue of Scotland's future and that of the UK—a failure illustrated in the election of 56 Scottish National Party (SNP) MPs to the UK Parliament in the UK General Election of May 2015. The idea of a federal redesign of the UK state had emerged in discussion as the 2014 Scottish Referendum approached: Unionist politicians in the 'Better Together' campaign alluded to the potential for the UK to move towards federalism. Gordon Brown, former Labour Prime Minister from 2007 to 2010, argued in the weeks leading up to the referendum that if a No vote was secured the UK would be a 'federal state within two years' with each territory and region across the UK having equal status and a UK federal government remaining responsible for defence and foreign affairs (Brown, 2014; Whitaker, 2014). The day after the Scottish Referendum, David Cameron spoke about the need to progress with plans for further devolution in Scotland, setting up the Smith Commission on further devolution of powers to the Scottish Parliament, which reported in November 2014 (Smith Commission, 2014).

However, Cameron stated that these plans for further devolution would be developed in tandem with reform in the Westminster Parliament aimed at ensuring English votes for English laws (BBC, 2014; UK Government, 2014b). For Cameron, further devolution for Scotland was linked to solving the problem presented by demands for 'English votes for English laws' (EVEL) in order, their supporters claimed, to give MPs in English constituencies rights to consider and vote on legislation only applying in England, in the same way as the Scottish parliament could debate and legislate on matters only relating to Scotland. This problem was pressing because it was an issue that UKIP (the Unitied Kingdom Independence Party) was likely to exploit in the May 2015 UK General Election, at the cost of Conservative votes. So the interest in EVEL was driven by the need for a quick political fix rather than conscious commitment to steps towards development of a federal UK state.

Following the referendum vote on 18 September 2014, Alex Salmond announced that he planned to resign from the posts of SNP party leader and First Minister of Scotland. Nicola Sturgeon, Deputy First Minister in the Scottish Parliament and putative successor to both of these posts, noted:

> In the few days before the referendum the language being used was the language of substantial radical change—devo max, something close to federalism, home rule. That is the expectation that has been generated [...]. Unless we end up with a package that is substantial, the backlash against the Westminster parties is going to be severe. (BBC, 2014)

We can see, then, that increasingly heterogeneous political projects have developed and are developing within the increasingly fragile UK polity; it is also apparent that the idea of federalism has been invoked as a resource that can be mobilised against the independence agenda, but without much attention to what federalism might mean for the redesign of UK governance. In any event, tension between the SNP governing 'project' of independence and the UK government's attempts to preserve the union exists not only on the fundamental issues of independence versus unionism and the UK's relationship with the EU, but in relation to a range of social and public policy directions, including deficit reduction, where the SNP government in Scotland opposes austerity. Further key areas where the SNP favours policies at odds with the UK government's position include implementing progressive personal tax-ation, ending the UK's Trident nuclear deterrent, using public funds to address poverty, including in mitigation of costs incurred by individuals as a consequence of the so-called bedroom tax, free state education including support grants for school, further and higher education students, opposition to privatisation of education or health provision, and increased pay and employment protection for public sector workers (SNP, 2015; Sturgeon, 2013). Post-September 2014 proposals for enhanced devolution set out in the Smith Commission Report and also the UK Coalition government's Command Paper *Scotland in the UK: the enduring union* further politicised debates about increasing interdependencies between devolved policy areas in Scotland and the UK government. The 2015 UK General Election campaign raised issues about the constitutional future of the UK. These issues drew attention to the inter-connectedness and inter-relationships within the asymmetrically devolved UK. Such issues included future devolved powers to Scotland including over welfare reform, fiscal powers, the respective voting powers of MPs from Scottish constituencies and MPs from English constituencies. Following the Smith Commission and the Scotland Bill 2015, interdependencies between devolved and reserved powers including education became more visible. Moreover, the introduction of 'English votes for English laws', which excludes MPs representing Scottish constituencies from votes on matters that are judged to be restricted to England, is seen by some Unionist politicians and commentators as inev-itably contributing to the eventual demise of the Union (Brown, 2015; Mason & Brookes, 2015). Developments in education policy in Scotland in recent years and currently need to be placed in the context of this tense and unsettled relationship.

Education, nationalism and the devolution 'settlement'

Historically, the relationship between education and the nation has been established as one in which education (more properly schooling) was well understood by governments as a significant contributor to their capacity to govern, through its creation of a common space of meaning, around identification with the nation. As Novoa puts it: 'education is, by defini-tion, the space for the construction of national identity' (2000, p. 46).

In Europe, most national education and training systems developed in the 19th and 20th centuries as negotiated settlements between nation-building states and organised labour, more or less advancing agendas driven by enlightenment commitments to individual equal-ity and collective progress. These agendas were framed by nation-building activities to which systems of schooling contributed through strengthening national economies, addressing social problems and influencing the distribution of individual life chances. Education systems also sought to 'define, replicate and ensure the national distinctiveness' of nation states (Dale, 2006, p. 373), a role that varied depending on the political history of the nation-state in question. In the UK, it was and is a key factor in sustaining the identity of the 'stateless nation' of Scotland (McCrone, 1992).

Indeed a distinctive narrative of education provision (Arnott, 2005, 2008) has distinguished education provision in Scotland from that of its larger, more powerful neighbour, despite Scotland's membership of the United Kingdom from the Union of the Parliaments in 1707. In the absence of a Scottish state, the key Scottish institutions (the law, the church and education) maintained a Scottish identity: education/schooling in Scotland was an element in the assertion of continued distinctiveness from England, supported by established and embedded myths and traditions that continued and continue to reference the public nature of schooling in Scotland and promote its contemporary role in both the construction of community and in driving progress.

The historically-embedded themes of 20th-century Scottish education—especially strong in the period of post-1945 social democracy (McPherson & Raab, 1988)—are reflected in the relative uniformity of school provision (through a comprehensive school system), greater social mobility, meritocracy, especially the recognition of talent and its fostering regardless of social class, a broad curriculum uniting sciences, arts and humanities and public support for teachers and for education more generally. These elements together are said to construct the 'Democratic Intellect' (Davie, 1961)—a combination of academic excellence and social openness that enables a career open to talents, or in the Scottish idiom, enables the career of the 'lad and lass o'pairts'. These themes can certainly be interrogated empirically: the point we are making here is that they create a mythology of Scottish education that offers powerful resources for the construction of a nationalist narrative. People in Scotland are offered the opportunity to identify as inheritors of a tradition that values fairness and inclusivity, while also achieving academic excellence, combined, since the introduction of the Curriculum for Excellence, with a judicious dose of personal and practical development.

In the immediate period following political devolution in 1999 these embedded references were somewhat muted by pressure for convergence in policy across the UK, because in that period the Labour Party was in power in both Holyrood and in Westminster, and as a consequence there were common themes in education policy in both Scotland and England—themes such as choice, privatisation and standards (Croxford & Raffe, 2007). These tended to be actively promoted by the Westminster UK government and reflected in policy in Scotland. However, even with this close relationship there were divergences: policy in Scotland sometimes conveyed an uneasy blending of rather contradictory approaches: for example in the field of education the 'Ambitious Excellent Schools' programme (Scottish Executive, 2004) echoed English based reforms in its apparent support for the introduction of more diversity in provision but within a framework that stressed the centrality of the principle of comprehensive provision. In fact, comprehensive provision remains the norm in Scotland, and the various forms of diversity in provision such as academies and Free Schools that characterise provision in England have not developed.

In the wider political arena, tensions emerged throughout the period from 2000 to 2007 about whether political devolution was to be understood as a 'settlement' or as a 'process'. Perhaps the key point is that the UK government understood devolution to the Assemblies/ Parliaments in the non-English UK as, indeed, a *settlement*, that would satisfy demands for greater autonomy and reduce support for nationalist political parties, including, especially, the SNP; but the asymmetrical nature of devolution (Arnott, 2015) and the untidiness of some of the arrangements resulted in continuous debate about areas of overlap and uncertainty. For example, among the areas of policy-making 'reserved' to the UK government are pensions, benefits, employment law, immigration and defence. Debates over, for example, policy for higher education and differences in arrangements for student support across the UK, along with difficulties in having two jurisdictions for policy for education and for employment, were exacerbated with the election of the first SNP administration (a minority government) to Holyrood in 2007, with a clear commitment to devolution as a process that offered opportunities for debate that could build support for independence. The arrival in Westminster of a UK Coalition government in 2010, with an agenda of reform of welfare arrangements and committed to deficit reduction, produced a situation of heightened tension, culminating in the independence referendum of 2014 in Scotland, a defeat for the SNP's independence agenda, which the UK government once again hoped marked a closing down of the debate and the establishment of 'an enduring settlement', a move strengthened by the promise of even greater devolution following the recommendations of the Smith Commission in the Scotland Bill currently going through Parliament. For our purposes in this paper, the important point is that there is no serious attempt to re-design the constitutional arrangements of the UK, in order to make something like a federal arrangement possible. Expectations that future reform of the governance of the UK following the Scottish Referendum would move towards a federal relationship between devolved nations and the UK government had featured prominently in the UK general election campaign in Scotland. Current Westminster arrangements and practices seem increasingly inappropriate in more fluid, networked and flexible governing practices and relations (Ball & Junemann, 2012; Grek & Ozga, 2010). Reflecting perhaps the feeling that at least *something* more was needed after the Referendum result, membership of the SNP more than quadrupled to 114,000 between 19 September 2014 and the time of the SNP annual conference in October 2015 (Sim, 2015). There is, then, a continuing instability in governing arrangements around the devolution 'settlement', and education—though formally devolved to the Scottish parliament—provides resources that may be mobilised to sustain a continuing debate. In the next section, we discuss our approach to governing, and the importance we ascribe to such resources.

The political work of governing

We understand governing to be a rather broader set of activities than is usually included in more conventional political science approaches to the governing of the UK, where formal, fixed entities and institutional arrangements form the cornerstone of most of the territorial, constitutional and regional studies of post-devolution governance (see, for example Jeffrey, 2015; Keating , 2013). We take a *political sociology* approach (Favell & Guiraudon, 2011; Smith, 2009) understanding governing as a set of practices which participate in the organisation and the orientation of social life and focusing on actors who do 'political work', i.e. work that 'both discursively and interactively seeks to change or reproduce institutions by mobilising values' (Smith, 2009, p. 13). This work mobilises or articulates political blocs; builds alliances, negotiates and reconciles interests, and assembles projects that define the direction and purpose of governing (Clarke, 2009, p. 2). The mobilisation of discourse is a highly significant element of the governing work that such actors do, not least because it attempts to provide coherence and meaning through the promotion of particular narratives, including narratives of civic nationalism, defined by Ignatieff (1993) 'as a community of equal, rights-bearing citizens, united in attachment to a shared set of practices and values' in an overarching 'project' of governance, in times where national states face insecurity and loss of power in the context of economic crises, global interconnectedness and 'loss of meaning' (Laidi, 1998; Ozga, 2011).

Discourse is a highly significant resource for the Scottish National Party in government: it was mobilised effectively in their first term where their minority status required them to position themselves as effective, competent and collaborative (Arnott & Ozga, 2012). It supported a presentation of the SNP's governing style as networked, decentralised and collaborative, in which government and people are discursively positioned as learning together to exercise increasing autonomy—for example in the 'Concordat' with Local Government and the National Performance Framework— these combine to build 'responsible autonomy' and provide a model of independent Scotland. There is a constant production of debate— from the 'National Conversation' to the Independence Referendum—aimed at generating an informed public, and building shared understandings of the relationship between government and citizens as a social contract, while also underlining claims to popular sovereignty:

> For many of the progress measures responsibility for success is shared between the Scottish Government and partners in local government, with our universities, the business community and in many cases with individual Scots ... Scotland Performs is an important part of our new approach, based on a distinct, and emerging Scotland-wide social partnership. It is about removing barriers between government and the people, and it recognises the fundamental truth that each and every person in this nation has a stake, a part to play, in growing Scottish success. (Scottish Government, 2008)

Indeed, analysis of key SNP policy texts (Arnott & Ozga, 2010a, 2010b) suggests two master discourses: the first is economy-driven, foregrounding economic growth, referencing skills, smartness and success. It is a discourse of competitiveness at a general level, and references 'outwards' to establish Scotland in a global competitive environment. The second links the economic drivers of policy to the idea of a 'flourishing' Scotland and an emphasis on community, fairness and inclusiveness—referencing 'inwards' to established embedded and collective narratives, including those embedded in education, as we see in the next section.

The SNP and education policy

> So it matters deeply to me personally that every young girl and boy growing up today—regardless of where they were born or what their family circumstances are—gets the same chances that I did. And of course it also matters to us as a nation. Scotland pioneered the idea of universal access to school education in the 17th and 18th centuries. Ever since then, a commitment to education has been part of our identity, part of our sense of ourselves as a country. (First Minister of Scotland, Nicola Sturgeon, August 2015)

Education is understood as a productive policy field by the SNP Government, indeed their first administration saw a considerable shift in policy towards a focus on Scotland, without reference to England, but referencing 'outwards' to other selected comparators and alongside a renewed interest in referencing 'inwards' to the national 'narrative' in education. Through *inward referencing*, implicit characteristics of the education system and the nation are mobilised (especially those that promote Scottish education as fair, equitable and socially just) and through *outward referencing* (to Europe and the Scandinavian and Baltic nations in particular) Scotland is repositioned and realigned in a global, competitive policyscape.

In 2011 the SNP won a majority in the Holyrood elections and it is predicted to comfortably maintain its majority in the Holyrood elections in May 2016. Education policy activity declined somewhat in the referendum year (2013–14), but there has been a recent acceleration of developments in the run up to the 2016 Holyrood election. We say more about these later in the paper.

The SNP government seems very aware of the need to manage the considerable tensions between globalising imperatives for modernisation and economic competitiveness while maintaining and sustaining ideas of national integrity and quality, and devotes considerable energy to combining these apparently competing pressures. This dual referencing, described by critics as 'speaking social democratic and acting neo-liberal' is threaded through the entire range of SNP government policy in education, which includes curriculum reform, establishing Education Scotland (which combines the Inspectorate with the curriculum and professional development agency), remodelling the relations between local authorities, schools and the inspectorate (Ozga, Baxter, Clarke, Grek & Lawn, 2013), restructuring provision from early years through to the College sector, as well as seeking to draw the universities and colleges into their project, through reform of university governance.

Thus, although there is an emphasis on economic growth in their statement of National Priorities for Education (The Scottish Government, 2007) as the creation of 'successful learners, confident individuals, effective contributors and responsible citizens', this emphasis is aligned with references to selected aspects of the national myth or tradition that connect to education's role as a key institution in maintaining and developing national identity. There is, then, a narrative that seeks to establish Scotland in a global competitive environment, but it is inflected with a sense of capacity and national resources and priorities. The economic drivers of policy are linked to the idea of a 'flourishing' Scotland and an emphasis on community, fairness and inclusiveness. This is seen, for example, in an extract from the National Performance Framework, setting out key objectives:

> Our young people are successful learners, confident individuals, effective contributors and responsible citizens. Our children have the best start in life and are ready to succeed. We live longer, healthier lives.
>
> We have tackled the significant inequalities in Scottish society. We have improved the life chances for children, young people and families at risk. We have strong, resilient and supportive communities where people take responsibility for their own actions and how they affect others. We take pride in a strong, fair and inclusive national identity. Our public services are high quality, continually improving, efficient and responsive to local people's needs. (The Scottish Government, 2007, p. 12)

Analysis of Scottish Government policy texts from 2007 to 2014, along with interviews with policy makers during the first SNP administration and continuing work on analysis of relevant and current policy texts reveals a shift over time from early statements dominated by economic imperatives towards a more complex mix. For example, early statements stress the need to tie education to the promotion of sustained economic growth, but this changes over time to an increased emphasis on incorporating education's capacity to address problems of poverty. Policy interventions are harnessed explicitly to the 'fairer' agenda: the Scottish government discursively references an education system that was successful and worked well for most, thereby underlining Scotland's tradition of meritocratic egalitarianism (Grek et al., 2009), while simultaneously underlining the obligation to help particular groups overcome their material disadvantages.

This way of characterising the education system is also to be found in the Scottish Government's adoption and adaptation of the 'Curriculum for Excellence' (CfE). In its previous existence as a product of the previous Labour administration, that programme of curriculum reform was described in terms that tended to reference the knowledge economy agenda of the Lisbon Council, and the policy discourse around CfE was very much that of modernisation in pursuit of economic growth. CfE was promoted as an example of a European—even global—policy agenda for increased 'personalisation' of learning with attention to building learners' confidence, enterprise and a range of intelligences in order to better align schooling with knowledge economy requirements for self-managing, responsible entrepreneurs.

The SNP administration does not neglect the economic imperatives, but it aligns the development and delivery of CfE more directly with ideas of using education to challenge inequalities. CfE marks a quite radical shift away from the traditional academic character of Scottish schooling (Paterson, 2009) that is being promoted through references to the need to extend opportunity and fairness, as well as ensure effective economic growth through education. The discursive shift is accomplished by foregrounding the social justice issue (i.e. we are well-schooled but the poorest pupils do very badly) and using that shared idea of Scottish education (as socially just and fair) to displace its meritocratic character and thus enable the dilution of academic curricula and the development of CfE. This discursive framing is not convincing to some educationalists (see, for example, Priestley & Humes, 2010). However, whether desirable or not, the referencing 'inward' to particular social democratic elements of 'shaping myths' has enabled a shift in a fundamental characteristic of Scottish provision, supported by international evidence, from particular European comparators—Finland, Lithuania, Norway and Poland.

The question of international comparisons also features in relation to the SNP government's use of the OECD as a point of reference. One of the most powerful forms of international assessment is OECD's Programme for International Student Assessment (PISA) test, which creates league tables of more or less successful nations. PISA has been a complex issue politically for the UK, as OECD originally recognised only one system (viz. the UK), but has shifted over time to acknowledge the separate Scottish system, which was entered separately in PISA in 2003 and 2006 (Scottish Executive, 2004; Scottish Government, 2007). Before the SNP election victory, PISA was often used by politicians in Whitehall and latterly in Holyrood to score points in an inter-UK competition for status as best performers in the OECD league. Since 2007, however, there is a shift in the discussion, which reflects a wider shift in 'referencing outward' to other systems. The UK—and specifically England—has been displaced discursively in the reception of PISA. Other comparators are referenced. As one of our informants, a senior policy officer, puts it:

> I think we should start really to look at some of the Baltic countries—say Estonia, Lithuania, Latvia—there are some other countries coming along … how those countries are developing, their economies and developing how they operate ... so we need to be looking at them ...

In other words, interviewees suggested that PISA can now be used to reinforce Scotland's distinctiveness (from England) and as a source of discursive framing of Scotland's education in relation to a new set of comparator nations, so that it is a resource in reinforcing Scottish distinctiveness while repositioning Scotland through new relations with small strong—and emergent—states. At the same time as referencing PISA to both reassure and move the international frame of reference, the Scottish Government began to extend the principles of comparison so that they were more generalised across social policy areas. More general

OECD data, not just PISA data, were used to create an independent research report—the Index of Children's Well-being in Scotland. Categories included suicide rates, dental health, child poverty, teenage pregnancy rates etc., and Scotland came almost last of 24 OECD comparator 'western' countries. Thus although PISA data looked healthy, other OECD derived data showed the severe problems in Scotland and the need for a more considered approach to children's services as a whole. This attention to the social indicators of health, wealth and well-being enabled the further development of the modernised nationalist narrative—one that takes some embedded myths or ideals about Scotland and brings them into relationship with continued social problems.

This has driven a shift in emphasis towards provision for the 'whole' child through integrated children's services (Grek & Ozga, 2010) rather than focusing on education as a separate policy sphere. This enhanced attention to problems of poverty and on efforts to break the link between poverty and underachievement in Scottish education is the focus of recent policy statements by the First Minister, as illustrated in the quotation at the beginning of this section. Despite evidence of an overall increase in the percentage of pupils achieving qualifications, school leavers from the least affluent areas of Scotland continue to underperform in comparison to those from the more affluent areas. The First Minister is herself taking the initiative in attempts to close this gap: in this case using inward referencing to illuminate the potential gap between the national narrative and the reality:

> My aim—to put it bluntly—is to close that attainment gap completely. It will not be done overnight—I accept that. But it must be done. After all, its existence is more than just an economic and social challenge for us all. It is a moral challenge. Indeed, I would argue that it goes to the very heart of who we are and how we see ourselves as a country. (Sturgeon, 2015)

There is, here, a blend of inward referencing to 'how we see ourselves' that is designed to appeal to the embedded mythology of fairness, but with a more focused attention to the gap between that myth and the actual attainment results of disadvantaged learners. The inward referencing seeks to harness public support—including from those for whom the system works—in order to devote resources to those whom the system is failing.

The field of Higher Education offers a further example of the blending of inward and outward referencing in education policy. The centrality of a particular idea or narrative of the university in Scottish cultural and political life, and its power as a resource in mobilising support is illustrated in the quotation below from a speech by the then First Minister of Scotland to the SNP conference in 2011, where he confirms the SNP's opposition to charging tuition fees for university education (which apply in England but not in Scotland). The text is given added force through the use of a well-known quotation (the rocks will melt wi' the sun) from the National Poet, Robert Burns. Note also the reference to a 'social contract'—a key term in SNP policy texts and speeches.

> And this nation pioneered free education for all, which resulted in Scots inventing and explaining much of the modern world. We called this the Scottish Enlightenment. And out of educational access came social mobility as we reached all the talents of a nation to change the world for the better.
>
> We can do so again—'the rocks will melt with the sun' before I allow tuition fees to be imposed on Scottish students—upfront or backdoor … this is part of the Scottish Settlement, our social contract with the people. (Salmond, Speech to SNP Conference March 2011).

Current SNP government policy seeks to draw the universities into their governing project. The public character of Scotland's universities stems not only from their public funding, but from their historical role as 'harvesters of talent' whatever its social origins. A recent review of university governance (von Prondzynski, Brotherstone, McWhirter & Parker, 2012) at the same time as the introduction of University Sector Outcome Agreements in 2012–13 could be interpreted as attempts to draw the higher education sector into a debate on its public role and responsibilities, and to make a public demonstration of the universities' acceptance of the forms of accountability they are required to meet. Considerable discursive resources have been mobilised by the Scottish Government around the 'public' nature of university governance (including the idea of the 'democratic intellect' mentioned above), stressing the need of society 'to protect its broader investment in education, knowledge and intellectual innovation in a way that makes the most of a long Scottish tradition adapted to the needs of the 21st century world' (Von Prondzynski et al., 2012). SNP policy for higher education uses inward referencing to embedded and shared ideas of the public nature of universities in Scotland and their democratic and intellectual traditions to help in 'steering' of the universities towards their identification with a national 'project'. 'The Learning Nation' has been employed as a discursive strategy within this 'project' (Russell, 2012). The attempted steering of the sector is revealed in the new funding arrangements that tie increased investment in teaching and research to 'working with us' (i.e. the government) and assessment of that work through the National Performance Framework (Russell, 2012), while the Scottish Funding Council, that allocates funds to the universities, is also calling for closer collaboration between universities in order to deliver TSG's agenda.

> The strength of Scottish university system is that we have diversity within the universities themselves and that is to be celebrated and supported and we will do that. That is one of the outcomes of the report but it also forced them to think of themselves as part of a collective responsibility. (Interview with senior policy maker)

Higher education policy continues to feature prominently in SNP policy agenda. In 2013 the Post-16 Education Bill was passed in the Scottish Parliament. Plans to widen access to post-16 education and to put widening access on a statutory basis were agreed. Opposition parties were critical of the Bill, with the Labour Party criticising the Bill for adopting a centralised approach and the Conservative Party for the 'unintended consequences of forcing universities to adopt prescriptive targets enshrined in legislation' (BBC, 2013). In June 2015 the Cabinet Secretary for Education and Lifelong Learning introduced the Higher Education Governance (Scotland) Bill. The Bill follows the von Prondzynski Review 2012 referred to above and outlines a number of proposals concerning higher education governance; these aim to reform four key areas: membership of governing body, chairing of governing body, academic freedom and also academic boards (MacPherson, 2015).

Conclusions

In this paper we have attempted to place some of the recent policy activity of the SNP government in the context of changing and unstable political and constitutional developments in the UK. We have not provided a comprehensive account of all of the SNP's education policy activity: rather our purpose has been to use selected examples from the policy field of education to show how the SNP 'does' governing in the complex and contested context of current UK arrangements—in particular to show how education offers a policy field in which both inward and outward referencing act to promote a version of the 'learning nation' in progress towards independence, despite the loss of the referendum in 2014. In selecting our examples, we are trying to show how the SNP works discursively to reference embedded assumptions and myths about education, as a means of engendering support. At the same time, we have also pointed to the ways in which they situate Scotland within a new frame of reference in the globalising and competition-driven contemporary setting, through selecting particular comparators, referencing the OECD, which has just completed a further review of Scottish education (OECD, 2015) and attempting to discursively blend tradition and modernisation. Our intention is neither to endorse nor condemn their activity, but to illuminate it as an example of how the education policy field may be implicated in governing projects.

Acknowledgements

This paper draws on the following funded research projects: Governing by Inspection: School Inspection and Education Governance in Scotland, England and Sweden (ESRC RES 062 23 2241A); Knowledge and Policy in the Health and Education Sectors in Europe (EUFP6 IP 028848-2); Education and Nationalism: The Discourse of Education Policy in Scotland (RES-000-22-2893). The article represents the authors' views, not those of the ESRC.

Disclosure statement

No potential conflict of interest was reported by the authors.

References

Arnott, M. A. (2005). Devolution, territorial politics and the politics of education. In G. Mooney & G. Scott (Eds.), *Exploring social policy in the 'New' Scotland*. Bristol: Policy Press.

Arnott, M. A. (2008). Public policy, governance and participation in the UK: A space for children ? *International Journal on Children's Rights, 16*, 355–367.

Arnott, M. A. (2015). The Coalition's impact on Scotland. In M. Beech & S. Lee (Eds.), *The Conservative-Liberal Coalition: Examining the Cameron-Clegg Government*. Basingstoke: Palgrave Macmillan.

Arnott, M. A., & Ozga, J. (2010a). Nationalism, governance and policy making: The SNP in power. *Public Money and Management, 30*, 91–97.

Arnott, M. A., & Ozga, J. (2010b). Education and nationalism: The discourse of education policy in Scotland. *Discourse, 31*, 335–350.

Arnott, M. A., & Ozga, J. (2012). Education and social policy. In G. Mooney & G. Scott (Eds.), *Social justice and social policy in Scotland*. Bristol: Policy Press.

Ball, S., & Junemann, C. (2012). *Networks, new governance and education*. Bristol: Polity Press.

BBC. (2013, 26 June). *MSPs back post-16 education reforms*. Retrieved from http://www.bbc.co.uk/news/uk-scotland-scotland-politics-23054513

BBC. (2014, 19 September). David Cameron statement on the future of the UK.

Brown, G. (2014). *My Scotland, our Britain: A future worth sharing*. London: Simon and Schuster.

Brown, G. (2015, 9 October). Tories must deliver on Vow promises, or forever be accused of betrayal. *Daily Record*. Retrieved from http://www.dailyrecord.co.uk/news/politics/gordon-brown-tories-must-deliver-6601261

Clarke, J. (2009). Governance puzzles. In L. Budd & L. Harris (Eds.), *eGovernance: Managing or governing?* (pp. 29–52). London: Routledge.

Croxford, L., & Raffe, D. (2007). Education markets and social class inequality: A comparison of trends in England, Scotland and Wales. In R. Teese, S. Lamb, & M. Duru-Bellat (Eds.), *Education and inequality: International perspectives on theory and policy*, Vol. 3. Dordrecht: Springer.

Dale, R. (2006). Policy relationships between supranational and national scales: Imposition/resistance or parallel universes? In J. Kallo & R. Rinne (eds.), *Supranational regimes and national education policies—encountering challenge. Finnish educational research association: Research in educational sciences, 24*, 27–52.

Davie, G. E. (1961). *The democratic intellect: Scotland and her universities*. Edinburgh: Edinburgh University Publications.

Favell, A., & Guiraudon, V. (Eds.). (2011). *Sociology of the European Union*. London: Palgrave Macmillan.

Gallagher, J., & Raffe, D. (2013). Higher education policy in post devolution UK: More convergence than divergence? *Journal of Education Policy, 27*, 467–490.

Grek, S., Lawn, M., Lingard, B., Ozga, J., Rinne, R., Segerholm, C., & Simola, H. (2009). National policy brokering and the construction of the European Education Space in England, Sweden, Finland and Scotland. *Comparative Education, 45*, 5–23.

Grek, S., & Ozga, J. (2010a). Re-inventing public education: The new role of knowledge in education policy-making. *Public Policy and Administration, 25*, 271–288.

Grek, S., & Ozga, J. (2010b). Governing education through data: Scotland, England and the European education policy space. *British Education Research Journal, 36*, 937–952.

Ignatieff, M. (1993). *Blood and belonging: Journeys into the new nationalism*. New York, NY: Farrar, Strauss & Giroux.

Jeffrey, C. (2015). Constitutional change—without end? *The Political Quarterly, 86*, 275–278.

Keating, M. (2013). *The Government of Scotland: Public policy making after devolution*. Edinburgh: Edinburgh University Press.

Keating, M., Cairney, P., & Hepburn, E. (2012). Policy convergence, transfer and learning under devolution. *Regional and Federal Studies, 22*, 289–307.

Laidi, Z. (1998). *A world without meaning*. London: Routledge.

MacPherson, S. (2015). Higher Education (Governance) Bill SPICe Briefing 15/54. Retrieved from http://www.scottish.parliament.uk/ResearchBriefingsAndFactsheets/S4/SB_15-54_Higher_Education_Governance__-_Scotland_Bill.pdf

Mason, R., & Brooks, L. (2016, 22 October). English votes for English laws plan branded 'charter for end of the union'. *The Guardian*. Retrieved from http://www.theguardian.com/politics/2015/oct/22/commons-passes-english-vetoes-for-english-laws-plan

McCrone, D. (1992). *A sociology of a stateless nation*. London: Routledge.

McPherson, A., & Raab, C. (1988). *Governing education*. Edinburgh: Edinburgh University Press.

Mitchell, J. (2014). *The Scottish question*. Oxford: Oxford University Press.

Nóvoa, A. (2000). The restructuring of the European educational space. In T. Popkewitz (Ed.), *Educational knowledge: Changing relationships between the state, civil society and the educational community*. New York, NY: State University of New York.

OECD. (2015). *Education at a glance 2015*. Retrieved from https://www.oecd.org/education/education-at-a-glance-19991487.htm

Ozga, J. (2011). Governing narratives: 'Local' meanings and globalising education policy. *Education Inquiry, 3* 05–318.

Ozga, J., Baxter, J., Clarke, J., Grek, S., & Lawn, M. (2013). The politics of educational change: Governing and school inspection in England and Scotland. *Swiss Journal of Sociology, 39*, 205–214.

Paterson, L. (2009). Does Scottish education need traditions? *Discourse, 30*, 269–281.

Priestley, M., & Humes, W. (2010). The development of Scotland's Curriculum for Excellence: Amnesia and déjà vu. *Oxford Review of Education, 36*, 345–361.

Russell, M. (2012, October). *Speech to SNP Conference*. Retrieved from http://www.snp.org/blog/post/2012/oct/snp-conference-address-michael-russell-msp

Scottish Executive. (2004). *Ambitious excellent schools: Our agenda for action*. Edinburgh: Scottish Executive.

Scottish Government. (2007). *Scotland performs: National outcomes*. Retrieved from http://www.gov.scot/About/Performance/scotPerforms/outcomes/youngpeople

Scottish Government. (2008). *Building the Curriculum 3: A framework for learning and teaching*. Edinburgh: Scottish Government.

Sim, P. (2015, October 16). SNP Conference 2015: Who are the party's new members? *BBC Scotland News*. Retrieved from http://www.bbc.co.uk/news/uk-scotland-scotland-politics-34553158

Smith, A. (2009, February). *Studying the Government of the EU: The promise of political sociology*. Paper presented to Edinburgh's Europa Institute seminar Practising EU Government. Edinburgh.

Smith Commission. (2014). *Report of the Smith Commission for further devolution of powers to the Scottish Parliament*. Edinburgh: The Smith Commission.

SNP. (2015) *Stronger for Scotland SNP manifesto*. Retrieved from http://votesnp.com/docs/manifesto.pdf

Sturgeon, N. (2013, November). *Speech to SNP Conference*. Perth. Retrieved from http://d3n8a8pro7vhmx.cloudfront.net/yesscotland/pages/3159/attachments/original/1382109831/18.10.13-NicolaSturgeonspeech-SNP_conference.pdf?1382109831

Sturgeon, N. (2015, August). *A world leader in education*. Speech. From http://news.scotland.gov.uk/News/A-world-leader-in-education-1c10.aspx

UK Government. (2014a). *The parties published proposals on further devolution for Scotland*, Cm. 8946. London: HMSO.

UK Government. (2014b). *The implications of devolution for England*, Cm. 8969. London: HMSO.

UK Government. (2015). *Scotland in the UK: An enduring settlement*, Cm. 8890. London: HMSO.

Von Prondzynski, F., Brotherstone, T., McWhirter, I., & Parker, R. (2012). *Report of the review of higher education governance in Scotland*. Retrieved from http://www.scotland.gov.uk/Resource/0038/00386780.pdf

Whitaker, G. (2014, 15 August). Gordon Brown backs federalism in the event of no vote. *Scotsman*. Retrieved from http://www.scotsman.com/news/politics/top-stories/gordon-brown-backs-federalism-in-event-of-no-vote-1-3511291#axzz3qdGTYUSe

The meaning of curriculum-related examination standards in Scotland and England: a home–international comparison

Jo-Anne Baird and Lena Gray

ABSTRACT

The ways in which examination standards are conceptualised and operationalised differently across nations has not been given sufficient attention. The international literature on standard-setting has been dominated by the psychometrics tradition. Broader conceptualisations of examination standards have been discussed in the literature in England, which has curriculum-related examinations at the end of schooling. There has, however, been little analysis of conceptualisations of examination standards in Scotland. Different education systems and examinations operate in Scotland and England, and the stated value positions and processes relating to examination standards differ markedly. This paper critically examines policy positions on assessment standards in Scotland and England through the lens of recent theories of standard-setting. By analysing public statements on standards, the paper illuminates similarities and differences in conceptual bases and operational approaches, and examines the effects of these on outcomes for candidates. We conclude that both systems are operationalising attainment-referencing, but with different processes in Scotland and England and these practices do not fit within previous examination standards classifications. As such, the paper moves examination standards theory forward by concluding that there is at least one superordinate definitional category that draws upon more than one definitional stance.

Introduction

The meaning of examination standards is slippery and has been much debated in the literature in England (Baird, 2007; Baird, Cresswell & Newton, 2000; Cresswell, 1996; Christie & Forrest, 1981; Coe, 1999, 2007a, 2010; Newton, 1997a, 1997b, 2003, 2005, 2010a). Oftentimes stakeholders discuss examination standards without realising they are talking at cross-purposes and using contradictory definitions. The international academic literature on standard-setting[1] has been dominated by the psychometrics tradition, which positions examinations standards as representing an underlying construct, a 'postulated attribute of people, assumed to be reflected in test performance' (Cronbach & Meehl, 1955, p. 283). The psychometrics tradition is often associated with tests that are disconnected from curriculum, such as the American SATs. Broader conceptualisations of examination standards have been discussed in the literature in England, which has curriculum-related national examinations at the end of schooling and for university entrance. In this article, we continue the debate on the meaning of curriculum-related examination standards. Because this literature has been dominated by the curriculum-unrelated psychometrics tradition and latterly developed in relation to examinations in England, very little has been written that documents and conceptualises the meaning of examination standards in high stakes national examinations. Given the importance of these examinations for people's life chances, this is a yawning gap in the literature which makes it difficult to understand examination systems internationally and to explain how they operate, how they are interpreted and why certain issues are a matter of public controversy in one country, but not in another. For example, when the results for Higher English declined in 2003, this was seen as evidence for falling educational standards in Scotland, whilst in the same year *rising* A-level pass rates were seen as declining standards in England.

Transparency of the meaning of examination standards matters to a wide range of educationalists, who are trying to enact them through teaching and other practices. Such transparency also matters to a wider group of stakeholders, including candidates, parents, politicians and the media. Each may have their own definition of what it means for standards to be 'comparable'. Curriculum-related examinations, which are used for high stakes purposes such as university entrance, provide a number of comparability challenges. A key challenge is deciding which factors are legitimate to take into account when making standards decisions (Baird, 2007, pp. 132–136).

Here, we focus upon a comparison of curriculum-related examination standards in Scotland and England for the school-leaving examinations. We contrast policy statements, standard-setting systems, controversies and cultural positioning of examination standards. Methodologically, we base our argument upon critical evaluation of published policy documents and the authors' insider experiences of standard-setting in Scotland and England (Sikes & Potts, 2008). Both authors have had professional responsibility for standards in an English examining board and one of the authors was formerly responsible for standard-setting policy at the Scottish Qualifications Authority (SQA). Our depictions of the standards policies in Scotland and England have been constructed in part through member-checking (Creswell and Miller, 2000) with senior examining body personnel who are now or were formerly responsible for standards. In this article we present our interpretations of the stated policies and have also discussed this with those senior practitioner-policy-makers as part of a collaborative contribution to the field (Creswell & Miller, 2000, p. 126). Examination boards have a tricky, political task in managing public and stakeholder perceptions of examination standards, so we do not claim that practitioners are necessarily in a position to make the kinds of public critiques of the system that are presented here.

As these countries are part of the United Kingdom, they represent a special case for comparative research, termed a home–international comparison (Raffe, 2007). With many things in common between the countries, such as similar economic settings, home–international comparisons help researchers to understand each system better, clarify alternative policy strategies, compare the impact of alternative policy strategies, understand policy issues better by observing greater variation and understand the processes of educational change (Raffe, 2007). We briefly outline the systems used to set standards in the two countries, but our focus is more upon the meaning of standards in policy documents. Cultural contexts of current examination reforms are considered to help explain the reasons for the different approaches to the meaning of examination standards. Evidence from the outcomes of the examinations is also used to help characterise examination standards. Our focus is on the Scottish system, but we use England as a contrasting case because more has been written about the meaning of examination standards in England.

Whilst some studies have compared the level of standard of the examinations in Scotland and England, that is not our purpose: this article's central theme is how the curriculum-related, school-leaving examination standards are construed, how that differs and what the consequences of this are for the literature. There are many aspects of educational standards that are not the focus of this paper, such as the quality of education provision, the experienced curriculum and equality issues.

Defining examination standards

Setting and maintaining examination standards are conceptually distinct, but in practice a new examination's standards are often set with reference to a previous standard. Therefore, much of the literature on the meaning of examination standards relates to the maintenance or comparability of standards across examinations. Over the past 20 years, there have been numerous attempts to set out typologies of examination standards definitions that might be useful within the UK system of curriculum-based examinations. Most articles have argued for the adoption of a particular definition (e.g. Baird, 2007; Baird et al., 2000; Coe, 2010; Cresswell, 1996; Wiliam, 1996). Newton (2010a) synthesised this literature and criticised previous work for confusing methods with definitions. He focused upon the claims regarding attainment that justify definitions of common standards between examinations, proposing three categories of definition (Table 1), essentially categorising ways of thinking about standards according to the type of factor it is legitimate to take into account within each type of definition. Each type of definition is making a different sort of statement about what students who have achieved 'comparable' standards have in common with each other. Definitions that rely upon attributes of students' performances are *phenomenal* definitions. If a standard-setting system is based on a phenomenal definition of comparability, we would expect policy statements and operational processes characterised by a focus on particular features of student performance. The demands of the questions that students have to answer or the performances students give in examination booklets might be used as evidence for this category of definition. A second, *causal*, category, justifies standards by pointing to evidence that students with similar background characteristics (such as prior attainment) gain similar results. If a standard-setting system is based on a causal definition, then policy statements and operational processes would stress the causes of similarities and differences in attainment. Newton's (2010a,b) third, *predictive*, category justifies common standards on the

Table 1. Categories of definitions of examination standards (Adapted from Newton, 2010a, 2010b).

Definitional category	Aspects of attainment which are maintained
Phenomenal	features, properties, or dispositions that comprise attainment: similarly graded students should share similar outcomes from learning
Causal	factors that result in attainment: similarly graded students should have had similar inputs to learning
Predictive	potential that is implicit in attainment: similarly graded student should have a similar likelihood of future success

grounds that students with similar grades are able to progress to similar achievements, such as degree results or job prospects, in the future. A standard-setting system based on a predictive definition of standards would show an emphasis on progression pathways and later success, and we would expect discussion of those progression patterns (and success in them) to be the main focus of debates about comparability. We adopt this categorisation scheme due to its focus upon the *kind of attainment factor* at the basis of definitions and its explanatory power to incorporate previous definitional approaches.

Newton's position is broader than that of Coe (2010), who argued that the fundamental view underlying all conceptions of comparable standards was 'construct comparability'. That is, Coe (2010) conceived of all standards definitions as essentially being based upon an underlying variable that provides a measure of educational attainment in the subject of the test, for example, proficiency in chemistry. Coe's (2010) position is consistent with a psychometric methodology and, as such, is in keeping with the philosophy in curriculum-unrelated testing. However, given the wide range of conclusions that test-users in the United Kingdom wish to draw from national examination standards and the purposes to which they put the tests, it is hard to sustain the argument that there is a single construct for each test that is used in all comparisons (Baird, 2010).

Further, some instances of standard-setting indicate that a much broader conception of comparable standards is in use. An illustrative example is the case of the General Certificate of Secondary Education (GCSE) examination in Welsh, which can be taken in two forms; for first language Welsh speakers or second language speakers. The results for 2008 showed that approximately 70% of each group was awarded at least a grade C in the two examinations. Given the different levels of construct attainment (i.e. Welsh language skill) that we would expect these groups of students to reach, it is clear that a conception of comparability other than construct comparability was in use (Newton, 2010b, p. 47). Psychometric 'technology' has arisen from psychological and educational testing. It sits most comfortably with a positivist world-view (Borsboom, 2005), in which constructs exist in people and we go out and measure them with our tests. These constructs then form a basis for conceptualising and deciding standards. Discussion of wider issues regarding the use of test scores does not sit so comfortably within the psychometric tradition. Since our aim is to investigate, present and critique the stated positions on the meanings of standards for particular examinations in Scotland and England, we need a conceptual framework that engages with the application of standards definitions in these contexts.

The categories of definitions in Table 1 are conceptually distinct, but as Newton (2010a,b) pointed out, they are not necessarily tied to a particular methodology. For example, expert judgment on whether attainment is the same could be used to marshal evidence for all three categories, as could statistical techniques. Different methods can be utilised to evidence claims and these could fail to converge on whether standards are the same across examinations. Even working within a definitional category, there can be disagreements regarding whether standards have been maintained due to different nuances in meaning in use. Moreover, national examinations in Scotland and England are expected to be comparable in a range of ways: standards are expected to be comparable over time, between subjects, between qualifications and sometimes between countries, to name a few. Evidence regarding standards over time for a qualification could indicate year on year comparability whilst data on between-subject comparability could show that standards have not been maintained. Thus, evidence regarding standards can be contradictory for reasons of definition, method or data. Our focus in this article is upon the conceptualisation of standards and we encountered methodological and data issues in applying them to policies and practices in Scotland and England, but we cannot explore those issues fully here. We return to the onto-logical status of standards later. Before presenting how standards are defined, operational-ised and debated in Scotland, we explain aspects of the broader educational culture and give some background information about the Scottish qualifications system.

Scottish education and the Higher Examinations

Education is an aspect of Scottish culture which has long been seen as distinctively Scots by custom and right. It has been uniquely defined since the Reformation, was enshrined as unique in the 1707 Act of Union, and was made a devolved power of the Scottish Parliament in 1999. The commitment to education for all in Scotland dates back to the First Book of Discipline in 1561 (Gray, McPherson & Raffe, 1983, p. 40). Ideas about Scottish education and assessment are central to Scotland's national identity as a meritocratic society that values educational success for all. This conception of Scottish education has been construed by some as an anthropological myth (Gray, McPherson & Raffe, 1983, p. xv). Humes and Bryce (2013, p. 139) summed up the myth and its centrality to Scottish identity as follows.

> Belief in the worth and purpose of education is linked to the sense of national identity which is regularly invoked to draw attention to the differences between Scottish and English society. This takes the form of a story or 'myth', shaped by history but not always supported by his-torical evidence, to the effect that Scotland is less class-conscious than England; that ability and achievement, not rank, should determine success in the world; that public (rather than private) institutions should be the means of trying to bring about the good society; and that, even where merit does justify differential rewards, there are certain basic respects—arising from the common humanity of all men and women—in which human beings deserve equal consideration and treatment.

The persistence of this national cultural positioning can be seen in the Scottish Government's (2015a, p. x) recent major education policy document, *A Draft National Improvement Framework for Scottish Education*. It reads:

> We are committed to a fairer Scotland and ensuring that every child is able to develop the knowledge, skills and attributes they will need to flourish in life, learning and work [...]

> This matters to us as a nation. Scotland pioneered the idea of universal access to school edu-cation in the 17th and 18th centuries and a commitment to universal education has been part of our identity ever since. Excellence in education will be essential to our success as a nation in the future.

Scotland can be argued to have 'pioneered the idea of universal access to school education' (Scottish Government, 2015a, p. 3), but achieving universal access is a separate matter. Some critics argue that the myth is simply untrue (H. Paterson, 1983), that it is a partial truth which masks complexity and prevents debate and change (Gray et al., 1983; McPherson, 1983), or that a more nuanced explanation is needed (Finn, 1983; L. Paterson, 2003). Comparisons of socioeconomic status effects upon educational outcomes and life chances between Scotland and England have complex findings. Whilst the *relationship* between socioeconomic status of pupils and educational outcomes at school is similar across the two countries (and stable over time), pupils at any given level of socioeconomic status gained higher educational outcomes in Scotland (L. Paterson & Iannelli, 2007).

One in five children in Scotland is living in poverty (Scottish Government, 2014), with the figure reaching one in three in the largest city, Glasgow (Child Poverty Action Group, 2014); this level of child poverty is similar to that in England (Social Mobility and Child Poverty Commission, 2014, p. 7). The bottom socioeconomic group had worse outcomes in school level qualifications in Scotland compared with England (L. Paterson and Iannelli, 2007). So the Scottish education system has not been better for the poorest in society's attainment at school.

The Scottish Higher examination, which was introduced in 1888 (Philip, 1992) is the standard entrance qualification for higher education. Young people in Scotland typically take Highers in their fifth year of secondary school, at around 17 years of age. Students can choose from a wide range of subjects, and typically take four or five (although some may be at lower qualification levels). Until the introduction of *Curriculum for Excellence*, most young people would take qualifications in English, mathematics, and two or three other subjects.

The Higher has been through several reforms (McVittie, 2008), but the most recent changes have a structure that remains similar to that introduced as part of the *Higher Still* development in 1999 (Scottish Office, 1994). Most Highers contain two or three Units which are assessed by teachers on a pass/fail basis, and an externally assessed synoptic assessment which is the basis of the grading for the course (SQA, n.d.). In the new Highers for *Curriculum for Excellence*, this external assessment is typically split into two components: an examination of up to three hours in length, and a controlled assessment, usually a project requiring investigation skills and allowing some choice of topic for the student (SQA, 2013). Highers are typically taken after a one-year course. In 2015, approximately 60% of school-leavers[2] gained at least one Higher (The Scottish Government, 2015b) and 29% gained five Highers (The Scottish Government, 2015c). The typical entry requirement for university entrance is four or five Highers at grade C or above. Grade C has traditionally been seen as a pass.[3]

Advanced Highers are taken at age 18, in the sixth year of secondary schooling. Whilst possession of Advanced Highers may allow some exemption or advanced standing, Advanced Higher is not itself an entry requirement for Scottish universities. Degrees are four-year courses in Scotland, reflecting the historical emphasis on breadth of study (Davie, 1961; L. Paterson, 2003). When Scottish students progress to universities in other parts of the UK, though, they may find that they must complete two or three Advanced Highers, particularly for entry to the higher status institutions.

The statistics for Higher examination outcomes that gain most public attention are the outcomes at the level of entries (rather than by pupil), as published by examination boards on results day. These results are part of the context in which examination boards operate and set standards, so we briefly depict them, comparing Higher results with those for A-level and later relating results to how standards play out in each country.

There has been a steady rise in Higher attainment over time (Figure 1), with a slow rise in the Higher pass rate, from 66% in 1986 to 78% in 2015 and a sharper rise in the proportion of entries awarded grade A, from 12% in 1986 to 30% in 2015.

Curriculum for Excellence *Highers*

In 2015, the SQA awarded new Highers developed to support the Government's 3–18 curriculum and assessment initiative, *A Curriculum for Excellence*. The Scottish government responded to the 2002 National Debate by establishing a Curriculum Review Group (Scottish

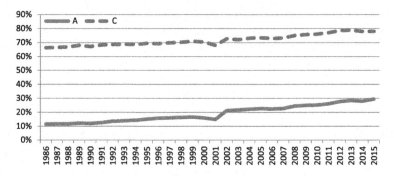

Figure 1. Proportion of Higher examination entries gaining grade C and above and grade A. Source: Scottish Qualifications Authority http://www.sqa.org.uk/sqa/64717.4239.html.

Executive, 2003). The group's report, *A Curriculum for Excellence*, was published in 2004, arguing for transformative change in Scottish education, and emphasising the need to 'Make sure that assessment and certification support learning' (Scottish Executive, 2004, p. 7). In 2008, *A Consultation on the Next Generation of National Qualifications in Scotland* was published, making four major proposals for qualifications reform (Scottish Executive, 2008). In contrast to recent qualifications reform in England, the Scottish reform was positioned as aiming to reduce the reliance on examinations, increasing the focus on skills rather than knowledge, and providing a qualifications system which allowed more personalised programmes to allow individual young people to reach their potential (Scottish Executive, 2008, p. 11).

The introduction of the new qualifications has not been unproblematic, in line with experience of previous qualifications reform in Scotland (Hayward, 2007, 2015; Hayward & Hutchinson, 2013). Reform of examinations is risky and systemic failures have been known to happen, such as in 2000 when the Highers were last reformed (Deloitte & Touche, 2000). However, the failure in 2000 was logistical, not related to standards, as has been the case in other countries, such as in England in 2002 and New Zealand in 2003 (Baird & Coxell, 2009).

The policy context for reform of the Highers was about increasing attainment and skills for all (Scottish Executive, 2008), following an OECD review which found that too many of Scotland's young people left school with few qualifications, and too many failed to be engaged by the general academic curriculum on offer (OECD, 2007). These aims are in keeping with the view of Scottish education as inclusive. The overall pass rate, taking into account students who sat the old Highers and the new examinations (as both were available in 2015) was 74.6%; a rise of 0.4% from the previous year. As such, there was not a dramatic change to attainment for all in Scotland in 2015, but the results were still welcomed. On results day, the SQA, Scottish Government, Directors of Education and Teacher Unions separately publicly welcomed the increased pass rates, each attributing them to the success of their own policies or practices (ADES, 2015; EIS, 2015; Scottish Government, 2015d; SQA, 2015a). Little dissention from this reaction is evident (although there is some discussion—see *The Telegraph*, 2015a).

Scotland has a single examination board, is a small country and its education system has been characterised by inter-agency partnership working (Hayward, 2007; Humes, 2013). Due to this interconnectedness, it is usually in everyone's interest to support increased pass rates as an indicator of rising standards. Bryce and Humes (2013) analysed the public reactions to pass rates in Scotland, claiming that the following pattern could be observed most years.

- The SQA highlights 'the best-ever levels' of results and asserts that they demonstrate the value of qualifications.
- Government politicians congratulate pupils and teachers on their well-earned achievements.
- Opposition politicians also congratulate pupils and teachers but claim there is public suspicion about a lowering of standards.
- Newspapers express 'fresh concerns' that qualifications are being 'dumbed down'.
- Perhaps a little too defensively, teaching unions point to the robustness of the qualifications framework and state that results inevitably fluctuate a bit from year to year.
- Local authorities claim that the results vindicate their commitments to raising standards and aspirations (with, in 2012, the directors of education in Glasgow and Edinburgh both pointing to better attendance rates in their city schools).
- Many teachers concede that increases in pass rates reflect their growing familiarity with courses and the demands of particular examinations. (Bryce & Humes, 2013, p. 685)

Periodically, overly difficult examination questions become a narrative in the Scottish press and this was the case in 2015 with the Higher Mathematics examination (e.g. *The Telegraph*, 2015b). Philip (1992) gave a historical account of the outrage at the first Higher Mathematics exam in 1888, and similar outrage at the level of demand of all subjects in 1946. These debates have a notion of inclusion at their heart.

Another enduring concern is that of social class equality in attainment. The issue featured in debates about standards in 2015, with the Conservative party education spokesperson noting on results day that 'The government must not lose sight of the fact that there is still a significant attainment gap between pupils from poorer and wealthier backgrounds' (The Scotsman, 2015). The issue was raised by all opposition parties at First Minister's Questions, and by members of the Education Committee in questioning the SQA's Chief Executive (Scottish Parliament, 2015a,b). A month after results day, the Scottish Government published the *Draft National Improvement Framework for Scottish education*, which set out four priorities for Scottish education, one of which is to close 'the attainment gap between the most and least disadvantaged children' (Scottish Government, 2015c, p. 8).

To summarise, introduction of the *Curriculum for Excellence* Higher examinations went well, with no systemic failure. Controversies related to lack of attainment for all, but more so to difficult questions on the mathematics paper. A small rise in overall attainment was welcomed by commentators, as is traditional and in keeping with the cultural position of the education and examination system in Scotland.

The meaning of standards in Scottish Highers

The Education (Scotland) Act (1996, p. 2), which established SQA, forefronted the notion of 'competence' in educational outcomes, giving SQA the right to,

    (a) determine what it is that a person is required to do and the level of competence he is required to demonstrate in order to attain the qualification;

    (b) determine the means of assessing whether he has done what is required or demonstrated the level of competence required.

Use of the word 'competence' is a signal that a criterion-referenced definition (Popham, 1971) of examination standards is in use. Such a definition encompasses the writing of statements regarding students' necessary examination performances for the award of certain

grades. Standard-setting methods which accompany such a definition are typically phenomenal (Newton, 2010a, 2010b), involving the judgment of artefacts such as question
papers and students' examination performances by examiners. SQA's standard-setting meetings focus upon the demands of the examination, with most emphasis being placed upon
whether the question paper and marking has functioned as intended (SQA, 2015b). This is
entirely consistent with a criterion-referencing approach, within a phenomenal definition
of standards. Additionally, it is in keeping with the media concern regarding difficulty of
questions.

The policy document describing the standard-setting procedure (SQA, 2015b) could apply
in large part to practices in Scotland or England. This is typical of such documents internationally, as they are written at a broad level for a national, educational, professional audience.
Scores required to be awarded particular grades are termed cut-scores (here 'cut-off scores')
or grade boundaries in SQA's nomenclature. The policy indicates that SQA ensures that the
cut-off scores set will reflect established standards by using the following sources of information, as appropriate to the qualification:

- performance/grade descriptions
- exemplar material
- the assessment and associated marking instructions
- candidate evidence
- statistical information (e.g. mark distributions, item statistics, cohort information)
- other relevant qualitative and/or quantitative information. (SQA, 2014, p. 10)

Statistical information is available in standard-setting meetings, but it is not forefronted. Of
course it would be a mistake to interpret the focus of meetings as a clear indication of the
prioritisation of information used in the decision-making process regarding standards and
therefore of the definition of standards in use. Preparation for the meeting or the cognitive
process of decision-making could prioritise different sources of evidence.

SQA's own published definition of standards is clearly a criterion-referenced, phenomenal
definition.

- Qualification standards are where we define the levels of knowledge and skills required to achieve
  a qualification. We apply these standards to evidence of learner achievement for the purpose of
  gauging if learners have achieved the requisite level of knowledge and skills (otherwise known
  as 'level of competence').
- Assessment standards are the levels of demand on learners (how difficult the assessment is
  for learners taking it) and what the assessment covers. (Retrieved from http://www.sqa.org.uk/
  sqa/74496.1559.html)

But while policy statements suggest that the definition in use is a phenomenal one, the
pattern of results suggests otherwise. If Scotland were truly using such a definition based
upon examiner judgments alone, then we would expect results to fluctuate, as forefronting
examiner judgement in standard-setting has this effect (Baird, 2007; Cresswell, 1997).
Fluctuations have not happened in Scotland, which means that statistics which are part of
the process (SQA, 2014, p. 10) *must* play more of a role than described in public
statements.

In fact, most national examination systems use both statistics and examiner judgment in
their standard-setting processes (Cizek & Bunch, 2007, p. 10). Lack of transparency regarding
how various sources of information are utilised in decision-making is also common. Baird
et al. (2000) argued that examining boards had to gauge the values of stakeholders in setting

standards and that the prioritisation of various sources of evidence was essentially subjective. In part, this was, they argued, due to the fact that no single source of evidence adequately captured the meaning of examination standards. Coming to an overall standards decision, utilising examiner judgment and statistical evidence, was termed 'weak criterion referencing' (Baird et al., 2000), though this approach has been renamed a number of times since (see Newton, 2010a). A better term is Newton's (2011) 'attainment referencing', which he defined as follows:

> Instead of judging students on the basis of their profile of attainment across sub-domains, in terms of clearly specified performance criteria, they are judged on the basis of their overall level of attainment in the curriculum area being examined. (Newton, 2011, p. 20)

Attainment-referencing embraces qualitative information about candidates' performances and statistical information. Although not forefronted in policy documents, statistics such as numbers sitting examinations in adjacent years, students' prior attainment, whether the schools entering students for the examinations are the same in both years, teachers' estimates of students' grades and so on, have played a role in standard-setting for Highers for some time (Elliot & Ganson, 1999; SQA, 2005). Whilst accepting that evidence, data and definitions are conceptually distinct, these sources of statistical information could not form part of a phenomenal definition of examination standards. They do not tell us about the features, dispositions or properties of students' attainments. Instead, they are related to causes of performances. We return to what this means for Newton's (2010a) categorisation scheme for examination standard definitions in the discussion section below. First, we contrast Scotland's conceptions and operation of national examination standards with those in England.

England's Advanced Level General Certificate of Education (GCE A-level)

England's A-levels were introduced in 1951, giving a single national examination system for university-entrance selection. At the time of writing there are three examination boards in England (AQA, OCR and Pearson), one in Wales (Eduquas) and one in Northern Ireland (the Council for the Curriculum, Examinations and Assessment). Each of these offers A-level examinations in England in a market.

Students choose from a wide range of subjects at A-level and are not constrained to particular subject combinations, except insofar as universities specify entrance criteria for particular courses. The A-level itself has been through several reforms over its history and is now being changed from a modular format to an end-of-course examination. Each subject is typically assessed through three written examination papers of two hour duration. A-levels are taken after a two year course, typically at age 18. Students normally need three A-levels for entrance to universities with an AAA requirement, or even the top A* grade for the most selective courses. Approximately 40% of the cohort take at least one A-level examination and 29% gain three A-levels.[4] Degrees are mainly three year programmes in England. Given the differences in the number of subjects taken and the duration of the courses, the comparison between Highers and A-levels is not straightforward. Qualifications frameworks[5] have been devised to help with drawing correspondences, but our purpose here is to compare conceptualisations of standards, so to a large extent differences between the examinations are moot.

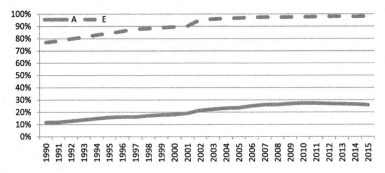

Figure 2. Proportion of A-level entries gaining grade E or above or grade A (or above from 2010). Source: Joint Council for Qualifications http://www.jcq.org.uk/examination-results/a-levels.

The English A-level examination system is less inclusive than Scottish Highers, with a lower proportion of the cohort entering the examinations. A-levels are graded A* to E, with an unclassified fail grade. Grade E is deemed a pass; the proportion of examination entries graded as passing has risen from 77% in 1990 to 98.1% in 2015 (Figure 2). The proportion of the cohort entered for the examination has also changed, alongside the expansion of participation in education more generally. The proportion of examination entries graded as an A or above has risen from 11.7% in 1990 to 25.9% in 2015. Note that the proportion of entries passing in A-level is higher than in Highers, due to the assignment of grade E as a pass (as opposed to grade C). However, the proportion of entries awarded a grade A is lower in England than in Scotland.

As noted above, A-level examinations are being reformed in response to a fear that standards are in decline (e.g. Coe, 2007b; Royal Society of Chemistry, 2008). The concern in England is that examination boards are competing commercially on the basis of standards, attracting customers by awarding grades more generously than competitors (House of Commons Education Committee, 2012). The prototypical media narrative in England on results day is that standards are in decline because examination results have gone up (Warmington & Murphy, 2004). Currently, culture (or at least, the media) in England seems to have an elitist stance regarding examinations, with their selective function being emphasised to a larger extent than in Scotland.

The meaning of standards in English A-levels

Examination boards set standards with reference to the regulator's *GCSE, GCE, Principal Learning and Project Code of Practice* (Ofqual, 2011). This list of 16 information sources is taken into account in standard-setting meetings, including qualitative and quantitative evidence and instructions from the regulators. At the time of writing, Ofqual is consulting on a replacement for this Code of Practice; the evidence that they propose to be included remains similar (Ofqual, 2015). Aside from the regulator's instructions, the list is similar to the kind of information used in Scottish standard-setting meetings. However, standard-setting meetings in Scotland typically involve a single examiner, whilst approximately 5–7 examiners are involved in standard-setting in England. This is more inclusive of a wider range of examiners' views.

There was a widespread belief that A-levels were norm-referenced in the past, meaning that no matter the quality of students' performances, a certain proportion were awarded each grade. As Newton (2011, p. 23) pointed out, norm-referencing does not fit into any of his categories (Newton 2010a,b). Norm-referencing requires a fourth category, that of 'competitive definitions', the underlying rationale being that grades are awarded on a competitive basis and testify to only a relative standard. However, the notion that A-levels were ever norm-referenced is a myth, as the outcomes data show (Newton, 2011). The misapprehension about how standards were set in the past flags the fact that it was under-conceptualised but also lacking in transparency.

Most of the time in A-level standard-setting meetings is spent on script scrutiny. This implies a phenomenal definition of examination standards. As with the Scottish system, much of the practice in England is derived from tradition, with the *Code of Practice* (Ofqual, 2011) changing incrementally. Standard-setting for A-levels in the 1990s was characterised by a predominance of the phenomenal definition and the prioritisation of evidence derived from examiners' expert judgments. However, problems with the precision of and biases in these judgments were found (Baird, 2000, 2007; Baird & Scharaschkin, 2002; Cresswell, 1996; Forster, 2005; Scharaschkin & Baird, 2000). This led to more emphasis upon statistical evidence in standard-setting.

The Joint Council for Qualifications (JCQ) is an umbrella association in which the examination boards work collaboratively to address industry-wide issues. With the added dimension of a requirement for common standards across examination boards, the JCQ and the regulator conducted a series of studies investigating inter-examination body standards (for a review see Elliott, 2011). These involved both qualitative and quantitative methods (see Newton, Baird, Goldstein, Patrick & Tymms, 2007 for a review). JCQ introduced a statistical comparison technique (Baird & Eason, 2004). The technique was based upon a methodology developed by Cresswell for AQA when the examination board was formed as a merger of the Associated Examining Board and the Northern Examinations and Assessment Board in 2000. AQA had to ensure that the standards were the same across the qualifications from each of the predecessor boards. Ofqual adopted and developed this technique for A-level from 2010 (Ofqual, 2014), terming it 'comparable outcomes' (following Cresswell, 2003). The method operationalises a causal definition of examination standards, as it predicts the outcomes for each syllabus on the basis of the candidates' prior attainment. The assumption is that, for syllabuses with a large number of candidates, the progress between examinations taken at age 16 and A-level outcomes is likely to be similar from one year to the next. Thus, it is now assumed in policy terms that there will be little change in the overall attainment at A-level from year to year and that is what we have seen in the statistics since 2010.

Systemically, there is a significant issue with joined-up government thinking with the adoption of a purely causal definition in England. Schools are subjected to accountability mechanisms with an expectation that they will improve the examination outcomes of their pupils. Given that the comparable outcomes policy constrains this, Ofqual has given consideration to their operation of the policy and to its formal definition of examination standards, which it states is attainment-referencing (Ofqual, 2014). Newton (2011) argued that attainment-referencing had always been in use, but more emphasis has been given to statistics over the past 20 years, and indeed Ofqual's position is that standards decisions should be formed by weighing all of the available evidence, both quantitative and qualitative, whilst recognising that the application of the comparable outcomes policy,

In practice … drives the final recommendations for grade boundary marks to be consistent with statistical predictions. (Ofqual, 2014)

Ofqual is grappling with the methodological issues in finding reliable indicators with sufficient precision to make confident claims of changes in outcomes between years.

Discussion

Although the literature is dominated by a curriculum-unrelated, psychometrics tradition, Newton (2010b) synthesised this with the curriculum-related literature on the meaning of examination standards published by scholars working within the English system. The current article has used Newton's (2010a,b) categorisation scheme for examination standards definitions as a basis for analysing the definitions used in practice for Scottish Highers and English A-levels. By applying the scheme to these cases, we have been able to conceptualise better the stated policy positions in each country. Further, the research literature on definitions and methods indicates patterns in outcomes that can be expected from the adoption of particular stances and has allowed us to evaluate critically whether the stated policy positions pertain in practice.

SQA has a phenomenal definition in many of its public policy statements about the meaning of standards in Higher examinations; with standards representing students' competences in the examination. This is in keeping with the wider cultural desire for inclusiveness and attainment for all in the education system. However, it is apparent from the outcomes data that the definition in use is not purely phenomenal, based upon a method of examiner judgment. Indeed, the fairness of purely phenomenal approaches has been questioned in the research literature because of its inconsistency (Baird, 2007; Cresswell, 1997). We conclude therefore that SQA has been operating an attainment-referencing approach, in which they have used both phenomenal and causal definitions. Such an approach will have made defence of standards more robust to challenges mounted from either of these definitions.

England has an explicit attainment-referencing definition for its A-levels, but the use of the comparable outcomes method implies that a causal definition is forefronted. Policy documents from the regulator discuss the tensions in finding precise and reliable methods for a more phenomenal approach (Ofqual, 2014).

Attainment-referencing might not be as publicly acceptable a standards definition in Scotland as in England. Use of statistics in the standard-setting process has its challenges in England: perhaps this would be seen as even more difficult in Scotland, but for different reasons. Scotland does not have the same accountability regime as England, but given the focus upon meritocracy, the prospect of statistical methods limiting students' attainment would be viewed negatively across the educational and political spectrum. Of course, statistical evidence does not have to constrain attainment as part of an attainment-referencing definition; it depends upon how the statistics are used in the decision-making.

Conclusion

Comparing the two systems has been enlightening, in the sense of Raffe's (2007) home–international comparison. At face value, the standard-setting processes for Scottish Highers and English A-levels appear similar, with the lists of evidence being taken into account looking the same. However, in contrasting these two cases, their different operations have been brought into better relief. In contrast to the English A-levels, the Scottish Highers have higher participation rates, there is wider cultural acceptance of rising outcomes and the standard-setting is positioned as being driven by examiner judgments of the demands of the question paper. Whilst it has been recognised that policy, politics, stakeholder values and wider culture influence standard-setting for national examinations (Baird, 2007; Baird et al., 2000; Cresswell, 1996; Wiliam, 1996), this has not been illustrated through the comparison of examination standards in two national settings previously. From our analysis, we conclude that despite the different cultural settings in these two countries in federal Britain, both systems adopt attainment-referencing definitions of standards for their main, high-stakes, university-entrance examinations. There are good reasons for this, as attainment-referencing attempts to carry forward a standard that represents what students know and can do, as well as maintaining stability of the system by considering what similar cohorts have achieved. Not only this, considering both sources of evidence means that an argument can be established for the validity of the standards with respect to potential challenges from phenomenal or causal definitional perspectives. Given this serious advantage, it would be interesting to extend the approach taken in this article to a wider range of examination systems to see whether other national examination systems adopt attainment-referencing definitions. Extension of the comparisons to other countries might challenge our thinking regarding the definition of examination standards further.

Atttainment-referencing strives for a culturally and politically acceptable definition of examination standards that is robust to challenges. Scotland and England have distinctive examination traditions, cultures and processes, yet both appear to be attainment-referencing. Different balances are struck, with Scotland's recent public policy statements appearing to be more phenomenal and England's recent policy appearing to be more causal. Acceptability of examination standards arguments differ radically in the two settings. The contexts of examination reforms in the two countries show how the interpretation of examination outcomes differs, and illuminates the different environments within which the examination boards are operating.

Our analysis was based upon Newton's (2010a,b) categorisation scheme for examination standards definitions, but we found that the definition in use was attainment-referencing in both cases. This raises theoretical matters. First, attainment-referencing is not easily classified using Newton's scheme because, as discussed above, by Newton (2011) and Ofqual (2014), phenomenal *and* causal evidence definitions are in operation in attainment-referencing. Tensions arising in practice from this situation were described in previous work (Baird, 2007). Concentrating on what it means for theory, attainment-referencing is a super ordinate category of examination standards definition, as it encompasses the phenomenal and causal definitional categories in the two cases presented here. Other forms of attainment-referencing might be evident in other countries and it is possible that other definitional categories and further superordinate categories would emerge from a wider consideration of countries.

Notes

1. We use the term standard-setting to include the annual process, which is sometimes termed maintenance, equating or linking.
2. Children can leave school in Scotland at ages 16, 17 or 18.

3. For example, see Robin (2014).
4. Calculated from Office for National Statistics figures and HEFCE (2015).
5. The Scottish Credit and Qualifications Framework (SCQF) http://www.scqf.org.uk/framework-diagram/Framework.htm and the Qualifications and Credit Framework (QCF). http://www.accreditedqualifications.org.uk/qualifications-and-credit-framework-qcf.html.

Disclosure statement

No potential conflict of interest was reported by the authors.

References

Association of Directors of Education in Scotland (ADES). (2015, 4 August). Directors welcome improving examination performance. Retrieved from https://adescotland.files.wordpress.com/2015/08/sqa-diet-2015.docx

Baird, J. (2000). Are examination standards all in the head? Experiments with examiners' judgments of standards in A-level examinations. *Research in Education, 64*, 91–100.

Baird, J. (2007). Alternative conceptions of comparability. In P. E. Newton, J. Baird, H. Goldstein, H. Patrick, & P. Tymms (Eds.), *Techniques for monitoring the comparability of examination standards* (pp. 124–156). London: Qualifications and Curriculum Authority.

Baird, J. (2010). What constitutes legitimate causal linking? *Measurement: Interdisciplinary Research and Perspectives, 8*, 151–153. doi: http://dx.doi.org/10.1080/15366361003748219.

Baird, J., & Coxell, A. W. (2009). Policy, latent error and systemic examination failures. *CADMO, 21*, 105–122.

Baird, J., & Eason, T. (2004). *Statistical screening procedures to investigate inter-awarding body comparability in GCE, VCE, GCSE, Applied GCSE and GCSE short courses*. AQA. Retrieved from P. E. Newton, J. Baird, H. Goldstein, H. Patrick, & P. Tymms (eds.), *Techniques for monitoring the comparability of examination standards*. London: Qualifications and Curriculum Authority.

Baird, J., Cresswell, M. J., & Newton, P. E. (2000). Would the real gold standard please step forward? *Research Papers in Education, 15*, 213–229.

Baird, J., & Scharaschkin, A. (2002). Is the whole worth more than the sum of the parts? Studies of examiners' grading of individual papers and candidates' whole A-level examination performances. *Educational Studies, 28*, 143–162.

Borsboom, D. (2005). *Measuring the mind: Conceptual issues in contemporary psychometrics*. Cambridge: Cambridge University Press.

Bryce, T., & Humes, W. (2013). The Scottish Qualifications Authority. In T. Bryce, W. Humes, D. Gillies, & A. Kennedy (eds.), *Scottish Education: Fourth edition: Referendum*. Edinburgh: Edinburgh University Press.

Child Poverty Action Group. (2014). *Percentage of children living in poverty in Scotland*. Retrieved from http://www.cpag.org.uk/content/percentage-children-living-poverty-scotland

Christie, T., & Forrest, G. M. (1981). *Defining public examination standards (Schools council research studies)*. London: Macmillan Education.

Cizek, G. J., & Bunch, M. B. (2007). *Standard setting. A guide to establishing and evaluating performance standards on tests*. California: Sage.

Coe, R. (1999). *Changes in examination grades over time: Is the same worth less? Paper presented at the annual conference of the British Educational Research Association, September 2–5*. Brighton: University of Sussex.

Coe, R. (2007a). Common examinee methods. In P. E. Newton, J. Baird, H. Goldstein, H. Patrick, & P. Tymms (Eds.), *Techniques for monitoring the comparability of examination standards* (pp. 331–367). London: Qualifications and Curriculum Authority.

Coe, R. (2007b). Changes in standards at GCSE and A-level: Evidence from ALIS and YELLIS (Report for the Office for National Statistics, April). Retrieved from http://www.cem.org/attachments/ONS%20 report%20on%20changes%20at%20GCSE%20and%20A-level.pdf.

Coe, R. (2010). Understanding comparability of examination standards. *Research Papers in Education, 25*, 271–284.

Cresswell, M. J. (1996). Defining, setting and maintaining standards in curriculum-embedded examinations: Judgemental and statistical approaches. In H. Goldstein & T. Lewis (Eds.), *Assessment: Problems, developments and statistical issues* (pp. 57–84). Chichester: John Wiley.

Cresswell, M. J. (1997). Examining judgments: Theory and practice of awarding public examination grades. Unpublished PhD thesis, University of London Institute of Education.

Cresswell, M. J. (2003). *Heaps, prototypes and ethics: The consequences of using judgements of student performance to set examination standards in a time of change*. London: Institute of Education.

Creswell, J. W., & Miller, D. L. (2000). Determining validity in qualitative inquiry. *Theory into Practice, 39*, 124–130. doi:http://dx.doi.org/10.1207/s15430421tip3903_2.

Cronbach, L. & Meehl, P. E. (1955). Construct validity in psychological tests. *Psychological Bulletin, 52*, 281–302.

Davie, G. (1961 [3rd edn. 2013]). *The democratic intellect, Scotland and her universities in the nineteenth century*. Edinburgh: Edinburgh University Press.

Deloitte & Touche (2000). *Scottish Executive*. Retrieved from http://www.scotland.gov.uk/library3/education/sqar-00.asp

Educational Institute of Scotland (2015) Scottish Exam Results – Pupils and Teachers should be praised. Retrieved from http://www.eis.org.uk/public.asp?id=2715

Elliot, D., & Ganson, H. (1999). *SEB findings on Scottish achievements. In Scottish Education*. Edinburgh: Edinburgh University Press.

Elliott, G. (2011). 100 years of controversy over standards: An enduring problem. *Research Matters*. Special Issue 2: Comparability, 3–8.

Finn, M. E. (1983). Social efficiency progressivism and secondary education in Scotland, 1885–1905. In W. Humes & H. M. Paterson (Eds.), *Scottish culture and Scottish education* (pp. 175–196). Edinburgh: John Donald.

Forster, M. (2005). *Can examiners successfully distinguish between scripts that vary by only a small range on marks? Unpublished internal paper*. Cambridge: Oxford Cambridge and RSA Examinations.

Gray, J., McPherson, A. F., & Raffe, D. (1983). *Reconstructions of secondary education: Theory, myth and practice since the War*. London: Routledge & Kegan Paul.

Hayward, L. (2007). Curriculum, pedagogies and assessment in Scotland: The quest for social justice. 'Ah kent yir faither'. *Assessment in Education: Principles, Policy & Practice, 14*, 251–268.

Hayward, L. (2015). Assessment is Learning: The preposition vanishes. *Assessment in Education: Principles, Policy & Practice, 22*, 27–43.

Hayward, L., & Hutchison, C. (2013). 'Exactly what do you mean by consistency?' Exploring concepts of consistency and standards in Curriculum for Excellence in Scotland. *Assessment in Education: Principles, Policy & Practice, 20*, 53–68.

HEFCE. (2015). *Young participation in higher education. A-levels and similar qualifications.* Higher Education Funding Council for England. http://www.hefce.ac.uk/media/hefce/content/pubs/2015/201503/HEFE2015_03.pdf.

House of Commons Education Committee. (2012). *The administration of examinations for 15–19 year olds in England. First Report of Session 2012–2013. Volume 1.*

Humes, W. (2013). Policy making in Scottish education. In T. Bryce et al. (eds.), *Scottish Education: Fourth edition: Referendum* (pp. 98–108). Edinburgh: Edinburgh University Press.

Humes, W., & Bryce, T. (2013). The distinctiveness of Scottish education. In T. Bryce et al. (eds.), *Scottish Education: Fourth edition: Referendum* (pp. 138–152). Edinburgh: Edinburgh University Press.

Knox, J. (1561). *The first book of discipline.* Presbyterian Heritage Publications. Retrieved from: http://www.swrb.com/newslett/actualNLs/bod_ch00.htm

McPherson, H. M. (1983). An angel on the geist: Persistence and change in the Scottish educational tradition. In W. Humes & H. M. Paterson (Eds.), *Scottish culture and Scottish education* (pp. 216–243). Edinburgh: John Donald.

McVittie, J. (2008). *National qualifications: A short history. SQA Policy and New Products Research Report 3.* Retrieved from http://www.sqa.org.uk/files_ccc/PNP_ResearchReport3_NationalQualificationsAShortHistory.pdf

Newton, P. E. (1997a). Examining standards over time. *Research Papers in Education, 12*, 227–248.

Newton, P. E. (1997b). Measuring comparability of standards between subjects: Why our statistical techniques do not make the grade. *British Educational Research Journal, 23*, 433–449.

Newton, P. E. (2003). *Contrasting definitions of comparability.* Paper presented at the QCA Standards and Comparability Seminar, April 3–4, Milton Keynes.

Newton, P. E. (2005). Examination standards and the limits of linking. *Assessment in Education: Principles, Policy & Practice, 12*, 105–123.

Newton, Paul E. (2010a). Contrasting conceptions of comparability. *Research Papers in Education, 25*, 285–292.

Newton, P. E. (2010b). Thinking about linking. *Measurement: Interdisciplinary Research and Perspectives, 8*, 38–56.

Newton, P. E. (2011). A level pass rates and the enduring myth of norm-referencing. *Research Matters.* Special Issue 2: Comparability, 20–23.

Newton, P. E., Baird, J., Goldstein, H., Patrick, H., & Tymms, P. (2007). *Techniques for monitoring the comparability of examination standards.* London: Qualifications and Curriculum Authority.

OECD. (2007, 11 December). *Reviews of national policies for education: Quality and equity of schooling in Scotland.* Paris: OECD. Retrieved from http://www.oecd.org/edu/school/reviewsofnationalpolici esforeducation-qualityandequityofschoolinginscotland.htm

Ofqual. (2011, May). *GCSE, GCE, principal learning and project code of practice.* Retrieved from https://www.gov.uk/government/uploads/system/uploads/attachment_data/file/371268/2011-05-27-code-of-practice.pdf

Ofqual. (2014). *Setting GCSE, AS and A Level grade standards in summer 2014 and 2015.* Ofqual/15/5759. Retrieved from https://www.gov.uk/government/uploads/system/uploads/attachment_data/file/451321/2015-08-05-summer-series-gcse-as-and-a-level-grade-standards.pdf

Ofqual. (2015). *Consultation on: Improving Reviews and Appeals of GCSE, AS and A level Marking; Withdrawing the GCSE, GCE, Principal Learning and Project Code of Practice; New Requirement on Setting BCSE, AS and A level Grade Boundaries.* Ofqual/15/5807. Retrieved from https://www.gov.uk/government/uploads/system/uploads/attachment_data/file/484076/Consultation_on_marking_reviews__appeals__grade_boundaries_and_Code_of_Practice.pdf

Paterson, H. M. (1983). Incubus and ideology: The development of secondary schooling in Scotland. In W. Humes & H. M. Paterson (Eds.), *Scottish culture and Scottish education* (pp. 1900–1939). Edinburgh: John Donald.

Paterson, L. (2003). *Scottish education in the twentieth century.* Edinburgh: Edinburgh University Press.

Paterson, L., & Iannelli, C. (2007). Social class and educational attainment: A comparative study of England, Wales and Scotland. *Sociology of Education, 80*, 330–358.

Philip, H. L. (1992). *The higher tradition: A history of public examinations in Scottish schools and how they influenced the development of secondary education* Dalkeith: Scottish Examination Board.

Popham, J. (Ed.). (1971). *Criterion-referenced measurement. An introduction*. Englewood Cliffs, NJ: Educational Technology Publications.

Raffe, D. (2007). *Learning from home–international comparisons: 14–19 policy across the United Kingdom*. In D. Raffe, & K. Spours, *Policy-making and policy learning in 14–19 education* (pp. 133–156). London Bedford Way Papers.

Robin, G. (2014). *University of Glasgow Curriculum for Excellence statement*. University of Glasgow. Retrieved from http://www.gla.ac.uk/media/media_273068_en.pdf

Royal Society of Chemistry. (2008, November). *The five-decade challenge. A wake-up call for UK Science Education?* Retrieved from http://www.rsc.org/images/ExamReport_tcm18-139067.pdf

The Scotsman. (2015, 4 August). Attainment gap fears over new and old Higher exams. *The Scotsman* online. Retrieved from http://www.scotsman.com/news/education/attainment-gap-fears-over-new-and-old-higher-exams-1-3848562

Scottish Executive. (2003). *Educating for excellence: Choice and opportunity*. The Executive's Response to the National Debate. Edinburgh. Retrieved from http://www.gov.scot/Publications/2003/01/16226/17177

Scottish Executive. (2004). *A Curriculum for Excellence*. Edinburgh. Retrieved from http://www.gov.scot/Publications/2004/11/20178/45862

Scottish Executive. (2008). *A consultation on the next generation of national qualifications in Scotland*. Edinburgh. Retrieved from http://www.gov.scot/Resource/Doc/226233/0061255.pdf

The Scottish Government. (2014). *Poverty and income inequality in Scotland: 2012/13*. National Statistics Publication. Retrieved from http://www.gov.scot/Resource/0045/00454875.pdf

The Scottish Government. (2015a, June). *A draft national improvement framework for Scottish education*. Retrieved from http://www.gov.scot/Publications/2015/09/7802/2

The Scottish Government. (2015b, June). *High level summary statistics. School education*. Retrieved from http://www.gov.scot/Resource/0048/00480271.pdf

The Scottish Government. (2015c). *Attainment and leaver destinations supplementary data*. Retrieved from http://www.gov.scot/Topics/Statistics/Browse/School-Education/leavedestla/follleavedestat/attainmentandleavers1314

The Scottish Government. (2015d). *Results day for students*. Retrieved from http://news.scotland.gov.uk/News/Results-day-for-students-1ba7.aspx

The Scottish Office. (1994). *Higher still: Opportunity for all*. Edinburgh: HMSO.

Scottish Parliament. (2015a). *Official report: Meeting of the Parliament 28 May 2015. Scottish Parliament*. Retrieved from http://www.scottish.parliament.uk/parliamentarybusiness/report.aspx?r=9973

Scottish Parliament. (2015b). *Education and Culture Committee 22 September 2015*. Retrieved from http://www.scottish.parliament.uk/parliamentarybusiness/report.aspx?r=10111

Scottish Qualifications Authority. (2005) The Scottish Standard: a Guide to Pass Mark Meetings for National Courses. Retrieved from http://www.sqa.org.uk/files_ccc/TheScottishStandard.pdf.

Scottish Qualifications Authority (SQA). (2013). *Assessment in the new national courses and units*. Retrieved from http://www.sqa.org.uk/sqa/files_ccc/Assessment_in_the_new_National_Courses_and_Units.pdf

Scottish Qualifications Authority. (2014). *SQA Awarding Body Code of Practice*. http://www.sqa.org.uk/files_ccc/SQA_Awarding_Body_Code_of_Practice.pdf. Publication Code: FA6723.

Scottish Qualifications Authority. (2015a). *Results for national courses and awards*. Retrieved from http://www.sqa.org.uk/sqa/74832.html

Scottish Qualifications Authority. (2015b). *A guide to grade boundary setting*. Retrieved from https://www.sqa.org.uk/sqa/files_ccc/A_Guide_to_Setting_Grade_Boundaries.pdf

Scottish Qualifications Authority. (u.d.). *Design principles for national courses*. Retrieved from http://www.sqa.org.uk/files_ccc/DesignPrinciplesNationalCourses.pdf

Scharaschkin, A., & Baird, J. (2000). The effects of consistency of performance on A level examiners' judgements of standards. *British Educational Research Journal, 26*, 343–357.

Sikes, P., & Potts, A. (2008). *Researching education from the inside. Investigations from within*. Abingdon: Routledge.

Social Mobility and Child Poverty Commission. (2014, October). *State of the Nation 2014: Social mobility and child poverty in Great Britain*. Presented to Parliament pursuant to section 8B(6) of the Child Poverty Act 2010.

The Telegraph. (2015a, 4 August). Questions over higher Scottish exam pass rate. The Telegraph online. Retrieved from http://www.telegraph.co.uk/education/secondaryeducation/11781251/Questions-over-higher-Scottish-exam-pass-rate.html

The Telegraph. (2015b, 9 October). Can you answer the tricky crocodile maths question, that left students 'in tears'. Retrieved from http://www.telegraph.co.uk/education/educationnews/11921671/Can-you-answer-the-tricky-crocodile-maths-question-that-left-students-in-tears.html

Warmington, P., & Murphy, R. (2004). Could do better? Media depictions of UK educational assessment results. *Journal of Education Policy, 19,* 285–299.

Wiliam, D. (1996). Standards in examinations: A matter of trust? *The Curriculum Journal, 7,* 293–306.

The politics of education and the misrecognition of Wales

Sally Power

ABSTRACT
This paper examines the positioning of the Welsh education system within contemporary policy debate and analysis. It begins by outlining some of the ways in which education policy and provision in Wales differs from that of its neighbour, England, and then goes on to critique how these differences have been represented in both the media and by members of the educational research community. Indeed, the paper argues that these representations constitute a form of misrecognition. It is tempting to counter this misrecognition with assertions of the superiority of the 'Welsh way'—and certainly pronouncements of a 'crisis' in Welsh education appear to be as much politically-driven as evidence-based. However, such an approach would underplay the very real challenges that face Wales—challenges which are both like and unlike those facing England, Scotland and Northern Ireland. The paper concludes that we need a serious engagement with national divergences across the four nations of the UK—as well as elsewhere. The case of Wales highlights the need to undertake not only comparative analysis but also *relational* analysis if we are to enhance our understanding of the changing politics of education.

Introduction

Education in Wales has long been the site of political struggle. Over the centuries, there have been ongoing confrontations, particularly around religion and language, as Wales was governed by administrations in London whose principal concerns were with England (Jones & Roderick, 2003). Not only did those in Westminster take little account of the differences between England and Wales, but after the electoral victory of Margaret Thatcher's Conservative Party in 1979, the Welsh found themselves subjected to reforms by a political party which had only ever received minority support in Wales.

In 1997, the people of Wales voted in favour of political devolution. As a result, the National Assembly for Wales was established in 1999 and given responsibility for the governance of key areas of policy, including health and education. It was therefore not surprising that the newly-formed Welsh Government sought to distance itself from the neoliberal politics which had characterised successive London-based governments, not only the new right agenda of Margaret Thatcher, but also the 'third way' New Labourism of Tony Blair. In 2002, Rhodri

Table 1. The 'clear red water' of contrasting policy discourses.

Wales	England
Good government is good for you	Government control should be minimal
Progressivism	Cultural restoration
Universalism	Diversification
Cooperation is better than competition	Competition is necessary to drive standards
Trust professionals	Challenge professionals
Ethic of participation	Ethic of consumerism
Greater equality of outcome	Greater equality of opportunity

Morgan, the First Minister, made his now famous 'clear red water' speech which outlined the different approach that Wales would take:

> Our commitment to equality leads directly to a model of the relationship between the government and the individual which regards that individual as a citizen rather than as a consumer. Approaches which prioritise choice over equality of outcome rest, in the end, upon a market approach to public services, in which individual economic actors pursue their own best interests with little regard for wider considerations. (Morgan, 2002)

These wider considerations have usually involved the pursuit of greater social justice. Drakeford (2007), former advisor to Rhodri Morgan and now Assembly Member and Minister, argues that the Welsh commitment to social justice is based on a series of core principles which include a belief that 'good government is good for you', a commitment to progressive universalism, high rather than low trust, a strong ethic of participation and a commitment to ensuring greater equality of outcome. Table 1 outlines, albeit somewhat crudely, some of the contrasts between the dominant political discourses in Wales and England in recent decades.

Even before parliamentary devolution, when Wales was subject to the same policy regimes and legislative measures as England, the Welsh political and cultural context gave Welsh education a distinctive complexion. Since devolution, this distinctiveness has become ever more apparent, as is evident in some of the key policies outlined in the next section.[1]

Good government is good for you

The Welsh starting point that 'good government is good for you' stands in stark contrast to the ideologies underpinning England's public sector reforms. Since the 1980s, education policies in England have been driven by an assumption that the notion of good government is oxymoronic and that, in general, government is 'bad for you'. Successive neoliberal administrations have tried to lessen what they saw as the 'dead hand of the state' on schools, teachers and parents and reduce the power of what were sometimes referred to as 'local education monopolies' (Flew, 1991). In England, the capacity of local authorities to redistribute resources and target areas of need has been significantly weakened as almost all funding is now devolved directly to schools. Conservative governments have sought to remove state-maintained schools from the control of their local authorities entirely through encouraging schools to operate independently of local government. Indeed, a significant number of local authorities in England have had their education services privatised.

Even before devolution, local authorities in Wales were seen as integral to the governance and administration of education. The Grant-Maintained (GM) Schools policy, ushered in with the National Curriculum as part of the 1988 Education Reform Act, applied to both England

and Wales. But only very few schools in Wales (less than 1.5% of the total number of GM schools) elected to 'opt out' of local authority control. And while schools in Wales have been given responsibility for budgets, a significant proportion of funding is still retained at local authority level to provide a range of supplementary services. In 2011, 90% of the total school budget was delegated directly to schools in England. In Wales, the figure was only 70%.[2] Furthermore, since parliamentary devolution, Wales has not sought to weaken the principle of local authority control either through privatisation or through encouraging schools to operate independently. Even where local authorities have been assessed by Estyn to be unsatisfactory, the solution is not seen to reside in *reducing* government control but rather in *strengthening* it.[3]

Progressivism

Over the last few decades, English education policy has increasingly been characterised by a need to return to the past, while the Welsh Government has upheld the virtues of progressivism. The contrasting orientations to traditionalism and progressivism can be seen in the extent to which England and Wales have developed different curricular and assessment regimes. As already mentioned, the 1988 Education Reform Act which ushered in the National Curriculum applied to both England and Wales—but the ways in which it was interpreted and implemented were subtly different in each context. In England, the National Curriculum can be seen as the start of a project of cultural restoration—celebrating 'English' culture and the 'curriculum of the dead' (Ball, 1993). In Wales, the project took a different direction—characterised by 'a democratic spin with an orientation towards a wider Europeanism' (Phillips & Sanders, 2000, p. 15).

In the years since parliamentary devolution, the gap between Wales's progressivism and England's restorationism has continued to widen. One of the clearest examples of this gap is early years education. In England, the former education minister, Michael Gove, vilified the 'progressive betrayal' of children and initiated a 'back to basics' curriculum for young learners (Gove, 2013). In Wales, the Foundation Phase programme, discussed by Chris Taylor in this issue, is unashamedly 'progressive' in orientation. Inspired by movements in Italy and Scandinavia that are based on the principles of child-centred education, the Foundation Phase is designed to offer children a 'rich curriculum' with a central focus on wellbeing (Aasen & Waters, 2006; Maynard et al., 2013). Even more fundamental differences are likely to emerge as a result of the recently published Donaldson Report on curriculum and assessment. The Report, *Successful Futures* (Welsh Government, 2015), recommends the thorough-going re-organisation of the curriculum into 'areas of learning and experience': the expressive arts; health and wellbeing; humanities; languages, literacy and communication; mathematics and numeracy; and science and technology. If these recommendations are fully implemented, we will see the erosion of traditional subject boundaries at secondary school level. The reforms will bring Wales further in line with Scandinavian-style arrangements and even further out-of-step with what is happening in England.

Associated with the moves towards a more progressive curriculum have been other changes in assessment. In general there is far less standardised testing in Wales than in England. In 2006 the Welsh Government abandoned many of the tests introduced as part of the 1988 Education Reform Act. Standardised assessment tests (SATs) for seven-year-olds were dropped in 2001 and those for 11 and 14-year-olds in 2004. In the words of the former education minister, Jane Davidson, it was important for Wales to move away from a system where 'each student was just a statistic' (Archer, 2008). In terms of the debates around standards in assessment, the English administration has tried to eliminate coursework from GCSE and A levels entirely, while Wales has continued to see coursework as a valuable component. The Welsh Baccalaureate, like the Foundation Phase, assesses self-directed learning through individual projects.

Universalism

In 2001, Alistair Campbell (2007), Tony Blair's Director of Communications, announced that 'the day of the bog-standard comprehensive school is over'. Based on the assumption that uniformity implies mediocrity, New Labour and Conservative administrations have encouraged the diversification of schools in England to the extent that it is now difficult to talk of an education 'system' at all. Wales, on the other hand, has continued to uphold the virtues of a comprehensive education system. Indeed Britain's first comprehensive school (Ysgol Uwchradd Caergybi) was opened in Wales in 1949. Speaking in 2013, the Welsh Minister for Education and Skills, Huw Lewis, reaffirmed his belief: 'in the worth and the potential of community-based, comprehensive education', adding that 'in their bones this is the way the Welsh people want things to be' (Lewis, 2013).

Unlike in England, where grammar schools continue to exist (and even expand), Wales has no academic selection by ability on entry to state-maintained secondary schools. Neither does Wales have the range of specialist schools nor academies which have mushroomed in England and which attract and select pupils on the basis of aptitude (Coldron, Willis & Wolstenholme, 2009). The only form of differentiation of schools within the state-maintained sector in Wales relates to the medium of instruction. Currently, over one fifth (22%) of seven-year-olds are taught in the medium of Welsh (Welsh Government, 2013). There is some fall-off in numbers as children progress to secondary education—where less than one fifth (17%) are assessed in Welsh as a first language at Year 9. However, there are no selective admissions procedures for these schools and the Welsh Government is committed to providing Welsh medium instruction for every parent that wishes it for their child. The lack of desire for either selective or specialist provision is evident in the very small number of private schools in Wales. In England, over 7% of pupils attend private schools. In Wales, the proportion stands at less than 2%.

Cooperation is better than competition

The explicit rejection of consumerism in the 'Clear Red Water' speech can be seen in the Welsh Government's attempt to reduce rather than heighten competition between schools. With reference to what is happening in England, Huw Lewis (2013), the Education Minister, commented:

> I want a Welsh educational system where we do not have the phenomenon that is starting to play out across the border in England where schools compete for the 'best' students, whatever they are, or they play the qualifications game between exam boards … to improve their public standing.

The Welsh Government does not publish primary and secondary school performance data through which 'league tables' can be compiled. There is currently a colour-coded 'national school categorisation system' which ranks primary and secondary schools. However, this categorisation is based on a range of hard and soft measures (including self-evaluation) and is designed to reflect a school's capacity to improve rather than simple attainment levels. It would certainly provide no simple yardstick on which to base school choice.

High trust rather than low trust

Relatedly, the Welsh Government claims that its relationships with education providers are based on collaboration rather than mistrust. The Government has traditionally worked *with* teachers—eschewing some of the more hostile portrayals of the teaching profession and the 'education establishment' which can be found in England (most famously characterised by Michael Gove as the 'blob'). For example, the former Minister for Education, Jane Davidson, is reported to have met with the teaching unions individually—as well as together—twice each year (Evans, 2015). More recently, Huw Lewis claims that the close relationships with teachers avoided strike action:

> …respect through dialogue and negotiation—an open door and a willingness to listen and so Wales has avoided what England is suffering this autumn in terms of a teacher dispute. It is not rocket science to hold on to a sense of respect and a willingness to listen. (Lewis, 2013)

Ethic of participation

It is not only dialogue with professionals which is sought after. Wales was the first, and remains the only, country in the UK to make school councils mandatory. The Schools Councils (Wales) Regulations introduced in 2005 require all schools to establish a council which will be convened at least six times each year and will enable pupils to discuss matters relating to their school, their education and any other matters of concern to them. Although Estyn inspections (2008) and other research (Farrell, 2010) indicate that these councils may not always be as effective or as participatory as many would like, they do provide a symbol of participatory democracy. In addition, pupils are routinely invited to contribute to policy consultations. For example, the recent consultation undertaken as part of the Donaldson Review elicited over 350 individual responses from school pupils. The Children's Commissioner recently undertook a major national survey called 'What Next?' inviting children to highlight issues which might help determine the key areas of work.

Greater equality of outcome

Finally, the Welsh education policy agenda emphasises the importance of reducing educational inequalities. The relationship between poverty and attainment is as strong in Wales as elsewhere, but the Welsh Government has tried to put in place measures to ameliorate the worst effects of poverty. Tackling the impact of poverty on attainment is Wales's 'top priority' (Lewis, 2013). In order to help more disadvantaged pupils, Wales has retained some of the targeted funding, such as the Educational Maintenance Allowance (a means-tested bursary provided for those from poorer backgrounds to stay in education after the leaving age of 16), which England has abandoned. Similarly, at higher education level, Wales has tried to soften the impact of raised tuition fees through subsidising the fees of

Welsh-domiciled students, avoiding the payment of up-front fees through making loans available and providing a wide range of means-assessed grants for those from poorer backgrounds.

Of course England is also concerned to minimise the impact of social background on attainment, but the discourse there tends to focus on equality of *opportunity*. In Wales, the emphasis is much more in equality of *outcome*. Huw Lewis claims: 'My ambition then, is to eradicate inequalities in learner outcomes' (Welsh Government, 2014, p. 4).

The representation of Wales: a case of misrecognition?

In spite of—or most probably because of—this growing divergence between England and Wales, developments in the Welsh education system have either been largely overlooked or derided. Indeed, it is possible to argue that Wales suffers the injustice of misrecognition. Fraser (1997) argues that misrecognition occurs when peoples or practices are rendered invisible (non-recognition), routinely derided and/or subject to cultural domination. Each of these dimensions can be found in the way in which Welsh education policy and provision features in current debates and analysis.

Non-recognition

Wales is often rendered largely invisible in media and academic coverage of education policy and practice. Most UK-wide newspapers make two common errors in their coverage of education. One is to not make any reference to the country to which the article relates—because it is just assumed it is England. The other is to lump England and Wales together as if they were a single polity. More surprising, though, is the relative neglect of Wales in academic writing on education policy.

Over 20 years ago, Phillips (1995, p. 103) commented that within the growing field of education policy sociology there was 'a tendency to avoid the Welsh agenda', noting that 'virtually no reference is made either to the Welsh education policy initiatives or to the unique debates over cultural expression'. It might have been thought that the subsequent emergence of even greater divergence within the UK as a result of parliamentary devolution would attract some attention. However, in general, post-devolution reform continues to be ignored by the field. An examination of education policy textbooks published recently shows that, with the commendable exception of Stephen Ball's (2013) *The Education Debate* (which is explicit about the use of 'England' and 'English' at the outset and recognises that there are significant differences between English education policy and what is happening elsewhere in the UK), Wales continues to be overlooked. Chris Chapman and Helen Gunter's (2008) edited collection *Radical Reforms: public policy and a decade of educational reform* contains no reference either to Wales or to Scotland—nor does it mention democratic devolution amongst its list of significant New Labour reforms. Abbott, Rathbone and Whitehead's (2012) *Education Policy* also makes no reference at all to devolution and does not acknowledge that the contents refer only to England.

In addition to overlooking Wales, there is a tendency to lump the two countries together—and nearly always with the assumption that what happens in England must also apply to Wales. As we have seen, even before parliamentary devolution, such an assumption was problematic and ignored the significant differences between the two nations. After devolution, eliding Wales with England is even more misguided. For example, a recent collection of essays published by Demos (Wood & Scott, 2014) claims to be about 'the education system in England and Wales' even though the contents only relate to policies and research in England. This is particularly disheartening given that Demos is an organisation which claims to be 'at the centre of policy debates'. Similarly, Paul Adam's (2014) textbook *Policy and Education* refers sometimes to the UK and sometimes to England without any precision. Students are given no indication that the book really only applies to England and that the policies discussed have no remit in Wales, Scotland or Northern Ireland.

Derision

Over the last five years, where Wales has come into the spotlight it is almost always cast in a negative light, as the following selection of headlines demonstrates:

Pisa tests show pupils in Wales falling behind (BBC News 7/12/10)

Wales worst in UK for global education rankings (Daily Post 3/12/13)

School standards in Wales 'causing concern' (The Guardian 29/1/13)

I have seen the Labour future and it doesn't work. It's called Wales (The Daily Telegraph 6/12/13)

The policies that have wrecked Wales – coming soon to a Miliband government near you (The Spectator 11/7/14)

As can be seen from the last two headlines, the judgments have a party political dimension. Speaking in 2012, Michael Gove, then England's Secretary of State for Education, told the House of Commons:

…it grieves me that the Welsh education system went backwards under Labour, and it grieves me even more that every objective assessment of what has happened under Labour in Wales shows that education has improved more quickly and effectively in England than in Wales. (Gove, 2012)

A year later in December 2013, Gove warned voters in England that 'you need only look over the Severn to see a country going backwards.' In 2014 he referred to Wales as 'an object lesson' in what happens when you abandon reform—claiming that 'This decline is traceable directly to the Labour Party's refusal to embrace reforms we've been pursuing in England. In fifteen years not a single academy or free school has opened in Wales'. In the run-up to the 2015 UK General Election, the Conservative-led coalition rarely seemed to miss an opportunity to pass negative judgement on what was going on in Wales to the extent that many Welsh politicians claimed that they had launched a 'War on Wales' (e.g. Williamson, 2014).

In some ways it is not surprising that those on the right in England should seek to gain political mileage out of maligning the more left-wing Welsh Government. Rees (2012) notes that there has been an interesting shift in perception in recent times from largely positive views of Wales' education reforms in the first few years of devolution to the current portrayal of these same reforms as being little short of disastrous. This shift may be less about the changing fortunes of the Welsh education system and rather more about the changing political climate in England. A Conservative-dominated coalition was hardly likely to view developments in Wales with a sympathetic eye. Michael Gove, known to be a keen supporter of private education, traditional teaching methods and a narrowly academic curriculum, could hardly be expected to warm to a system based on progressivism and a commitment to comprehensive schooling and a broad-based curriculum.

However, the discourse of derision is not only about party politics but reflects a more fundamental cultural domination of Wales by its larger neighbour. There are several dimensions to this. One simply relates to scale. It is not surprising that most media coverage and academic analysis of education policy refers to England, simply because that is where the greater number of readers are to be found. However, it is not only about numbers. England is much larger and more economically and politically powerful than Wales. It is English priorities which dominate, with the agendas of Wales and the other small home nations being largely by-passed. The inequality between the nations is clearly illustrated in Leighton Andrews' (2014) account of the debacle around the re-grading of English GCSE assessments in the summer of 2012. Andrews, who was then Minister for Education, outlines the disrespect with which Wales and Northern Ireland were treated by the English regulatory agency, Ofqual, and Conservative politicians. His successor comments on how the Westminster-based government's approach to Wales reveals 'the seemingly indestructible colonial attitudes buried in the dark heart of the Conservative Party in England' (Lewis, 2014).

The dominance of England, coupled with the almost hegemonic hold that neoliberalism enjoys over education policy in Anglophone countries (Rizvi & Lingard, 2009), gives the impression that to take an alternative path is nothing less than perverse. For example, Reynolds argues that what he calls the 'producerism' of Wales goes against the grain of 'policies seen as axiomatic internationally' (2008, p. 754). He claims that rather than being based on evidence, Welsh reforms have been driven instead by 'hostility to the English policies ... marked by a principle of not doing what England did' (2008, p. 756). In a similar vein, Prowle (2012) in an article headlined 'Bottom of the Class' asserts that 'Welsh collaboration gets poorer results than English competition.' He goes on to advise us that:

> Wales must be careful of dismissing initiatives from England on the basis of political ideology or nationalistic pride and instead consider their effectiveness on the evidence available.

Both Reynolds and Prowle imply that Wales has somehow diverged from a steady reform course being ploughed in England. In reality, the continuities with the past are much stronger in Wales than they are in England. It is possible that the growing gap between England and Wales may be explained less by Wales's 'deviation' from some internationally accepted norm and rather more by the distinctive and ideologically narrow policy path which England is pursuing. What both Reynolds and Prowle also ignore is the significant amount of doubt and debate about the efficacy of market-led reforms in education—and their rejection by governments of some of the highest performing countries. Both Reynolds and Prowle overlook the fact that Welsh reforms *do* have an evidence base. The Foundation Phase, for example, is based on the Scandinavian model which is widely acclaimed as one of the most successful models of early childhood education.

A politics of recognition for Wales?

If it is the case that Wales is subject to the cultural injustice of misrecognition, one strategy would be to develop a politics of recognition (Taylor, 1992). This might involve a number of approaches, but is likely to include countering the discourse of derision, exposing its ideological underpinnings and re-affirming the worth of the Welsh approach.

There are many grounds on which the evidence used to deride Wales's education system can be challenged. The 'objective assessments' to which Michael Gove refers are certainly less robust than his confident claims assert and are often based on a lack of acknowledgment of different levels of resourcing, different levels of scale, different assessment regimes and different educational aims.

In terms of resources, there is a significant and growing discrepancy in per capita funding with levels of educational expenditure lower in Wales than in England. In 2011, the spend per pupil in Wales was £604 less than in England. As Gorard (2002) noted over ten years ago, if one controls for socio-economic factors, differences in attainment between the two countries are far less marked. There are also differences in scale which make simple England–Wales comparisons rather problematic—it is unsound to compare a country with a population of nearly 55 million with one of 3 million, not least because it discounts significant within-country variation. Rees and Taylor (2014) have modelled a 'synthetic Wales' through matching the 22 local authorities in Wales with the 22 (of 353) local authorities in England that most closely resemble them in terms of economic and social characteristics. This kind of matching significantly reduces the attainment gap between England and Wales. The issue of scale may also be a significant aspect of the apparent 'underperformance' of Wales in the PISA tests. PISA tests are undertaken in only a sample of classes, and because Wales is a much smaller country than England a far greater proportion of Welsh pupils are sampled than English pupils. Given all that we know about sampling, response rates and systematic bias, it is almost certain that the test data from England will be less reliable than that from Wales. Moreover, it may well have led to a significant over-estimation of the test scores for England (Micklewright, Schnepf & Skinner, 2010).

However, even controlling for resources and scale there are still important differences which make comparisons difficult. As already mentioned, Welsh school children no longer take the standardised key stage tests which would enable straightforward comparisons with England to be made—and which might also give them equivalent experience of being tested (Goldstein & Leckie, 2016). But the wider context has also meant that English and Welsh schools prioritise different activities. There is little doubt that the emphasis on league tables and targets in England has led to a significant amount of 'gaming' which can artificially 'inflate' school-level performance. For example, an oft-quoted study by academics in England claims to show that the 'policy reform in Wales reduced average GCSE performance and raised educational inequality' (Burgess, Wilson & Worth, 2013). However, data from the English schools include a significant number of vocational qualifications which have only approximate equivalence with GCSEs. As Rees and Taylor (2014) point out, if the comparison is based on GCSEs alone, there is actually very little difference between England and Wales.

More robust data are available from the Millennium Cohort Study (MCS), which has followed the progress of approximately 19,000 children born in 2000 and tested them on a wide array of aptitudes at the ages of three, five and seven years. Sophisticated cross-country statistical comparisons (Taylor, Rees & Davies, 2013) show the complex nature of relative progress. For example, at aged seven, it does appear that children in England have made greater gains in literacy than their counterparts in Scotland and Wales. However, this pattern is not replicated in other important areas of cognitive development. In terms of maths ability, Welsh children score just as well as comparable children in England and better than comparable children in Scotland. In terms of measures of pattern construction, children in Wales do significantly better than their counterparts in either England or Scotland. Moreover, despite their lower level of literacy attainment, analysis of the MCS data also shows that 'poor' children in Wales and Scotland generally report greater levels of wellbeing than comparable children in England. Taylor et al. (2013, p. 301) speculate that 'attention on developing literacy skills in England could come at the expense of children's subjective wellbeing.'

Similarly, Wales's 2012 PISA scores may be lower than England's, but there are ways of examining the data which emphasise different aspects. For example, the OECD note that:

> Wales has a relatively equitable education system ... The performance of 15-year-old students is not as closely related to their socio-economic background as it is in most other OECD countries. A student's socio-economic background explains 10.4% of the variance in students' performance in mathematics, which is considerably lower than the OECD average of 20.8% .... (OECD, 2014, p. 21)

As Rees (2012) points out 'it is instructive that the bench-marks against which Welsh educational performance have been judged are *external* ones'. On criteria of equity and wellbeing—both of which are components of Wales's 'progressive' reform agenda—it could be argued that the MCS and PISA analyses indicate that Wales is actually doing *better* than England. From this perspective, it is tempting to counter the kind of discourse of derision which has been levelled at Wales with assertions that the 'Welsh way' is better. Indeed, many commentators *do* hold Wales up as an admirable bastion against the global tide of neoliberalism (e.g. Toynbee, 2014).

However, valorising the 'Welsh way' runs the risk of ignoring the very real challenges facing Wales. The policy directions outlined earlier are only aspirations and are a long way from being achieved. Education in Wales is not making significant progress towards realising even its own objectives. For instance, despite a political preference for collaboration, competition exists for places in the 'best' state schools. And despite attempts to move towards greater equality of outcomes, the connection between poverty and low educational attainment remains strong (Taylor et al., 2013).

What this suggests, and in contrast to Conservative-led critiques of what has happened in Wales, is that we are experiencing not the efficacy of the devolved government to effect change, but its *inefficacy*. Focusing on the lack of capacity of the Welsh Government to effect change draws our attention away from the specifics of the policies themselves and onto the social and political landscape in which they have been implemented. In Wales, this landscape is characterised by social and economic disadvantage and the legacy of post-industrialisation. Wales is also subject to complex, and often conflicting, layers of governance—pressured by the needs of many small local authorities, a relatively new devolved parliament and the funding and legislative controls of Westminster.

Looked at from this perspective, Wales needs more than simply a politics of recognition. As Fraser (2000) argues, misrecognition is rarely a 'free-standing cultural harm'. Wales' misrecognition is linked to other forms of injustice—participatory and economic—which inhibit its capacity for transformative change. Wales may not need a politics of recognition, it might need other kind of political remedies—a politics of redistribution and/or a politics of representation.

Repositioning Wales

In terms of analytical ways forward, rather than address the injustice of misrecognition with a politics of recognition which affirms the 'Welsh way', it is probably more fruitful to reposition Wales—and the other small home nations—to a more central role in policy debate and research. Wales, like Scotland and Northern Ireland, has been subjected to the 'peripheralisation of Britain' (Lovering, 1991) and needs to be brought in from the margins to mainstream analysis. Such a repositioning will be of benefit not only for those of us working in Wales, but also for the educational research community more widely. Rather than seeing Wales as some kind of peripheral distraction, its reform trajectory can be used to improve our analyses from policy science to policy scholarship (Grace, 1991, p. 3). In general, parliamentary devolution can tell us not only about education policies, but about the politics of education (Dale, 1989).

The issue of how Wales can be repositioned within policy research brings us back to longstanding and fundamental debates about the different ways of framing and analysing educational policies and processes. Thirty years ago, Dale (1986) outlined three different projects of policy research: the 'policy analysis' project, the 'social administration' project and the 'social science' project. Each of these different projects—which have different purposes and different audiences—might benefit from looking across the UK.

The 'policy analysis' project, according to Dale, seeks to evaluate specific initiatives without necessarily questioning the underlying direction or assumptions embedded within a policy. This project is perhaps most closely embodied in the 'what works' agenda which underpins evaluations such as those funded through the Education Endowment Fund in England. Even these very focused evaluations might be enhanced through a more comparative dimension.

The 'social administration' project can be epitomised by the political arithmetic approach (Halsey, Heath & Ridge, 1980) in which systems (and system change) is charted. Although, as Ozga (2000) argues, this kind of approach tends to focus on and within a national system, the increasingly divergent systems of the UK offer huge and as yet largely unrealised potential for political arithmetic through the use of 'home international' comparison proposed by Raffe, Brannen, Croxford & Martin (1999). As Taylor et al. (2013) remark, the shared characteristics of the four nations means that there is greater control for exogenous factors than with many 'fully' international comparisons—enabling a greater confidence in the attribution of relationships between policies and outcomes.

However, it is to the 'social science' project that the repositioning of Wales and the other 'peripheral' nations might contribute most. Rather than being tied to the concerns of policy-makers—whether they be in Cardiff, Edinburgh, Belfast or London—the social science project seeks to understand *how* policy works rather than simply *whether* it works (Ozga, 2000). In trying to understand the nature and direction of shared characteristics and national divergence we need to look not only at the trajectories of the four nations as if they were independent entities but at the historical, political and cultural relations *between* them. Thus, the repositioning of Wales will foster not only comparative research but *relational* analysis.

What has hopefully been made clear from the analysis offered here is that narratives of what is happening in Wales can *only* be understood in relation to what is going on elsewhere— and particularly in England. The recent debates around the relative performance of Wales highlights the very *political* nature of education policy and education policy research. The Conservative Party's so-called 'War on Wales' in the run-up to the UK General Election was as much about legitimating what was happening in England as it was about effecting any change in Wales—at least at that point in time.

The experience of Wales also illuminates some of the consequences of the 'governance by data' charted by Ozga (2009). Attainment data have been used by the UK government to influence not only what goes on in England but what goes on elsewhere. As Rees and Taylor (2014, p. 3) argue, the narrative of Welsh underperformance has had major impacts not only on how Welsh schools are perceived inside and outside the country but also on the actual form of policy-making in Wales. Although it would be hard to describe the Welsh Government's education reform agenda as especially radical, its politically dominant neighbour has sought to mobilise the 'tyranny of numbers' (Ball, 2015) to squeeze out alternative conceptions of what might constitute a 'successful' education system.

Notes

1. Because it is impossible to cover the range of policies that have been introduced in Wales at all phases since 1999, the analysis is based on only a selection of what might be seen as the 'key' policies in the compulsory phase.
2. This proportion has increased since 2011 (DfE, 2014), but the subsequent diversification of school types in England makes it impossible to make direct comparisons between the two countries.
3. Two reports into local governance have recently been commissioned which have raised a number of issues about the 'viability' of such a small country having 22 local authorities. The Williams Report and the Hills Report have recommended a number of strategies including greater use of regional consortia to deliver educational services and reducing the number of authorities.

Disclosure statement

No potential conflict of interest was reported by the author.

References

Aasen, W., & Waters, J. (2006). The new curriculum in Wales: A new view of the child? *Education 3–13. International Journal of Primary, Elementary and Early Years Education, 34*, 123–129.

Abbott, I., Rathbone, M., & Whitehead, P. (2012). *Education policy*. London: Sage.

Adams, P. (2014). *Policy and education*. London: Routledge.

Andrews, L. (2014). *Ministering to education: A reformer reports*. Cardigan: Parthian Books.

Archer, J. (2008, December 20). Wales eliminates national exams for many students. *Education Week, 26*, 10.

Ball, S. J. (1993). Education, Majorism and 'the curriculum of the dead'. *Curriculum Studies, 1*, 195–214.

Ball, S. J. (2013). *The education debate (policy and politics in the twenty-first century)* (2nd ed.). Bristol: Policy Press.

Ball, S. J. (2015). Education, governance and the tyranny of numbers: Editorial. *Journal of Education Policy, 30*, 299–301.

Burgess, S., Wilson, D., & Worth, J. (2013). A natural experiment in school improvement: The impact of school performance information on pupil progress. *Journal of Public Economics, 106*, 57–67.

Campbell, A. (2007). *The Blair years: Extracts from the Alastair Campbell Diaries*. London: Hutchinson.

Chapman, C., & Gunter, H. (Eds.). (2008). *Radical reforms: Perspectives on an era of educational change*. London: Routledge.

Coldron, J., Willis, B., & Wolstenholme, C. (2009). Selection and aptitude in English secondary schools. *British Journal of Educational Studies, 57*, 245–264.

Dale, R. (1986). Perspectives on policy making. In *Policy-making in education course E333 module 1, part 2*. Buckingham: Open University.

Dale, R. (1989). *The state and education policy*. Buckingham: Open University.

DfE (2014). *Government evidence to the STRB: The 2015 pay award*. London: Department for Education. Retrieved from https://www.gov.uk/government/uploads/system/uploads/attachment_data/file/370590/141027_DfE_Evidence_to_STRB.pdf

Drakeford, M. (2007). Social justice in a devolved Wales. *The Policy Press, 15*, 172–178.

Esytn, (2008). *Having your say—young people, participation and school councils*. Cardiff: Estyn.

Evans, G. (2015). *A class apart: Learning the lessons of education in post-devolution Wales*. Cardiff: Welsh Academic Press.

Farrell, C. (2010). *Pupil participation and School Councils*. Pontypridd: University of Glamorgan. Retrieved from www.pupilvoicewales.org.uk/uploads/publications/487.doc

Flew, A. (1991). Educational services: Independent competition or maintained monopoly. In D. Green (Ed.), *Empowering the parents: How to break the schools monopoly* (pp. 15–54). London: Institute of Economic Affairs.

Fraser, N. (1997). *Justice interruptus: Critical reflections on the 'postsocialist' condition*. New York, NY: Routledge.

Fraser, N. (2000). Rethinking recognition. *New Left Review*, 107–120.

Goldstein, H., & Leckie, G. (2016 in press).Trends in examination performance and exposure to standardised tests in England and Wales. *British Educational Research Journal*.

Gorard, S. (2002). *Education and social justice*. Cardiff: University of Wales Press.

Gove, M. (2012). *House of Commons Hansard debates* 17 Sept. 2012: Column 660.

Gove, M. (2013, February 5). The progressive betrayal. Speech to the Social Market Foundation. Retrieved from http://www.smf.co.uk/media/news/michael-gove-speaks-smf/

Grace, G. (1991). Welfare Labourism versus the New Right: The struggle in New Zealand's education policy. *International Studies in Sociology of Education, 1*, 25–42.

Halsey, A. H., Heath, A. F., & Ridge, J. M. (1980). *Origins and destinations: Family, class and education in modern Britain*. Oxford: Oxford University Press.

Jones, G. E., & Roderick, G. W. (2003). *A history of education in Wales*. Cardiff: University of Wales Press.

Lewis, H. (2013, October 16). Reform, rigour and respect. Ministerial Speech. University of South Wales. Retrieved from http://learning.wales.gov.uk/news/speeches/reform-rigour-respect/?lang=en

Lewis, H. (2014, June 28). Making bald comparisons between England and Wales ignores our vastly different demographics. *Wales Online*. Retrieved from http://www.walesonline.co.uk/news/news-opinion/education-minister-huw-lewis-accuses-7339401

Lovering, J. (1991). Southbound again: The peripherilization of Britain. In G. Day & G. Rees (Eds.), *Regions, nations and European Integration: Remaking the Celtic periphery* (pp. 11–38). Cardiff: University of Wales Press.

Maynard, T., Taylor, C., Waldron, S. M., Rhys, M., Smith, R., Power, S., & Clement, J. (2013). *Evaluating the Foundation Phase: Policy logic model and programme theory (Social Research No. 37/2012)*. Cardiff: Welsh Government.

Micklewright, J., Schnepf, S. V., & Skinner, C. J. (2010). *Non-response biases in surveys of school children: The case of the English PISA samples (Discussion Paper No. 4789, February)*. Bonn: IZA.

Morgan, R. (2002). Clear red water. Speech to the National Centre for Public Policy, Swansea. Retrieved from http://www.sochealth.co.uk/the-socialist-health-association/sha-country-and-branch-organisation/sha-wales/clear-red-water/

OECD (2014). *Improving schools in Wales: An OECD perspective*. Paris: OECD.

Ozga, J. (2000). *Policy research in educational settings*. Buckingham: Open University Press.

Ozga, J. (2009). Governing education through data in England: From regulation to self-evaluation. *Journal of Education Policy, 24*, 149–162.

Phillips, R. (1995). Education policy making in Wales: A research agenda. In Fourth International (Ed.), *Colloquium on education: British and American perspectives*. Swansea: Department of Education, University of Wales.

Phillips, R. & Sanders, L. (2000). Contemporary education policy in Wales: Theory, discourse and research. In R. Daugherty, R. Phillips, & G. Rees (Eds.), *Education policy-making in Wales: Explorations in devolved governance* (pp. 9–23). Cardiff: University of Wales Press.

Prowle, M. (2012, March 30). Bottom of the class. *Public Finance*. Retrieved from http://www.publicfinance.co.uk/2012/03/bottom-class

Raffe, D., Brannen, K., Croxford, L., & Martin, C. (1999). Comparing England, Scotland, Wales and Northern Ireland: The case for 'home internationals' in comparative research. *Comparative Education, 35*, 9–25.

Rees, G. (2012). *PISA and the politics of Welsh education (WISERD Policy Briefing PBS/007)*. Retrieved from http://www.wiserd.ac.uk/files/4913/9574/4727/WISERD_PBS_007_-_PISA_and_the_Politics_of_Welsh_Education.pdf

Rees, G., & Taylor, C. (2014). *Is there a 'crisis' in Welsh education? A review of the evidence*. London: Honourable Society of Cymmrodorion.

Reynolds, D. (2008). New Labour, education and Wales: The devolution decade. *Oxford Review of Education, 34*, 753–765.

Rizvi, F., & Lingard, B. (2009). *Globalizing education policy*. London: Routledge.

Taylor, C. (1992). *Multiculturalism and the politics of recognition*. Princeton: Princeton University Press.

Taylor, C., Rees, G., & Davies, R. (2013). Devolution and geographies of education: The use of the Millennium Cohort Study for 'home international' comparisons across the UK. *Comparative Education, 49*, 290–316.

Toynbee, P. (2014, March 7). Here's some lessons in real job creation from much-maligned Wales. *The Guardian*. Retrieved from http://www.theguardian.com/commentisfree/2014/mar/07/lessons-real-job-creation-wales

Welsh Government (2013). *Welsh medium education strategy: Annual report 2012–13*. Cardiff: Welsh Government.

Welsh Government (2014). *Rewriting the future: Raising ambition and attainment in Welsh schools*. Cardiff: Welsh Government.

Welsh Government (2015). *Successful futures: Independent review of curriculum and assessment arrangements in Wales*. Cardiff: Welsh Government. Retrieved from http://gov.wales/docs/dcells/publications/150317-successful-futures-en.pdf

Williamson, D. (2014, July 7). 'Dear Mr Cameron… please stop this Tory war on Wales': Shadow Welsh Secretary Owen Smith's fiery letter to the Prime Minister. *Wales Online*. Retrieved from http://www.walesonline.co.uk/news/wales-news/dear-mr-cameron-please-stop-7380450

Wood, C., & Scott, R. (Eds.). (2014). *Harnessing what works in eliminating educational disadvantage: A tale of two classrooms*. London: Demos.

Implementing curriculum reform in Wales: the case of the Foundation Phase

Chris Taylor 🆔, Mirain Rhys and Sam Waldron

ABSTRACT

The Foundation Phase is a Welsh Government flagship policy of early years education (for 3–7 year-old children) in Wales. Marking a radical departure from the more formal, competency-based approach associated with the previous Key Stage 1 National Curriculum, it advocates a developmental, experiential, play-based approach to teaching and learning. *The learning country: A paving document* (NAfW, 2001) notes that, following devolution, Wales intended to take its own policy direction in order to 'get the best for Wales'. Building on a three-year mixed methods independent evaluation of the Foundation Phase we discuss in detail the aims and objectives of the Foundation Phase, including the context to its introduction, the theory, assumptions and evidence underlying its rationale, and its content and key inputs. We then contrast this with how the Foundation Phase was received by practitioners and parents, how it has been implemented in classrooms and non-maintained settings, and what discernible impact it has had on young children's educational outcomes. The paper concludes with a critical analysis of the policy process and identifies a number of contextual issues during the inception of the Foundation Phase that has, it could be argued, constrained its development and subsequent impact. We argue that these constraints are associated with an educational policy landscape that was still in its infancy. In order for future education policy to 'get the best for Wales' a number of important lessons must be learnt.

Introduction

The Foundation Phase is the statutory curriculum for all 3–7 year-olds in the maintained and funded non-maintained[1] education sectors in Wales. It represents one of the 'flagship' education policies of the first ten years of the Welsh Government following parliamentary devolution in 1999. The Foundation Phase is symbolic for three reasons. First, it demonstrated a commitment to the use of the 'best' international evidence for education policy-making. Second, it constitutes a radical departure from its predecessor, the National Curriculum Key Stage 1, both in terms of curriculum and pedagogy. And third, it provided one of the first examples of how the education system in Wales differed from that of England following devolution. The Foundation Phase is also a very important example of education policy in Wales because of its scale—it universally applies to all primary schools and funded non-maintained settings across Wales—and breadth—it has involved a wide range of inputs and changes (see later).

It is argued that the origins of the Foundation Phase actually predate parliamentary devolution. Wincott (2006) maintains that it arose from the politicising of early childhood education and care amongst Welsh MPs in the UK Government and the establishment and prominence of a number of child-centred advocacy organisations in Wales. But it was the appointment of Margaret Hanney in 2000 as an expert advisor on early years provision that helped pave the way to ensure that curriculum was central to nursery provision, that three-year-olds should be part of any new curricula developments, and that international evidence was called upon. The then Assembly Minister for Education and Lifelong Learning, Jane Davidson, a keen advocate of the importance of early childhood education, set out a commitment to undertake a consultation on what was later called the Foundation Phase for 3–7 year-olds(NAfW, 2001). The resulting consultation, *The learning country: the Foundation Phase: 3 to 7 years* (NAfW, 2003) identified ten 'shortcomings' in early years education and eight 'shortcomings' in Key Stage 1. But underlying the need for reform of early years education, both in England and Wales, was the persistent underachievement of approximately 20% of the primary school age population over a number of years (see Figure 1, for example).

Whilst the overarching aim of the Foundation Phase was to provide a new statutory curriculum for 3–7 year-olds to replace the pre-existing National Curriculum Key Stage 1, the main aims for the Foundation Phase during its inception were to:

- raise children's standards of achievement;
- enhance their positive attitudes to learning;
- address their developing needs;
- enable them to benefit from educational opportunities later in their lives; and
- help them become active citizens within their communities. (NAfW, 2003, p. 6)

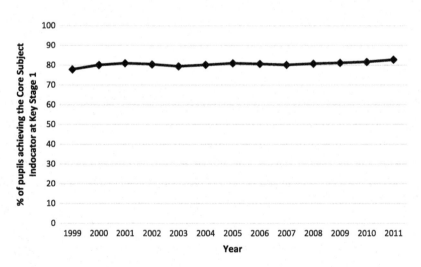

Figure 1. Levels of achievement in Key Stage 1 Core Subject Indicator (CSI) in Wales, 1999 to 2011.
* The Core Subject Indicator (CSI) represents the proportion of pupils achieving Level 2 or above in English or Welsh (first language), Mathematics and Science in combination.

However, a key argument underpinning the introduction of the Foundation Phase was a concern about formal approaches to teaching and learning in the first few years of schooling and a desire to introduce more developmentally appropriate practices into classrooms and settings. For example, in the original consultation exercise it was argued that 'teachers introduce formal learning too soon, before some pupils are ready' (NAfW, 2003, p. 5) and that this could result in 'some children underachieving and attaining lower standards' (2003, p. 14). This was seen as particularly concerning in relation to the teaching of reading and writing: 'an over-emphasis on making children read and write, before they are ready to do so, can be counter-productive' (2003, p. 11) with a risk that children will 'lose both confidence and a love of learning' (2003, p. 5).

Drawing particularly from early years education in Scandinavia, New Zealand (Te Whāriki) and Reggio Emilia in Northern Italy (see OECD, 2004 for an overview of each), the Foundation Phase is underpinned by constructivist theories of learning (i.e. is explicitly developmental with a clear focus on the individual child) and highlights socio-cultural ideas of empowerment and play in children's learning (Maynard et al., 2013). As a result it advocates a developmental, experiential, play-based approach to teaching and learning. However, the Foundation Phase deviates from these international comparisons and their associated theories of learning in at least three key ways. First, despite encouraging developmentally appropriate practice there remains a strong requirement for children to develop key skills or outcomes, particularly in literacy and numeracy, and by a certain age (i.e. at the end of the Foundation Phase). Second, the Foundation Phase does not entirely remove the need for direct, formal, teaching. Instead it encourages a balance of continuous, enhanced and focussed provision (as outlined in the Foundation Phase National Training Pack Module on Experiential Learning in Practice). And finally, the role of parents in the Foundation Phase is largely seen as requiring intervention (e.g. to mitigate the impact of educational disadvantage in the home) rather than seeing parents and families as co-producers of the curriculum or the learning experience. Many of these divergences underline the importance of the Welsh Government's more recent emphasis on raising standards and through greater performance management of schools (Rees & Taylor, 2015). It could be argued, therefore, that the Foundation Phase offers a unique attempt to bridge a child-centred approach to education within a standards-driven education system. Whether that is possible is something we will return to later in the paper.

The main aim of this paper is to outline how the Foundation Phase has been implemented, the impact it has had in maintained schools and funded non-maintained settings, what impact it has had on practitioners and what impact it has had on pupils. The findings are based on a three-year independent evaluation of the Foundation Phase that was commissioned and funded by the Welsh Government (and led by the authors of this paper).

The evaluation employed a stepped wedge design (Brown & Lilford, 2006). This exploits the sequential roll-out of the Foundation Phase by comparing the implementation and impact of the Foundation Phase at various stages of its introduction. The evaluation used a variety of mixed methods and included data collection and analysis at (a) a national level—including the use of national pupil data, a national survey of head teachers and setting managers, interviews with all local authority early years advisors and interviews with key Welsh Government personnel—and (b) at a local level. The latter involved the stratified random selection of 41 primary schools and a further 10 funded non-maintained settings. These case studies were selected on the basis of region, stage of roll-out, and medium of instruction (i.e. to ensure the selection included Welsh-medium schools and English-medium schools). Other than these criteria schools were then randomly selected to minimise any forms of selection bias. The case study schools and settings involved interviews with all headteachers or centre managers, over 150 teacher interviews, over 120 interviews with additional practitioners, a further 24 interviews with staff in funded non-maintained settings, and systematic observations of over 3,300 3–7-year-olds across 131 classrooms or settings. In addition to this over 1,000 parents who had children in the Foundation Phase in these case study schools and settings were surveyed and over 600 Year 2 pupils participated in a self-completion survey. The final report of the evaluation was published by the Welsh Government in spring 2015 and made 29 recommendations (Taylor et al., 2015a).

In this paper we provide a critical analysis of the policy and implementation process for the Foundation Phase. In particular we highlight a number of contextual issues that appear to have impeded or constrained its delivery, and subsequently its possible impact. Focussing on the process of design and implementation is important for two main reasons. First, this provides an excellent case study of Welsh Government policy development during the first ten years of political devolution. Secondly, the Welsh Government is about to embark on an even more radical overhaul of curriculum and assessment across all compulsory schooling in Wales. Following an independent review by Professor Donaldson (the 'Donaldson Review') a new blueprint, entitled Successful Futures, outlines proposals for the reorganisation and redesign of curricula and assessment from Foundation Phase to Key Stage 4 (Donaldson, 2015). The Minister for Education and Skills, Huw Lewis AM, has since accepted all the recommendations of the Donaldson Review and intends to implement them fully. Crucially they will (a) build upon the developments in the Foundation Phase and (b) require a similar breadth and scale of change to the curriculum and pedagogy that has been seen in the Foundation Phase. There are, therefore, important lessons that can be learnt from the implementation of the Foundation Phase for these future educational reforms.

The implementation of the Foundation Phase is presented in three main parts. First we outline the main resource implications of the Foundation Phase, including the substantial changes to the teaching workforce, the training that the introduction of the Foundation Phase necessitated and the capital developments required to improve teaching and learning environments for young learners. The second main section outlines the changes to the curriculum and the attempt to 'guide' practitioners to adopt 'new' pedagogical practices. The third main section then considers the impact of the Foundation Phase on pupils' learning. The paper concludes with a discussion of the challenges to the implementation of the Foundation Phase and suggests ways in which these could have been mitigated or avoided completely.

Investing in the Foundation Phase

The introduction of the Foundation Phase has not come without significant cost to the Welsh Government. Overall it is estimated that the total cost of primary years education in Wales has increased from £25,241 to £28,019 per pupil (based on 2012–13 figures) as a result of the Foundation Phase. This is an estimated 11% increase in costs and equates to just under £100 million per year in additional costs.

The main cost of the Foundation Phase has been to improve adult-to-child ratios. The Foundation Phase was introduced with recommended ratios of 1:8 for 3–5 year-olds (i.e. in funded non-maintained settings and Nursery and Reception classes/groups) and 1:15 for 5–7 year-olds (i.e. in Year 1 and Year 2 classes). This was strongly welcomed by practitioners (Taylor et al., 2014). Between 2004/05 and 2011/12 this has in effect doubled the practitioner workforce working in the Foundation Phase (or Key Stage 1). Despite this, less than half of nursery and reception classes/settings met the recommended ratio of 1:8 in 2011/12 (Taylor et al., 2015b).

The second main cost of the Foundation Phase has been in the provision of training and support for practitioners. The range of training and support provided by the Welsh Government has been extensive, and primarily involved the design and production of eight training modules (with a particular focus on pedagogy), a number of guidance materials (with a focus on curriculum and assessment), the employment of one full-time Training and Support Officer (TSO) in each local authority to support the training of staff, and in funded non-maintained setting, access to 10% of time (full time equivalent) from a Link Teacher to support children and practitioners in those settings. Between 2004–05 and 2013–14 the Welsh Government spent just under £46 million on training and support in the Foundation Phase (just under £7 million per year in the past five years—between 6% and 7% of the total additional cost of the Foundation Phase) (Taylor et al., 2015a).

The majority of the training and guidance materials were developed during a pilot stage of the Foundation Phase. This initially involved 22 maintained schools and 19 funded non-maintained (one of each per local authority). The role of the pilot schools was to intro-duce the Foundation Phase and simultaneously develop and test the materials required for the subsequent roll-out to all other schools and settings. However, the selection of the pilot schools was not random, and although the final selection of the pilot schools and settings rested with the Welsh Government, the process of nominating them differed considerably between local authorities (Siraj-Blatchford, Sylva, Laugharne, Milton, & Charles, 2005). Furthermore, despite an evaluation of the implementation of the Foundation Phase in the pilot schools at the time (Siraj-Blatchford et al., 2005) there was no detailed record taken of how the design and content of the Foundation Phase was developed. Nor was there any attempt to empirically 'test' the key components of the Foundation Phase as they were being developed. There was certainly no comparison made against non-pilot schools who contin-ued to deliver the Key Stage 1 curriculum in the traditional way.

Nevertheless, this important process of implementation, using pilot schools and settings to develop a deeper understanding of the curriculum and pedagogies of the Foundation Phase, constitutes a bottom-up approach to educational policy development. With hindsight it could be argued that many of the pilot schools, settings and practitioners lacked the necessary depth of knowledge and understanding of the educational theories underpinning the Foundation Phase. Indeed, the pilot evaluation recognised that despite a general endorsement of the Foundation Phase principles there was, amongst this key group of pilot schools and settings, still 'the need for clear guidance materials on AOLs [Areas of Learning] and associated pedagogy [and] better planned and funded training' (Siraj-Blatchford et al., 2005, p. 3). The pilot evaluation also raised a concern about the use of some of the key ter-minology used in the initial guidance materials. But it appears that this was not adequately addressed, since a further systematic review of the training and guidance materials over six years later raised almost precisely the same concerns (Maynard et al., 2013).

The more recent evaluation did find, however, that the vast majority of practitioners welcomed the support and training they received, and found it very useful (Rhys, Waldron

& Taylor, 2014). However, in this evaluation's case study schools and settings still only half of teachers and 30% of additional practitioners had accessed all eight training modules. Crucially, a greater level of training amongst staff was found to be associated with a greater implementation of the Foundation Phase pedagogies in classrooms and settings.

Finally, the Welsh Government also invested approximately £36 million of additional capital grants between 2004–05 and 2011–12 to help schools and funded non-maintained settings improve their learning environments (Taylor et al., 2015a). It was recognised very early on that many educational establishments lacked the facilities to deliver a more practical, play-based and experiential form of learning, particularly in the use of the outdoor environment (WAG, 2009; Welsh Government, 2014a).

Pedagogy and curriculum in the Foundation Phase

The introduction of the Foundation Phase has not just been about the need for additional resources and investment. It required the introduction of an entirely new curriculum for 3–7 year-olds. Replacing Key Stage 1 subjects for 5–7 year-olds and Desirable Outcomes for 3–5 year-olds the Foundation Phase introduced seven new statutory Areas of Learning:

  i.   Personal and Social Development, Well-Being and Cultural Diversity;
  ii. Language, Literacy and Communication Skills;
  iii. Mathematical Development;
  iv. Welsh Language Development (in English medium schools and settings);
  v.   Knowledge and Understanding of the World;
  vi. Physical Development; and
  vii. Creative Development.

Central to these curricula reforms was the Personal and Social Development, Well-Being and Cultural Diversity Area of Learning (Aasen & Waters, 2006). This provides a strong focus on pedagogical practice, since many of the outcomes from this Area of Learning are dispositions rather than skills, motivations rather than competencies.

Alongside these curricula changes was an explicit attempt to direct practitioners to use and adopt particular pedagogical practices. For example, in the Foundation Phase Framework (Welsh Government, 2015) there is a strong emphasis on the holistic development of a child, whereby 'practitioners must understand how children develop, and plan an appropriate curriculum that takes account of children's developmental needs and the skills that they need to grow to become confident learners', that children must be 'at the heart of any planned curriculum' and that 'children learn through first-hand experiential activities with the serious business of "play" providing the vehicle' (2015, pp. 3–4). A more detailed content analysis of the Framework and other guidance materials (including the core eight training modules for the Foundation Phase) suggested a number of key pedagogical practices that practitioners are encouraged to use in their classrooms and settings. These can be summarised as the following:

  (1) Participation: Children should be given the opportunity to initiate and direct their own learning activities.
  (2) Continuous/Enhanced/Focussed: Continuous provision should form the bedrock of Foundation Phase pedagogy, whereby an array of different learning activities are constantly available within the learning environment. Adults should enhance

provision further by adding/supplementing specific learning opportunities within the continuous provision. Focussed provision remains important, but should be used less frequently than continuous and enhanced.

(3)   First-hand: Children should be given the opportunity to learn from first-hand (direct) experiences.

(4)   Practical: Children should be given the opportunity to learn from practical (hands-on) experiences.

(5)   Explorative: Children should be given the opportunity to learn from explorative experiences.

(6)   Active: Children should be given the opportunity to learn through physically active experiences.

(7)   Learning zones: A Foundation Phase learning environment should offer a variety of different learning areas/activities for children to engage with.

(8)   Using the outdoors: Learning should take place indoors *and* outdoors.

(9)   Thinking skills: Adults should extend children's thinking by asking open (rather than closed) questions, and also by engaging children in sustained interactions/discussions.

(10) Reflection: Adults should encourage children to think about and reflect on their learning experiences.

(11) Observing progress: Adults should monitor children's progress predominantly through observations.

(12) Individual needs: All children should be challenged and supported appropriately, depending on their stage (not age) of learning.

These 12 pedagogical practices or 'elements' were formally used in the evaluation of the Foundation Phase through systematic child and practitioner observations. During lessons the researchers would observe to what extent each of these pedagogical elements were present or being used. Typically a one-hour lesson would involve the observation of 14 randomly selected children for two minutes each and the observation of all practitioners every 15 minutes. These observations were undertaken for one Nursery, Reception, Year 1 and Year 2 class in both the morning and the afternoon in each case study school. Additional one-hour observations were also undertaken in the morning and afternoon in the case study funded non-maintained settings.[2] In total across 41 case study schools and 10 case study funded non-maintained settings we observed 131 classes, 239 lessons (or sessions), 3,343 children and 824 practitioners. All observations were undertaken during the spring and summer terms of 2012–13.

Despite the breadth and depth of change required, the overwhelming majority of practitioners surveyed and interviewed welcomed changes to the curriculum. For example, 89% of all Foundation Phase lead practitioners surveyed said that the introduction of the Personal and Social Development, Well-Being and Cultural Diversity (PSDWCD) Area of Learning was an improvement from the previous Key Stage 1 National Curriculum. However, whilst the majority of Foundation Phase lead practitioners reported that they thought the new Language, Literacy and Communication and Mathematical Development Areas of Learning were an improvement on their predecessors (69% and 67% respectively) a much greater proportion of practitioners felt that there was no real difference (19% and 22%) or that the new Areas of Learning were actually worse than the Key Stage 1 National Curriculum (12% and 11%).

Of course it is notable that these two Areas of Learning include literacy and numeracy, and are the focus of much attention by the Welsh Government through its National Literacy and Numeracy Framework (LNF) for all learners aged 5 to 14. The LNF was introduced in September 2013, four years after the Foundation Phase had been rolled out to all primary schools and funded non-maintained settings. Crucially it introduced annual national assessments in literacy and numeracy for all 5–14 year-olds, overlapping with the Foundation Phase in Years 1 and 2. Although the LNF (Welsh Government, 2013) recognises that 'not all children progress in the same way' (p. 9)—a key theory underpinning the Foundation Phase—it attempts to argue that 'the year-by-year nature of the LNF allows teachers to ensure that they are incorporating the appropriate skills into their delivery of the curriculum and its content' (p. 9). However, the LNF does not clearly define what is 'appropriate'. Within the Framework frequent reference is made to age-appropriate learning and skills and age-appropriate contexts, 'In developing the LNF we have had to carefully consider what the appropriate expectations at *each age and key stage should be*' (2013, p. 7) (our emphasis). On only one occasion does the Framework refers to something more akin to developmentally appropriate practice, 'The LNF focuses on the learners' acquisition of and ability to apply the skills and concepts they have learned to complete realistic tasks appropriate for *their stage of development*' (2013, p. 8) (our emphasis). A similar level of uncertainty surrounds the introduction of the national literacy and numeracy assessments for all 5–7 year-olds in the Foundation Phase. Each pupil is provided with an age-adjusted score, demonstrating how they achieved against the average child of their same age (in months). Not only does this mean that 50% of all pupils will always be 'below average', it also reinforces the notion that learners, even as young as 5 years old, are expected to reach certain levels of ability based on their age rather than their stage of development.

The importance of literacy and numeracy within the education system in Wales has had two significant consequences for the Foundation Phase. The first is that these Areas of Learning continue to dominate the curriculum, particularly as children get towards the end of the Foundation Phase (Figure 2)—reflecting both (a) the 'overlap' with the LNF from age 3 years and (b) a 'readiness' for the Key Stage 2 National Curriculum.

The second consequence is on pedagogical practice. The majority of practitioners continue to believe that the most appropriate way of developing literacy and numeracy skills is through direct and often didactic learning. This is best illustrated in the use of continuous/enhanced/focussed provision, a central tenet of the Foundation Phase pedagogy. Figure 3 illustrates the 'balance' between the use of continuous, enhanced and focussed provision in the delivery of the three Areas of Learning. The Foundation Phase guidance materials state that continuous provision should be used most of the time and focussed provision the least of the time. As Figure 3 illustrates, in practice this 'balance' is heavily skewed in favour of focussed provision when delivering Language, Literacy and Communication and Mathematical Development Areas of Learning. This contrasts markedly from Personal and Social Development, Well-Being and Cultural Diversity—although even here focussed provision still tends to dominate.

To further illustrate this point Figure 4 attempts to show the use of all 12 Foundation Phase pedagogical 'elements' (indicated by a combined measure of their use from session/lesson observations) by the age or year group of the children. This clearly shows that the

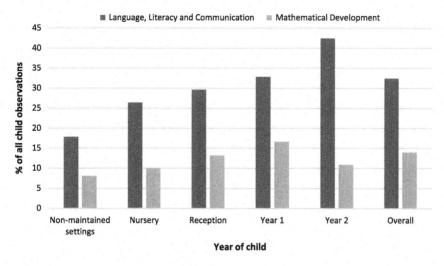

Figure 2. Prevalence of Language, Literacy and Communication and Mathematical Development Areas of Learning by Foundation Phase year group.

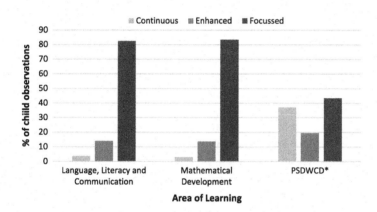

Figure 3. Use of continuous/enhanced/focussed provision by Area of Learning.
*Personal and Social Development, Well-Being and Cultural Diversity (PSDWCD).

older the learners the less likely that Foundation Phase pedagogies are being used in classrooms.

Impact of the Foundation Phase

As the aims of the Foundation Phase demonstrate above, it was intended to have a wide range of impacts on pupils and their learning, including attainment, attendance, classroom wellbeing and involvement and perceived benefits amongst practitioners, parents and children themselves (Taylor et al., 2015a; Waldron, Rhys & Taylor, 2014a, Waldron, Rhys & Taylor, 2014b). The evaluation attempted to measure all these outcomes objectively. In summary, the Foundation Phase is associated with a significant improvement in pupil attendance in the majority of schools. The evaluation also found that where schools had successfully implemented the Foundation Phase it observed higher levels of pupil involvement and wellbeing

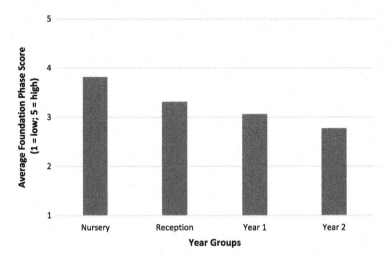

Figure 4. Use of Foundation Phase pedagogies by year group.

during their learning. Furthermore, the vast majority of practitioners surveyed and interviewed thought that there had been a positive impact on children and learning, including pupil behaviour, wellbeing and attitudes to learning.

However, raising pupil attainment was one of the most important objectives of the Foundation Phase. In this section we consider, in more detail, the impact the Foundation Phase has had on pupil's levels of attainment, with a particular focus on their achievements in literacy and numeracy.

There are two ways in which it has been possible to examine the impact of the Foundation Phase on levels of achievement. Each has their own advantages and disadvantages, but when combined provide valuable insights into how the Foundation Phase appears to benefit (or otherwise) learners. The first analytical approach is to compare National Curriculum Key Stage 2 outcomes (teacher assessments) of pupils at the end of Year 6 (at age 10–11 years) who attended the 22 Foundation Phase with outcomes of pupils of the same age and in the same year groups who attended non-pilot schools and who continued to follow the National Curriculum Key Stage 1. This allows us to compare the outcomes of three cohorts of pupils (1,491 in total) who experienced the Foundation Phase during its pilot stage. Using Key Stage 2 outcomes provides a common assessment framework to compare outcomes. Unfortunately the demographics of pupils who attended Foundation Phase pilot schools in the first three years are not representative of the wider pupil population. Therefore, to make any comparison 'fair' we have to control for their socio-economic circumstances, gender and special educational needs (i.e. based on their individual characteristics). We also account for the school intake characteristics (i.e. compositional characteristics). We do this by statistically matching pupils from the pilot schools with similar pupils in non-pilot schools. To ensure the comparison is as robust as possible the analysis compares the relative achievement of 'matched' pupils in pilot schools *prior* to the introduction of the Foundation Phase with the relative achievement of 'matched' pupils in pilot schools *after* the introduction of the Foundation Phase. This helps limit the influence of other unobserved factors, such as standards in teaching in the pilot schools prior to the introduction of the Foundation Phase.[3]

Table 1. Differences in achievement between pupils in Foundation Phase Pilot schools and 'matched' pupils in other schools achieving Level 4 or above in Key Stage 2 (age 11 years).

	Prior to Foundation Phase	After Foundation Phase
KS2 English	+0.02	+0.08
KS2 Maths	+0.06	+0.07
KS2 Science	+0.02	+0.05

The second analytical strategy compares the Foundation Phase outcomes of pupils at the end of Year 6 (at age 10–11 years) by how well the schools have implemented the Foundation Phase (using a measure based on systematic classroom observations). This is only possible for pupils who attended 41 case study schools for which we have detailed information about the use of Foundation Phase pedagogies. Unlike the first analytical approach it is not possible to compare National Curriculum Key Stage 2 outcomes because 2015–16 will be the first year that pupils in the final roll-out of the Foundation Phase will reach the end of Key Stage 2. However, these 41 case study schools are more representative of all other schools in Wales than the 22 pilot schools and include a representative sample of Welsh medium schools, schools from the four regions of Wales and schools of different sizes, intakes and geographical location. Despite being more representative we still control for individual and compositional characteristics, but this time using more conventional regression techniques.

Both analytical strategies are designed to provide equivalent comparisons, but each approach attempts to reveal two different, but complementary, 'effects' of the Foundation Phase:

i. Foundation Phase versus National Curriculum Key Stage 1

ii. High use of Foundation Phase pedagogies versus low use of Foundation Phase pedagogies.

Table 1 shows the differences in levels of attainment (achieving Level 4 or above) in three Key Stage 2 subjects before and after the introduction of the Foundation Phase between pupils attending pilot Foundation Phase schools and equivalently 'matched' pupils attending other schools. The figures in Table 1 are presented as proportions. The first column of results show that prior to the introduction of the Foundation Phase pupils attending pilot schools were slightly more likely to achieve Level 4 or above in all three core Key Stage 2 subjects than their equivalent peers in other schools. For example, in KS2 English and KS2 Science two percentage point more pupils achieved Level 4 or above, and six percentage point more pupils achieved Level 4 or above in KS2 Science in what became the pilot Foundation Phase schools. It is important to recall that in these comparisons we are comparing pupils who followed both the same National Curriculum at Key Stage 1 and Key Stage 2. Therefore, this would suggest that, on balance, the 22 pilot schools were relatively high achieving schools once the characteristics of their pupils had been taken into account. Importantly they do not appear to be representative of the wider school population based on levels of attainment achieved by their pupils.

Using the same matching techniques it is also possible to compare the relative achievement of pupils in these pilot schools after the Foundation Phase was introduced. This time the comparison being made is with equivalent pupils in other schools who continued to follow the previous Key Stage 1 National Curriculum. Of course both sets of pupils experienced the same Key Stage 2 National Curriculum from age 7 years onwards. The outcomes of these comparisons are presented in the second column of results in Table 1. In all three core subjects the proportion of pilot school pupils achieving Level 4 or above continues to be greater than the proportion of their equivalent peers in other schools. And crucially these 'gaps' or differentials are greater in all three subjects *after* the introduction of the Foundation Phase than they were *prior* to its introduction.

These results would suggest that, at least for the first three cohorts of pupils who experienced the Foundation Phase during the pilot stage, there has been a relative improvement in levels of achievement at the end of Key Stage 2. However, the initial evaluation of the pilot phase (Siraj-Blatchford et al., 2005) and the more recent evaluation (Taylor et al., 2015a) both showed that there has been considerable variation in the implementation of the Foundation Phase, particularly in terms of pedagogical practice, even amongst the pilot schools. Therefore the second set of results looking at the impact on attainment according to how well the Foundation Phase has been implemented is of critical importance.

For this second approach we are comparing Foundation Phase outcomes at the end of Year 2 when pupils are aged 6–7 years. Here we use the Foundation Phase Indicator (FPI). The FPI is achieved if a pupil achieves Outcome 5 or above in all three statutory Areas of Learning: Language, Literacy and Communication (English or Welsh); Mathematical Development; and Personal and Social Development, Wellbeing and Cultural Diversity. Using binary logistic regression the analysis attempts to predict the likelihood that a pupil will achieve the FPI depending on a range of individual and school-level variables. The results of this model and the variables considered are presented in Table 2.

To represent the implementation of the Foundation Phase we include the variable *Foundation Phase Score*. This is an aggregated score based on all the systematic classroom observations undertaken in each of 41 case study schools. The higher the score the more we observed the 12 Foundation Phase pedagogical elements, identified above, being used in classrooms (for more details about this measure see Taylor et al., 2015a). The aggregated score is then standardised so that the odds ratio relates to an increase in one standard deviation in the Foundation Phase Score.

Table 2. Estimating the likelihood of achieving the Foundation Phase Indicator (FPI), 2011/12.

Binary Logistic Regression Model		Exp (B) (Odds Ratios)		95% Confidence Intervals	Frequency in valid sample
Valid cases	1,065				
Cox & Snell R^2	0.275				
Constant		20.60			
Foundation Phase Score (standardised)		*1.55*******		*1.22, 1.96*	
Gender	Male		ref		535
	Female	1.37		0.93, 2.00	530
Free School Meals	Non-FSM eligible		ref		823
	FSM eligible	0.61*		0.39, 0.95	242
Ethnicity	White British		ref		968
	Not White British	0.76		0.36, 1.58	97
SEN provision	No SEN		ref		785
	SEN	0.05***		0.03, 0.07	280
Regional consortia in Wales	North		ref		143
	South West & Mid	0.54		0.28, 1.06	294
	Central South	0.65		0.34, 1.23	369
	South East	1.58		0.74, 3.38	259
School intake characteristics (% of school pupils)	Eligible for FSM	0.97***		0.96, 0.98	
	With SEN	1.03***		1.01, 1.04	
	Not White British	1.00		0.98, 1.02	

*p<0.05; **p<0.01; ***p<0.001.

The results of the binary logistic regression in Table 2 show that there is a significant relationship between the Foundation Phase Score and the likelihood that pupils achieved the Foundation Phase Indicator. Indeed, a one standard deviation increase in the Foundation Phase Score increases the probability that a pupil achieved the FPI by 55% on average. A one standard deviation increase in the Foundation Phase Score is the equivalent of moving from an 'average' school to a school in the top 20% of schools implementing the Foundation Phase.

Both sets of analyses on the impact of the Foundation Phase on pupil attainment carry with them a number of important limitations. One of the limits of both sets of analyses is that they are both based on relatively small samples of pupils. Furthermore, neither set of samples is randomly selected nor entirely representative of the wider pupil and school population. However, we use a variety of statistical techniques to try to control for any potential biases in the samples. And lastly, there will be, inevitably, many other factors that could account for differences in levels of attainment that have not been considered in these models.

Despite this, we are able to demonstrate using measures of educational attainment at two different age points, using two different statistical techniques, and with two very different samples of pupils, that there is a positive association between levels of attainment and the presence of the Foundation Phase.

Challenges to the implementation of the Foundation Phase

In this paper we have attempted to focus on the implementation of the Foundation Phase and the impact that it appears to have had on pupil attainment. We conclude this discussion by outlining the key challenges to its implementation.

The first key challenge of any curricula reform relates to staffing. The vast majority of additional costs associated with the Foundation Phase relate to improvements to the recommended adult-to-child ratios for 3–7 year-olds. As we have seen, this has led to a doubling in the number of additional practitioners working in schools in Wales. However, in its implementation there was a greater preoccupation with adult-to-child ratios than there was with the kind of expertise that would be required in settings and classrooms. For example, with the same additional costs it would have been possible to have employed additional qualified teachers instead of NVQ Level 3 additional practitioners, albeit with slightly worse adult-to-child ratios. Although the presence of more adults in a classroom or setting has been widely welcomed we find that there has been a clear division of labour between qualified teachers and additional practitioners—qualified teachers spend significantly more of their time involved in direct teaching (and indoors), whilst it is the additional practitioners who are engaged in more continuous, play-based, experiential and outdoors learning. It is perhaps unsurprising, then, to find that enhanced provision (i.e. the scaffolding of learning from more play-based experiential learning) has been the least observed form of provision in classrooms and settings.

This also demonstrates the importance of ensuring new staff are fully trained in the new curriculum and pedagogical approaches being encouraged. Again, despite being ten years since the Foundation Phase was first introduced the recent stocktake undertaken by Professor Siraj found 'the differences and inequalities in training and their accessibility to all appropriate staff concerning and the level and content of the initial training at least was lacking' (Welsh Government, 2014b, p. 38). As discussed above, we find that teachers who have participated in more of the Foundation Phase training are more likely to have implemented Foundation Phase pedagogies.

Another key challenge to the implementation of the Foundation Phase has been in securing a clear understanding of the theories and reasoning behind the changes to early years education. Of course it could be argued that the Foundation Phase represents such a radical departure from its predecessor that it was always going to be a significant challenge to develop a detailed understanding of its underpinning theories amongst practitioners in a short timescale. However, the development of the guidance and training materials was largely done in pilot schools and settings, with existing practitioners centrally involved in their development. The selection of those settings was, therefore, quite instrumental in the initial development of the Foundation Phase. Despite this there is no consistent account of how they were selected, and the pilot stage evaluation found considerable variation in the implementation of the Foundation Phase across these schools and settings (Siraj-Blatchford et al., 2005). Furthermore, some of the main features of the Foundation Phase, such as the pedagogy of play, are relatively new areas of teaching and learning with a limited research base from which to develop 'best' practice (Wood, 2009). The expectation that a largely practitioner-led development of such theories was the most appropriate way of developing new practice was always going to be problematic.

Our analysis above also suggests that pupils in these pilot schools were more likely, on average, to achieve Level 4 or above in Key Stage 2 teacher assessments than equivalent pupils in other schools with similar intakes before the Foundation Phase was introduced. The selection, inadvertently or consciously, of piloting the development of new curricula in generally high achieving schools does pose significant problems, particularly in relation to the challenges of developing a new curriculum that supports disadvantaged learners in schools that are already struggling to ensure their pupils reach expected levels before they enter secondary schools. Indeed, a major concern about the Foundation Phase has been the very limited impact it has had on reducing differences in attainment of key groups of pupils— especially for boys and pupils eligible for free school meals (Taylor et al., 2015a).

Many of the arguments for the introduction of the Foundation Phase and its associated pedagogical approaches resulted from a frustration with the appropriateness of its predecessor, the Key Stage 1 National Curriculum, and deep concerns that many practitioners were not adopting developmentally appropriate practices in the early years. Similar concerns and a desire for reform have been seen in many countries (Walsh, Sproule, McGuiness, Trew, & Ingram, 2010). However, what appears to have been lacking in Wales was the necessary understanding of the 'conditions' and 'contexts' in which this radical overhaul of the early years curriculum was to take place. A major objective of the reforms was to increase the proportion of children achieving expected levels in literacy and numeracy by the end of primary years, particularly those from disadvantaged backgrounds. In both cases there was little evidence that adopting developmentally appropriate practice or pedagogies of play was the most appropriate solution to these circumstances.

This leads on to the final key challenge in the implementation of the Foundation Phase. Many practitioners and key stakeholders have argued that there is a tension between the use of more child-centred developmentally appropriate practices whilst at the same time embarking on a major programme of reforms designed specifically to raise educational standards in schools. We have discussed above the possible adverse effects of the Literacy and Numeracy Framework on the implementation of the Foundation Phase. Despite these concerns the analysis presented above suggests that pupils in schools that do implement the Foundation Phase well are slightly more likely to achieve good outcomes in literacy and numeracy. But the reluctance amongst many practitioners, particularly those teaching in Year 1 and Year 2, to fully adopt the Foundation Phase stems from their concerns about an assumed tension or perceived contradiction in the theories underpinning both the Foundation Phase and the Literacy and Numeracy Framework. We would argue it is easy to see why. The pace of change expected or required in improving pupil attainment does not give practitioners much time to experiment or risk new pedagogical approaches. And with only a superficial understanding of the Foundation Phase and its underlying theories practitioners are very likely to mistakenly assume they 'know' how the Foundation Phase is meant to be taught, without recognising the importance of, for example, an appropriate balance between continuous, enhanced or focussed provision or using techniques to 'scaffold' pupils' learning. It also raises a more fundamental question about whether it is possible to combine a child-centred approach to education within a standards-driven education system. But as Goldstein (2007) argues, this 'contradiction, tension, inconsistency, and uncertainty, while difficult to manage, are a non-negotiable part of teaching young children. Acknowledging and embracing the unforgiving complexity of [early years] teaching would help us to reposition seemingly intractable problems and to perceive many of our challenges as positive opportunities for professional growth' (pp. 52–53). The dual role of encouraging something akin to 'developmentally appropriate practice' alongside a standards agenda simply contributes to the already complex nature of early years education.

Many of these issues will also be true of curricula and assessment changes that result from the comprehensive Donaldson review of education in Wales. Practitioners need to be aware that there are no 'easy' ways for policy-makers to design and deliver a successful education system, and that identifying, understanding and responding to new pedagogical challenges are just part of their continued professional development. Similarly, the Welsh Government needs to consider carefully the challenges that the implementation of the Donaldson recommendations will encounter. A key aspect of that will be to give considerable attention to the context and circumstances in which those recommendations will be implemented. The use of 'pioneer' schools as the basis of the new reforms will also be critical—these are 68 schools (primary and secondary, urban and rural, English-medium and Welsh-medium) that have been selected to design and develop the new curriculum for Wales. In much the same way as the 'Pilot' schools were central to the design and implementation of the Foundation Phase, so too will these 'Pioneer' schools for the new curriculum. Their selection and the expertise of practitioners working within these schools will determine the quality of the curriculum and associated resources. It is imperative, therefore, that any new developments require (a) a full and proper examination of those circumstances underpinning the need for change, (b) the involvement of a wide range of expertise (and not just practitioners in 'Pioneer' schools), and (c) much greater use of experimentation and design research in the development of new curricula materials.[4]

Notes

1. Some provision for three and four year-olds in Wales is provided in the non-maintained sector but funded by the Welsh Government. The Foundation Phase is not statutory for other private providers of childcare or education.
2. For more information about the methodology used in the evaluation of the Foundation Phase, including the tools used in the observation of practitioners and children see Taylor et al., 2015c.

3. For further information about how this technique, propensity score matching, is used see Taylor et al., 2015b.
4. See Middleton, Gorard, Taylor & Bannan-Ritland (2008) for further details of such an approach.

Acknowledgements

This article is based on research supported by the Wales Institute of Social & Economic Research, Data & Methods (WISERD). WISERD is a collaborative venture between the Universities of Aberystwyth, Bangor, Cardiff, South Wales and Swansea. The research that this publication relates to was undertaken through 'Evaluating the Foundation Phase' and was funded by the Welsh Government. The authors would like to thank all those involved in the research, most notably the practitioners and pupils in the 41 schools and 10 funded non-maintained settings that allowed us to spend a substantial amount of time with them. We would also like to thank the anonymous reviewers and Launa Anderson in the Welsh Government for their comments. However, all responsibility for the analysis and interpretation remains solely with the authors.

Disclosure statement

No potential conflict of interest was reported by the authors.

ORCID

Chris Taylor 🄳 http://orcid.org/0000-0002-9146-9167

References

Aasen, W., & Waters, J. (2006). The new curriculum in Wales: A new view of the child? *Education 3–13: International Journal of Primary. Elementary and Early Years Education, 34,* 123–129.

Brown, C. & Lilford, R. (2006). The stepped wedge trial design: A systematic review. *BMC Medical Research Methodology, 6,* doi:http://dx.doi.org/10.1186/1471-2288-6-54.

Donaldson, G. (2015). *Successful futures: Independent review of curriculum and assessment arrangements in Wales.* Cardiff: Welsh Government.

Goldstein, L. (2007). Beyond the DAP versus standards dilemma: Examining the unforgiving complexity of kindergarten teaching in the United States. *Early Childhood Research Quarterly, 22,* 39–54.

Maynard, T., Taylor, C., Waldron, S., Rhys, M., Smith, R., Power, S., & Clement, J. (2013). *Evaluating the Foundation Phase: Policy logic model and programme theory, Social Research No. 37/2012.* Cardiff: Welsh Government.

Middleton, J., Gorard, S., Taylor, C., & Bannan-Ritland, B. (2008). The 'compleat' design experiment. In A. Kelly, R. Lesh, & J. Baek (Eds.), *Handbook of design research methods in education* (pp. 2–46). New York, NY: Routledge.

NAfW (2001). *The learning country*. Cardiff: National Assembly for Wales.

NAfW (2003). *The learning country: Foundation Phase: 3 to 7 years*. Cardiff: National Assembly for Wales.

OECD (2004). *Five curriculum outcomes (starting strong, curriculum and pedagogies in early childhood education and care)*. Paris: OECD.

Rees, G., & Taylor, C. (2015). Is there a 'crisis' in Welsh education? *Transactions of the Honourable Society of Cymmrodorion, 2015*, 97–113.

Rhys, M., Waldron, S., & Taylor, C. (2014). *Evaluating the Foundation Phase: Key findings on training, support and guidance, Social research summary 54/2014*. Cardiff: Welsh Government.

Siraj-Blatchford, I., Sylva, K., Laugharne, J., Milton, E., & Charles, F. (2005). *Monitoring and evaluation of the effective implementation of the 128 Foundation Phase (MEEIFP) project across Wales: Final report of Year I pilot*. Cardiff: Welsh Assembly Government.

Taylor, C., Waldron, S., & Rhys, C. (2014). *Evaluating the Foundation Phase: Key findings on staffing, Social Research Summary 95/2014*. Cardiff: Welsh Government.

Taylor, C., Maynard, T., Davies, R., Waldron, S. Rhys, M., Power, S., Moore, L., Blackaby, D., & Plewis, I. (2015a). *Evaluating the Foundation Phase: Final report, social research no. 25/2015*. Cardiff: Welsh Government.

Taylor, C., Davies, R., Rhys, M., Waldron, S., & Blackaby, D. (2015b). *Evaluating the Foundation Phase: The outcomes of Foundation Phase pupils up to 2011/12 (Report 2), Social Research No. 01/2015*. Cardiff: Welsh Government.

Taylor, C., Maynard, T., Davies, R., Waldron, S., Rhys, M., Power, S., Moore, L., Blackaby, D., & Plewis, I. (2015c). *Evaluating the Foundation Phase: Technical report, social research no. 16/2014*. Cardiff: Welsh Government.

Waldron, S., Rhys, M., & Taylor, C. (2014). *Evaluating the Foundation Phase key findings on reported impacts social research summary 42/2014*. Cardiff: Welsh Government.

Waldron, S., Rhys, M., & Taylor, C. (2014). *Evaluating the Foundation Phase key findings on child involvement and wellbeing social research summary 44/2014*. Cardiff: Welsh Government.

Walsh, G., Sproule, L., McGuiness, C., Trew, K., & Ingram, G. (2010). *Developmentally appropriate practice and play-based pedagogy in early years education: A literature review of research and practice*. Belfast: Queen's University Belfast.

WAG (2009). *Foundation Phase Outdoor Learning Handbook*. Cardiff: Department for Children, Education, Lifelong Learning and Skills, Welsh Assembly Government.

Welsh Government (2013). *National Literacy and Numeracy Framework, information document No. 120/2013*. Cardiff: Welsh Government.

Welsh Government (2014a). *Further steps outdoors: Making the most of your outdoor spaces*. Cardiff: Welsh Government.

Welsh Government (2014b). *An independent stocktake of the Foundation Phase in Wales*. Cardiff: Welsh Government.

Welsh Government (2015). *Curriculum for Wales: Foundation Phase framework*. Cardiff: Welsh Government.

Wincott, D. (2006). Devolution and the welfare state: Lessons from early childhood education and care policy in Wales. *Environment and Planning C: Government and Policy, 24*, 279–295.

Wood, E. (2009). Developing a pedagogy of play for the 21st century. In A. Anning, J. Cullen, & M. Fleer (Eds.), *Early childhood education: Society and culture* (2nd ed.) (pp. 17–30). London: Sage.

Education in England – a testbed for network governance?

Geoff Whitty and Emma Wisby

ABSTRACT

Since devolution in the late 1990s, education policy in England has diverged further from that in Scotland and also from policy in Wales and Northern Ireland. In this paper we review the roots and trajectory of the English education reforms over the past two decades. Our focus is the schools sector, though we also touch on adjoining reforms to early years and further and higher education. In so doing, we engage with various themes, including marketisation, institutional autonomy and accountability. Changes in governance arrangements for schools have been a defining feature of education reforms since devolution. This has been set against an evolution in national performance indicators that has put government priorities into ever sharper relief. In theorising the changes, we pay particular attention to the suggestion that the English education system now epitomises the concept of 'network governance', which has also been applied to education in a global context. We question the extent to which policies have in practice moved beyond the well-established mechanisms of 'steering at a distance' and undermined the very notion of an education system in England. We conclude by considering possible futures for education policy and how they may position England in relation to other parts of the UK and the wider world.

Introduction

English and Scottish education policies were markedly different well before parliamentary devolution in 1998, especially in relation to schools policy, which had long been a devolved responsibility in administrative terms. Education policies in Wales and Northern Ireland had hitherto been much more similar to those in England, although with some distinctive characteristics of their own. However, a peculiarly English approach to education reform had already begun to emerge since the 1988 Education Reform Act (ERA) and 1992 Education (Schools) Act. Although other jurisdictions had their own watered down versions of the ERA, devolution in 1998 allowed them to break free and follow their own paths. England, however, continued to follow the direction set by the Thatcher government in the 1980s.

During the 1970s there had been growing antipathy in England towards the 'swollen state' of the immediate post-war years. This was largely for economic reasons concerning the level of public expenditure. But under the 1979 Thatcher government it became coupled with a market choice critique of public sector management. In the case of education this focused increasingly on the role of the so-called 'educational establishment'—principally left-leaning teaching unions, inspectors and teacher trainers—who seemed to favour what the Conservatives saw as highly questionable 'progressive' or 'child-centred' approaches to teaching. Local Education Authorities (LEAs) were also implicated, their central role in the allocation of school places seen as stifling the need for schools to innovate or to respond efficiently, if at all, to parental concerns (Shleifer, 1998). Taken together, the Conservatives argued, 'progressive' teaching methods and state allocation of places had brought a dull uniformity to the system and a levelling down of standards. Accordingly, throughout their time in office, the Conservative governments of Margaret Thatcher and John Major acted to increase the power of the 'consumer' and reduce that of the 'producer'. They did so through the introduction of greater parental choice over the school their children would attend, and increased differentiation of the types of schools parents could choose from. This was achieved in part by introducing new types of school, such as grant maintained schools and city technology colleges, autonomous from local authorities. Another new type of school—the specialist school—was permitted to select up to 10% of pupils on the basis of aptitude for the school's specialism. These schools also had greater freedoms in relation to the curriculum. This was coupled with per capita funding and the devolution of many LEA responsibilities, including funding decisions, to virtually all schools so that they could respond to the market.

However, while the Conservatives were enthusiastic about making schools more receptive to parents' wishes, they were unwilling to relinquish control over the outcomes that schools should achieve. In this, Conservative education policy provides a clear illustration of the tendency for liberal democracies to develop along the lines of the 'strong state' and the 'free economy' (Gamble, 1988) and the associated shift in the way the public sector is co-ordinated and controlled by government, to what can be characterised as 'steering at a distance'. While devolution of responsibilities to individual organisations appears to offer them greater autonomy, the state retains overall strategic control by setting the outputs that providers need to achieve and publishing details of their performance against them (Neave, 1988; Whitty, Power & Halpin, 1998). These indicators arguably influence the priorities of service users, who in turn reinforce the pressure on providers to work to them (Adnett & Davies, 2003). Examples of such central steering mechanisms under the Conservatives included the establishment of the National Curriculum and its associated system of assessment, and the introduction of a new and more intensive approach to school inspection through the Office for Standards in Education (Ofsted), a new non-ministerial government department. Given the relationship between the profile of a school's pupil intake in terms of prior ability and its performance in league tables, these policies made the issue of school autonomy over admissions one of growing significance within the English system.

In the 1997 general election the Conservative party was heavily defeated by New Labour, under the leadership of Tony Blair. There was, however, a good deal of continuity between the two parties' education policies in England. Indeed, in some respects, the New Labour government took both competition and central steering much further than the Conservatives had. Under New Labour this basic policy framework was presented in terms of furthering social justice through a modernised public sector. This reflected New Labour's founding commitment to the 'Third Way', a concept that Tony Blair adopted enthusiastically as part of his modernisation of the Labour party and abandonment of what were regarded as outdated ideologies (Blair, 1998). Formulated by the sociologist Anthony Giddens, the Third Way was a pragmatic approach that sought to marry social democracy and the market.

In schools policy there were major new investments intended to raise standards, under the banner of 'a high quality education for all'. These supported a significant extension of early years provision, successive area-based interventions to address poorly performing schools (e.g. Education Action Zones, Excellence in Cities, London Challenge), as well as efforts to improve the wellbeing of children and young people—delivered through a constellation of policies known as *Every Child Matters*. In New Labour's second and third terms of office there was a shift in emphasis, from that of simply raising standards to also narrowing the socio-economic attainment gap between pupils from advantaged and disadvantaged backgrounds. The result was the introduction of more targeted interventions in order to focus additional resources on pupils who needed greater support, one example being the literacy scheme Reading Recovery. A notable feature of this policy landscape was the way in which New Labour worked through a number of existing and new 'quangos' to take forward its policies, including the Qualifications and Curriculum Development Agency, Training and Development Agency for Schools, and the British Educational Communications and Technology Agency. All this sat, though, against the backdrop of a continued push for a greater diversity of autonomous schools, publication of performance data, and parental choice. Meanwhile, building on the National Curriculum, a series of 'national strategies', first for literacy and numeracy and then for the primary and secondary phases as a whole, provided the basis for further shaping the work of schools in a marketised system. Early years provision received the same treatment, including the introduction of the Early Years Foundation Stage and related standards.

In higher education policy New Labour placed a strong emphasis on widening participation, the 'flagship' target being to achieve a 50% participation rate in higher education among the 18–30 age group (see Whitty, Anders, Hayton, Tang & Wisby, 2016, ch. 5). This was combined with the dramatic development of introducing tuition fees for UK first degree students. The latter was based on the principle that students were as much a beneficiary of attending university as wider society and should therefore make a direct contribution to the costs of their study; the funding of higher education through general taxation was presented as being regressive. When Scotland subsequently abolished fees for its own students, English and Scottish higher education policy diverged, while the other UK jurisdictions adopted variants of the English approach, albeit with limited enthusiasm.

In post-compulsory education the New Labour administration will be most remembered for its rejection of the Tomlinson Report of 2004 and the recommendation to create a single diploma qualification for the 14–19 phase. The later 'compromise' of introducing a 14–19 Diploma to sit alongside A-levels was short-lived, though the policy to raise the participation age was more positively received. More generally, New Labour's governance of the further education and skills sector often appeared to lack coherence: in particular, in many instances it was seemingly unable or unwilling to steer the sector more decisively—not least in relation to the repeated calls for a better fit between provision and economic and employer need (Lupton, Unwin &Thomson, 2015).

Overall, in the immediate years following devolution, education policy in England was characterised by a continued shift away from two long established planks of social democratic thinking about education that remained more firmly intact in many other parts of the UK—comprehensive secondary schooling and free higher education. But there were many tensions, compromises and nuances in this drift away from the other UK nations under New Labour. These centred first and foremost on selection and school autonomy, especially in relation to admissions. The tuition fees policy arguably generated somewhat less overt soul searching within the Labour party at large, even though it led to one of the largest revolts in the Parliamentary Labour Party during the passage of the 2004 Higher Education Act. Higher Education policy is covered in detail in another contribution to this special issue (Hillman, 2016), so will not be addressed further in this article. In schools policy, the effects of successive Coalition and Conservative education policies after 2010 would pose a fresh challenge to the Labour party's commitment to social democratic principles in schools policy and even conflict within the party as a whole.

The demise of social democracy?

After Labour's failure to end academic selection at 11+ during its periods in office in the 1960s and 1970s, the extent of its continuing commitment to comprehensive education had by the 1990s become a vexed issue. Party sound bites from the 1992 general election suggested a renewed commitment to the abandonment of any selection within the state education system and the re-assertion of LEA control over maintained schools (see, for example, *The Independent*, 26 February 1992). It was following Labour's fourth successive general election defeat that the party moved towards a position that accepted, and then embraced, a version of the diversity and choice policies that were being pursued by the Conservatives. These were often based on—or certainly accepted—elements of overt selection across the secondary schools system; in other respects, this policy also raised concerns about covert selection.

Although the New Labour government did not support the creation of new state-funded grammar schools (and abolished the Assisted Places Scheme that had provided support for children of modest means to attend academically selective private schools), it was in the name of parental choice that the party side-stepped the so-called 'grammar school question' (Crook, Power & Whitty, 2000). As Blair told an audience in Birmingham during the 1997 general election campaign, 'so far as the existing … grammar schools are concerned, as long as the parents want them, they will stay. … We will tackle what isn't working, not what is' (Blair, 1997). Accordingly, immediately after its election victory, New Labour published proposals to allow parents to decide the fate of existing grammar schools or of area-wide selection where it still existed. The 1998 School Standards and Framework Act thus included provisions by which local communities could petition for a ballot to end academic selection. Several petitions were launched but only one received the signatures of 20% of eligible parents, the threshold needed to trigger a ballot. In this ballot, which was for Ripon Grammar School, parents rejected an end to selection by a ratio of 2:1. There therefore remained 164 grammar schools in England, located in 36 of the 150 local authorities; of these 36, only the 15 fully selective local authorities had substantial numbers of pupils attending grammar schools.

New Labour went on to endorse implicitly the principle of overt selection in other ways. The 1997 White Paper, *Excellence in Schools* (DfEE, 1997), and the aforementioned 1998 School Standards and Framework Act that followed it, continued the previous administration's support for specialist schools; while the Act placed rather less emphasis on these schools' selective character, it nevertheless permitted any school to select 10% of pupils on aptitude if the governing body was satisfied that the school had a specialism. Coldron, Willis & Wolstenholme (2009) note that although the great majority of specialist schools did not use selection, the potential was there for them to do so.

There were continuing calls from organisations such as the Campaign for State Education (CASE) and Comprehensive Future throughout the period of New Labour government—and beyond—for the Labour party leadership to tackle the remaining grammar schools. However, the more ambiguous territory of 'choice and diversity' had won out. Some in the party went so far as to dismiss the comprehensive school altogether as 'an institution of the past—part of the social democratic agenda of the Sixties and therefore of no relevance to the world of the Nineties' (cited in Chitty, 1994, p. 89). Other contributions from centre-left writers at this time saw benefit in overt selection: in their 1997 publication, *A Class Act*, Adonis and Pollard argued that 'for all the good intentions, the destruction of the grammar schools ... had the effect of reinforcing class divisions' (p. 61).

Accordingly, the amount of differentiation among schools grew under New Labour, and its rhetoric increasingly emphasised a supposed link between school diversity and higher standards. This was made clear by Tony Blair in a 2006 speech, where he commented that 'over time I shifted from saying "it's standards, not structures" to realising that school structures could affect standards' (Blair, 2006). As under the previous Conservative government, the key ingredient for linking differentiation to standards and excellence remained choice; this was illustrated by the 2005 schools White Paper, which had argued against ignoring 'the reality that the vast majority of parents want a real choice of excellent schools' (DfES, 2005, p. 8). New Labour chose to maintain something of the Conservative distinction between local authority and grant maintained status, albeit under the new titles of 'community' and 'foundation' schools. In addition, it retained the city technology colleges (CTCs), to which were added (city) academies, and trust schools. Many of these schools were also specialist schools, and so the number and proportion of these schools increased significantly; others were also faith schools. A new Schools Commissioner would act as a 'champion' of increased diversity and choice.

Academies in particular became a totemic policy for New Labour (and for the Coalition and Conservative administrations that followed). Their origins lay in the aforementioned CTCs, a new form of state-funded secondary school for the inner city that sat entirely outside the influence of LEAs. The plan was for CTCs to be run by independent trusts, with capital funding coming from the private sector and the state providing recurrent funding. In practice, however, few business sponsors came forward, the Thatcher government covered virtually all funding, and the number of CTCs remained small (Whitty, Edwards & Gewirtz, 1993). Under New Labour, academies were introduced explicitly to tackle failing local authority run schools, which were typically in deprived areas (NAO, 2007). Some academies were new schools; others were existing schools that had not responded to earlier 'turnaround' initiatives. All had sponsors, typically with business connections, who in these early days of academies were required to contribute to capital costs.

As Education Minister, Estelle Morris (2001) stated that specialist schools were 'only modern comprehensive schools', implying that they had no special advantages. But at least until they became the majority of secondary schools, the specialist school label clearly differentiated them from what Tony Blair's official spokesman, Alastair Campbell, termed 'bog-standard' comprehensive schools (Campbell, 2007). While the apparently superior performance of specialist schools added impetus to the policy of differentiation (Jesson &

Crossley, 2006), the fact that this performance may have been partly due to the nature of their pupil intakes was not always acknowledged (Sutton Trust, 2006). Although it had always been the case that all sorts of schools that were nominally comprehensive lacked balanced intakes, either socially or academically or indeed both, the charge was that school choice and school autonomy, including over admissions, would now make it possible for far more schools to select covertly as well as overtly (Gewirtz, Ball & Bowe,1995; Newsam, 2003). Academies became an important category of school in this regard, while selection by faith schools also came under the spotlight (Penlington, 2001).

So, for a time, the debate about overt academic selection took second place to a debate about whether covert social selection, and by implication covert academic selection, was taking place in the new diverse school system. A major issue of contention between the proponents and opponents of diversity was the effect of some but not all schools being their own admissions authorities. For example, Tough and Brooks (2007) found that schools that were their own admissions authorities had intakes that were far less representative of their surrounding areas than schools where the local authority was the admissions authority. In 2005 and 2006, the Sutton Trust looked at the social composition of the 'top 200' comprehensives in England and identified a group of high attaining schools that were more socially exclusive than the national average and other schools in their areas (Sutton Trust, 2006). It concluded that this mismatch could be explained by a number of factors, including covert social selection.

Such covert selection was an area of concern for the House of Commons Education and Skills Committee in its review of the 2005 schools White Paper, and its report to government prompted some significant concessions on admissions policy, mainly around the status of the admissions code (DfES, 2006; House of Commons Education and Skills Committee, 2006). In an attempt to address covert selection (whether intended or unintended), the new code prohibited schools from giving priority to children on the basis of their interests or knowledge, and this was combined with free school transport to open up choice to less advantaged families, and 'choice advisers' to assist these families in negotiating their child's transition to secondary school (DfES, 2005). Later research by Allen, Coldron & West (2012) has suggested that the 2003 and 2007 admission codes did reduce social segregation between schools to a limited extent.

Left of centre opponents of New Labour continued to argue that such measures would not be enough to overcome covert selection and 'playing the system' by knowledgeable middle-class families, so they united around a call for 'good schools in all areas, for all children' (e.g. Education Alliance, 2006). However, any attempt to return to traditional catchment areas after two decades of choice was unlikely to be attractive politically. An attempt by one local authority, Brighton, to run admissions lotteries as an alternative way of dealing with covert selection proved even more contentious (see Laville & Smithers, 2007)—as well as relatively ineffective in changing pupil sorting (Allen, Burgess & McKenna, 2010).

In June 2007, Gordon Brown replaced Tony Blair as leader of the Labour Party and Prime Minister. There were some initial signs that the Brown government might have been willing to confront some of these issues—with talk of an 'egalitarian project' even being heard in the Brown camp (Wilby, 2007). As Fiona Millar pointed out at the time, 'the words "diversity" and "choice", the mantras of education policy through the Thatcher, Major and Blair years' did not even feature in the first Commons statement by Ed Balls, Brown's Secretary of State for Children, Schools and Families (Balls, 2007a; Millar, 2007). Furthermore, that same minister's first major speech outside parliament indicated that a wider children's agenda would be as important as the standards agenda in his newly-created department and high-lighted the important links between them (Balls, 2007b). In particular, the new government also signalled a greater role for local authorities in the planning of new academies and indicated that such schools should be seen as part of their local family of schools rather than lying outside them. This change of focus appeared not to be merely rhetorical, backed as it was by Public Service Agreement delivery targets for the Department for Children, Schools and Families that related in large part to narrowing the gap in educational achievement between pupils from different backgrounds (Baker, 2007). Nevertheless, little substantive change in policy or outcomes could be detected. It was unclear how far a stronger social justice agenda could be reconciled with the electoral logic that had so influenced the policies of the Blair government. As Peter Wilby (2007) put it, 'a Brown government will need courage and ingenuity to reconcile egalitarian ambitions with political realities', and, in the end, it proved unable to do so.

The Conservative–Liberal Democrat Coalition 2010–15

At the time New Labour left office in 2010 the socio-economic attainment gap remained very real. The Coalition government that was elected to replace New Labour set an ambitious goal of 'closing' this gap as part of a wider commitment to increasing social mobility, which it claimed had stalled under New Labour (HM Government, 2011). The general thrust of its policies was to continue and accelerate the emphasis on seeking improvement through school autonomy, competition and choice that, as we have seen, had been pioneered by Margaret Thatcher's Conservative government and continued by New Labour under Tony Blair and, if not with quite the same enthusiasm, under Gordon Brown (Whitty, 2008).

While the academies policy of the Blair government had sought to use academy status mainly to prioritise the replacement or improvement of failing schools in disadvantaged areas, the Conservative-led Coalition potentially extended this status to virtually all schools. Schools highly rated by Ofsted, a disproportionate number of which were in more affluent areas, could be granted academy status automatically if they so desired. Meanwhile, parents, teachers and others were encouraged to open publicly funded 'free schools', which, like academies, were outside local authority jurisdiction. Neither academies nor free schools are bound by statute to teach the National Curriculum, nor do they have to employ qualified teachers (though most do both at the moment). They are their own admissions authorities. This policy has been reinforced by a wider emphasis on establishing a 'schools-led system' in which improvement is fostered through school-to-school support.

It remains an open question whether such policies (subsequently continued by the major-ity Conservative government elected in 2105) will help to 'close' the attainment gap or, as some critics have suggested, effectively 'open' it up again. So far, around 60% of English secondary schools and nearly 10% of primary schools have academy or free school status, and an increasing number of them are being linked in academy 'chains'. Recent attempts to assess the evidence have come to no firm conclusions about the impact of these policies. The House of Commons Education Committee argued that 'current evidence does not allow us to draw conclusions on whether academies in themselves are a positive force for change' and 'agree[d] with Ofsted that it is too early to draw conclusions on the quality of education provided by free schools or their broader system impact (House of Commons Education

Committee, 2015; see also McNally, 2015). What is clear is that, although some of these new schools are in disadvantaged areas or where there is a shortage of school places, others are in middle-class areas and where there is already a surplus of places, while those free schools located in disadvantaged areas have not necessarily attracted disadvantaged children (Green, Allen & Jenkins, 2014; Morris, 2015).

Nevertheless, some of the other policies adopted by the Coalition government reflected the social justice agenda of the Liberal Democrat party whose votes gave the Coalition a majority in parliament. Among the policies that were strongly influenced by Liberal Democrat thinking was a commitment to address the attainment gap through a 'pupil premium' to be paid on top of the normal grant for every school age pupil in receipt of free school meals in state schools. This was consistent with the earlier trend under New Labour of linking resources to individuals in need, regardless of the neighbourhood in which they received their schooling. The premium was subsequently increased and extended and, although the money was not ring-fenced or mandated for particular purposes, monitoring of its use by Ofsted was intended to ensure that it was used to benefit the education of the disadvantaged. Early surveys were not particularly encouraging in this respect, and suggested that too little of the money allocated through the pupil premium was being spent on activities known to boost attainment (Ofsted, 2012; Sutton Trust, 2012). However, later surveys were somewhat more positive about its role in narrowing the gap (Ofsted, 2014). Unfortunately, the pupil premium was introduced at a time of expenditure cuts in other areas, which is likely to undermine its potential impact (Lupton et al., 2015). Ultimately, the level of the premium was never such that it would act as an incentive for schools, in a marketised system, to enrol a more diverse intake of pupils in terms of socio-economic background or prior attainment.

There was also considerable controversy about whether the Coalition government's curriculum policies would help to close the gap. As well as admissions, this is another area in which the effects of marketisation have been evident within the English system. One Coalition policy was to reduce the number of 'equivalent' qualifications that are permitted to be used in school performance tables as alternatives to the GCSE qualifications at age 16. Schools' use of these qualifications, many of them poorly regarded, had mushroomed under the New Labour government, particularly so among academies (de Waal, 2009), and particularly to the detriment of more disadvantaged pupils. The Coalition's intention was to reverse this trend and place a much stronger emphasis on a return to conventional academic qualifications—for all pupils. Following the Department for Education-commissioned Wolf review, the Coalition removed a large number of vocational qualifications deemed to be of poor quality and in little demand among employers. It also strengthened the requirements for English and mathematics, asking all young people to achieve GCSE grade C or above by age 18. But perhaps the flagship curriculum reform under the Coalition was the 'English Baccalaureate' (EBacc), which was introduced in 2011. This is an award to pupils, but also effectively a new performance measure for secondary schools, based on the percentage of pupils achieving high grades in specified subjects, i.e. English, mathematics, sciences, history or geography, and a foreign language. This seems, initially at least, to have affected socially disadvantaged students adversely as they are more likely to have been exposed to alternative curricula than more advantaged students on a university entrance track (DfE, 2014). Gillborn (2014) has suggested that the introduction of the EBacc, 'restored White odds of success to 2.20 (more than double the Black rate), a rate not seen since 2003'.

Coalition and subsequent Conservative government ministers have claimed that they are encouraging the development of high quality vocational qualifications and that this is reflected in their championing of apprenticeships as an alternative (and/or an alternative route) to university. In its governance of the further education sector, aside from ring-fencing funding for apprenticeships, the Coalition removed any role for central planning, and funded provision on the basis of student demand and outcomes alone. In adult skills, it discontinued central funding and introduced the expectation that employers and individuals would co-invest, including through income-contingent loads as per the funding model for higher education. Alongside this, the Coalition introduced new performance indicators to inform the 'consumer'. The Conservative government has continued this approach. The priority since 2015 has been to expand apprenticeship at scale, for which the government intends to use a new levy on employers. On paper, this would appear to offer a more coherent set of policies than has been the case in the further education sector for some time.

A new era of network governance?

In recent evidence to a House of Commons committee, Stephen Gorard stated that 'there is strong evidence that diversification and fragmentation of what is intended to be a national system is linked to higher socio-economic segregation between schools, and all of the dangers that this entails' (House of Commons Public Bill Committee, 2015).

At the end of the period of Coalition government, the socio-economic attainment gap certainly remained a defining feature of the English education system. There were plaudits for the success of education policy in London in this regard (albeit debate continues as to the relative significance of the apparent contributory factors—see Whitty et al., 2016, chapter 4), as well as for those academy chains that have built their names on turning around the performance of the schools with which they work (Hutchings, Francis & de Vries, 2014). But there were also continuing concerns about the lack of progress in narrowing the gap elsewhere in the system (Wilshaw, 2013). The question that not only Gorard but many commentators are now raising—after three decades of policy underpinned by diversity and choice agendas—is whether England still has an education system in place in the sense that had existed between the landmark 1944 Education Act and the 1979 Thatcher government.

David Bell, a former Permanent Secretary at the education department under New Labour and the Coalition, has offered his own reflections on the English school reforms of recent decades. He has suggested that, with the ever reducing role of local authorities, we are probably moving towards a 'system of many small systems':

> 'Messiness' in terms of structures will be a natural by-product of radical structural reform as we move from a standardised national system to a system of many small systems. I don't have a single solution to offer, nor do I necessarily think there should be one, as the end-point of these school reforms hasn't been reached yet. (Bell, 2012)

He was thinking here of small systems of schools in particular, with academy chains, a few effective local authorities, and federations of schools led by teaching schools or successful individual school leaders. Interestingly, his use of the term 'messiness' resonates with Stephen Ball's characterisation of postmodern education systems as 'untidy' (Ball, 2011).

Greany (2015) regards the new landscape of education, particularly as it developed under the Coalition government, as 'more fragmented, and yet more networked' (p. 125). This applies both at the level of schools and the new policy players that have been encouraged by successive governments. Ball and Junemann (2012) discuss such trends in the governance of education in England in terms of 'network governance'. In particular, they channel our attention to the range of actors now involved in the governance of education in England, including the growing influence of business and philanthropy. Drawing eclectically on various types of network theory, Ball and Junemann show the links between leading individuals and institutions involved in debates around and the formulation of education policy. We can see in their account evidence of new actors sometimes steering policy, setting directions and influencing the terms of debate in a way that arguably was the province of government and just a few key partners in the past. These actors do so directly, contributing to the debate, but they also have influence through their involvement in sponsoring and running schools.

In our view, however, it is questionable that Ball's and Junemann's examples of network governance constitute a step change in education policy making and one that is here to stay. For example, it is unclear how far and in what sense network governance and multiple partnerships have actually replaced, as opposed to complemented, older ways of governing or even the so-called new public management. Ball and Junemann themselves warn of the dangers of overstating the case. It may be that we are seeing an increasingly complex version of the 'steering at a distance' framework that we identified earlier in this paper as the emergent mode of governance under Thatcherism and New Labour. Furthermore, new actors who fail in the eyes of governments do not survive as key players for long: the dramatic decline of the Specialist Schools and Academies Trust/The Schools Network as a significant voice provides just one illustration of this. The 'partnering state' can change its partners and reassign contracts as it wishes.

It can also close its own 'arm's length' agencies. Very soon into the Coalition administration, very little of the architecture of the New Labour years remained: all of the quangos we listed earlier were, among others, swiftly closed. Other agencies were merged, including, for example, the Training and Development Agency for Schools and the National College for Leadership of Schools and Children's Services. Some of these organisations' functions were taken back within the education department itself. The jury is still out on whether these changes reflected a genuine desire to remove unnecessary bureaucracy and hand power to the people or an audacious attempt to centralise it in the hands of the secretary of state.

With the increasing marginalisation of local authorities in education policy making and delivery, together with this 'bonfire of the quangos' (or NDPBs), direct government control does appear to have increased. The question is then how the state retains sufficient capacity to manage what is left of the 'system'. Accountability in the form of performance indicators and tables remains the primary lever—the only lever—through which the centre can direct and shape the focus of autonomous schools. We have indicated how use of these indicators has evolved. In addition, it became apparent early on that the centre cannot manage tens of thousands of schools alone. Whether for reasons of 'efficiency' or 'local democratic accountability', there have been mounting calls for the recreation of a 'middle tier' of education governance in England (e.g. Blunkett, 2014). To date, the Conservative government's response has been to establish Regional Schools Commissioners, although how they fit in to the overall system of accountability is still unclear (see, for example, House of Commons Education Committee, 2016). The English approach is a far cry from the still significant role of democratically elected local government in Scotland or Wales (West, 2015).

Future policy

2015 saw the replacement of the Coalition with a majority Conservative government and, accordingly, a more clear-cut policy agenda on schools: moving even more to a system of 'autonomous' and competing schools/chains, working to stronger accountability levers.

At the centre of schools policy remains the further acceleration of the academisation of secondary—and now primary—schools, including through the free schools policy. There will be forced conversion to academy status for 'coasting' or 'failing' schools. All 'good' schools, including grammar schools, will be allowed to expand. In October 2015 the Secretary of State authorised the expansion of a Kent grammar school—the first such expansion in 50 years—once again putting the grammar school question and overt selection centre stage in education policy.

The possible brakes on schools' and chains' enthusiasm to expand include a dearth of effective sponsors, and the risks of expanding (for chains and individual schools) under the new accountability measures. These measures include baseline tests and tests for pupils who do not reach expected levels in English and mathematics at the end of Key Stage 2; the requirement that virtually all pupils take GCSEs in the EBacc subjects; compulsory resits for those not reaching Level 4; Progress 8 (pupils' progress across eight subjects, including at least five EBacc subjects); and performance measures and inspection for academy chains. The party's manifesto pledge was that Ofsted would be unable to award its highest ratings to schools that refused to teach the EBacc subjects.

The aforementioned recent decision by Nicky Morgan to allow the Kent grammar school to expand by opening an annex in a nearby town is of considerable symbolic importance. Seen by critics as effectively opening a new grammar school, this move sits in stark contrast to the politics of Jeremy Corbyn, the newly elected leader of the Labour Party, who reportedly separated from his then wife due to her decision to send their child to a grammar school. Corbyn's position also stands in contrast to that of New Labour ministers who sent their children to a variety of new types of school, including in the case of Harriet Harman, a grammar school a considerable distance from her home.

It is therefore possible that the strong sense of continuity in policy and practice between successive governments of different political hues has run its course and we are witnessing a return to sharp differentiation between the parties of a sort we have not seen since the 1980s. If this is the case and a Labour Party under Corbyn's leadership were to be elected to government in 2020, it is possible that England might return to a more social democratic approach to education governance, and therefore once again have more in common with other UK jurisdictions. Labour's education spokesperson has already suggested that local authorities in England would be given greater powers over all their local schools under a Labour government.

At the time of writing, it seems more likely that England will continue along the trajectory favoured by all its governments since the 1980s and the question will be whether it remains an outlier or sets a precedent for the rest of the UK and perhaps the world beyond.

Acknowledgements

We are grateful to Nick Hillman and two anonymous reviewers for their encouraging comments and their suggestions for amendments and additions to the text of an earlier version.

Disclosure statement

No potential conflict of interest was reported by the authors.

References

Adnett, N., & Davies, P. (2003). Schooling reforms in England: From quasi-markets to Co-opetition? *Journal of Education Policy, 18*, 393–406.

Adonis, A., & Pollard, S. (1997). *A class act: The myth of Britain's classless society*. London: Hamish Hamilton.

Allen, R., Burgess, S., & McKenna, L. (2010). *The early impact of Brighton and Hove's school admission reforms* (MPO Working Paper Series No. 10/244). Bristol: Centre for Market and Public Organisation. Retrieved from http://www.bristol.ac.uk/media-library/sites/cmpo/migrated/documents/wp244.pdf

Allen, R., Coldron, J., & West, A. (2012). The effect of changes in published secondary school admissions on pupil composition. *Journal of Education Policy, 27*, 349–366.

Baker, M. (2007, October 20). Look where the target is pointing. *BBC News online*. Retrieved from http://www.news.bbc.co.uk/1/hi/education/7052798.stm

Ball, S. J. (2011). Attempting a theory of untidiness: An interview with Stephen. J. Ball. *Studia Paedagogica, 16*, 159–169.

Ball, S. J., & Junemann, C. (2012). *Networks, new governance and education*. London: Policy Press.

Balls, E. (2007a). Statement to the House of Commons from Ed Balls, Secretary of State for Children, Schools and Families, 10 July. Retrieved from http://www.dfes.gov.uk/speeches/speech.cfm?SpeechID=666

Balls, E. (2007b). National Children's Bureau speech—Every Child Matters, 18 July. Retrieved from http://www.dfes.gov.uk/speeches/speech.cfm?SpeechID=670

Bell, D. (2012, May). *Tribal annual education lecture: Reflections on reform*. Retrieved from http://www.tribalgroup.com/aboutus/events/Documents/Reflections%20on%20Reform.pdf

Blair, T. (1997, April). 21 steps to 21st century education. Lecture at The Barber Institute of Fine Arts, University of Birmingham. Retrieved from http://www.prnewswire.co.uk/news-releases/21-steps-to-21st-century-education—blair-156240055.html

Blair, T. (1998). *The third way: New politics for the new century (Fabian Pamphlet 588)*. London: Fabian Society.

Blair, T. (2006, November). Education is the most precious gift. Speech at Specialist Schools and Academies Trust Conference. Retrieved from http://www.number10.gov.uk/output/Page10514.asp

Blunkett, D. (2014). Review of education structures, functions and the raising of standards for all: Putting students and parents first. London: Labour Party. Retrieved from http://www.yourbritain.org.uk/uploads/editor/files/130514_Report_FINAL.pdf

Campbell, A. (2007). *The Blair years: Extracts from the Alastair Campbell diaries*. London: Hutchinson.

Chitty, C. (1994). Thirty years on. *Forum, 36*, 89–90.

Coldron, J., Willis, B., & Wolstenholme, C. (2009). Selection by attainment and aptitude in English secondary schools. *British Journal of Educational Studies, 57*, 245–264.

Crook, D., Power, S., & Whitty, G. (2000). *The grammar school question: A review of research on comprehensive and selective education*. London: Institute of Education.

de Waal, A. (2009). *The secrets of academies' success*. London: Civitas. Retrieved from http://www.civitas.org.uk/pdf/secrets_success_academies.pdf

DfE (Department for Education) (2014). *Statistical first release: GCSE and equivalent attainment by pupil characteristics in England, 2012/13*. London: Department for Education.

DfEE (Department for Education and Employment) (1997). *Excellence in schools*. London: TSO.

DfES (Department for Education and Skills) (2005). *Higher standards, better schools for all*. London: TSO.

DfES (2006). *The Government's response to the House of Commons Education and Skills Committee report: The Schools White Paper: Higher standards, better schools for all*. London: TSO.

Education Alliance (2006). A good local school for every child: Will the Education Bill deliver? Conference report, 25 March.

Gamble, A. (1988). *The free economy and the strong state*. London: Macmillan.

Gewirtz, S., Ball, S., & Bowe, R. (1995). *Markets, choice and equity*. Buckingham: Open University Press.

Gillborn, D. (2014). Changing benchmarks restore black/white inequality. Presentation to the Centre for Research in Race and Education, University of Birmingham.

Greany, T. (2015). More fragmented, and yet more networked: Analysing the responses of two Local Authorities in England to the Coalition's 'self-improving school-led system' reforms. *London Review of Education, 13*, 125–143.

Green, F., Allen, R., & Jenkins, R. (2014). Research briefing summary: The social composition of Free Schools after three years. London: LLAKES, Institute of Education. Retrieved from http://www.llakes.org/wp-content/uploads/2014/08/Free-Schools-briefing-document.pdf

Hillman, N. (2016). The Coalition's higher education reforms in England. *Oxford Review of Education, 42*.

HM Government (2011). *Opening doors, breaking barriers: A strategy for social mobility*. London: TSO. Retrieved from https://www.gov.uk/government/uploads/system/uploads/attachment_data/file/61964/opening-doors-breaking-barriers.pdf

House of Commons Education Committee (2015). *Academies and Free Schools. Fourth report of session 2014–15*. London: TSO. Retrieved from http://www.publications.parliament.uk/pa/cm201415/cmselect/cmeduc/258/258.pdf

House of Commons Education Committee (2016). *The role of Regional Schools Commissioners. First report of session 2015–16*. London: TSO. Retrieved from http://www.publications.parliament.uk/pa/cm201516/cmselect/cmeduc/401/40102.htm

House of Commons Education and Skills Committee (2006). *The Schools White Paper: Higher standards, better schools for all. First report of session 2005–06*. London: TSO. Retrieved from http://www.publications.parliament.uk/pa/cm200506/cmselect/cmeduski/633/633.pdf

House of Commons Public Bill Committee (Education and Adoption Bill) (2015). Written evidence submitted by Stephen Gorard, Professor of Education and Public Policy, Durham University, UK (EAB 19). Retrieved from http://www.publications.parliament.uk/pa/cm201516/cmpublic/educationadoption/memo/educ19.htm

Hutchings, M., Francis, B., & de Vries, R. (2014). *Chain effects: The impact of academy chains on low income students*. London: Sutton Trust. Retrieved from http://www.suttontrust.com/wp-content/uploads/2014/08/chain-effects-july-14-final-1.pdf

Jesson, D., & Crossley, D. (2006). *Educational outcomes and value added by specialist schools—2005*. London: SSAT/iNet.

Laville, S., & Smithers, R. (2007, March 1). War over school boundaries divides Brighton. *Guardian*, p. 4.

Lupton, R., & Thomson, S. (2015). Socio-economic inequalities in English schooling under the Coalition Government 2010–15. *London Review of Education, 13*, 4–20.

Lupton, R., Unwin, L., & Thomson, S. (2015). *The Coalition's record on further and higher education and skills: Policy, spending and outcomes 2010–15* (Working Paper 14). University of Manchester/Centre for Analysis of Social Exclusion, LSE.

McNally, S. (2015). *Schools: The evidence on academies, resources and pupil performance*. London: Centre for Economic Performance, LSE.

Millar, F. (2007). Admitting fault. *Fabian Review, 119*, 12–13.

Morris, E. (2001). We need your help to make a difference. *Education Review, 15*, 4.

Morris, R. (2015). Free schools and disadvantaged intakes. *British Educational Research Journal, 41*, 535–552. Retrieved from http://onlinelibrary.wiley.com/doi/10.1002/berj.3168/abstract

NAO (National Audit Office). (2007). *The Academies programme*. London: TSO.

Neave, G. (1988). On the cultivation of quality, efficiency and enterprise: An overview of recent trends in higher education in Western Europe, 1968–88. *European Journal of Education, 23*, 7–23.

Newsam, P. (2003). Diversity and admissions to English secondary schools. *Forum, 45*, 17–18.

Ofsted (2012). *The pupil premium: How schools are using the pupil premium funding to raise achievement for disadvantaged pupils*. London: Ofsted.

Ofsted. (2014). *The pupil premium: An update*. London: Ofsted.

Penlington, G. (2001). Why New Labour found itself converted to church schools. *Parliamentary Brief, 2*, 42–43.

Shleifer, A. (1998). State versus private ownership. *Journal of Economic Perspectives, 12*, 133–150.

Sutton Trust (2006). *The social composition of top comprehensive schools: Rates of eligibility for free school meals at the 200 highest performing comprehensive schools*. London: Sutton Trust.

Sutton Trust (2012). *The use of the Pupil Premium, NFER Teacher Voice omnibus 2012 survey*. Slough: NFER.

Tough, S., & Brooks, R. (2007). *School admissions: Fair choice for parents and pupils*. London: IPPR.

West, A. (2015). Education policy and governance in England under the Coalition Government (2010–15): Academies, the pupil premium, and free early education. *London Review of Education, 13*, 21–36.

Whitty, G. (2008). Twenty years of progress? English education policy 1988 to the present. *Educational Management Administration Leadership, 36*, 165–184.

Whitty, G., Anders, J., Hayton, A., Tang, S., & Wisby, E. (2016). *Research and policy in education: Evidence, ideology and impact*. London: IOE Press.

Whitty, G., Edwards, T., & Gewirtz, S. (1993). *Specialisation and choice in urban education: The City Technology College experiment*. London: Routledge.

Whitty, G., Power, S., & Halpin, D. (1998). *Devolution and choice in education: The school, the state and the market*. Buckingham: Open University Press.

Wilby, P. (2007, May 14). Why education remains the priority. *New Statesman*, p. 14.

Wilshaw, M. (2013, June). Unseen children. Speech given by Sir Michael Wilshaw, Her Majesty's Chief Inspector, at Church House, Westminster. Retrieved from http://webarchive.nationalarchives.gov.uk/20131216154121/https:/www.ofsted.gov.uk/resources/unseen-children-hmci-speech

The Coalition's higher education reforms in England

Nicholas Hillman

ABSTRACT

The Coalition Government of Conservatives and Liberal Democrats in office from 2010 until 2015 sharply increased the maximum tuition fees for UK and EU undergraduates at English universities to £9,000. Although this is often portrayed as a radical change, it is argued that the reform was an evolution rather than a revolution. Common pessimistic predictions, such as the claim there would be a big fall in the number of full-time students, were wrong. However, the policymaking behind the increase in the fee cap was rushed, and this contributed to shortcomings such as a decline in part-time students. The article considers a series of political mistakes made by the Liberal Democrats, including making the abolition of tuition fees a key part of their election strategy in 2010 when the party's leaders lacked faith in the policy. The article also notes that critics of the Coalition's higher education reforms were largely ineffectual because they lacked a strong intellectual case or a clear alternative and fixated on fees to the exclusion of other important issues. The piece ends by asserting that the Coalition's plan to remove student number controls was a change of overlooked importance.

Introduction

Higher education in England has undergone dramatic change in recent years, particularly in relation to the funding of undergraduate study and, as with schooling, the diversity of provision. The Coalition Government's (2010–2015) reforms reduced public spending on university teaching by around £3 billion a year and enabled tuition fee income to rise from £2.6 billion to £8.1 billion.[1] Fees, which were backed by income-contingent loans, were capped at a maximum of £9,000—almost three times higher than before—for full-time students at higher education institutions with an Access Agreement acceptable to the Office for Fair Access (OFFA). The loan and fee caps for part-time students, who were newly entitled to tuition fee loans, were set at £6,750 at the same time.

These changes meant students of classroom-based disciplines who secured well-paid work would be expected to repay the entire cost of their tuition—or sometimes, given the 3% real rate of interest applied to the loans of students and the highest-earning graduates, a little more. As direct public funding to institutions was less important, so alternative providers not in receipt of grants from the Higher Education Funding Council for England (HEFCE) found more viable business models. While their students' tuition fee loans were capped at a lower amount (£6,000), due to the absence of Access Agreements, this left a smaller shortfall between the size of the available loans and the cost of providing courses. Indeed, it was sometimes enough to run courses without incurring any loss.

These changes have typically been portrayed by both policymakers and academics as a complete reversal of approach. When the crucial votes on tuition fees happened in December 2010, Labour's Shadow Minister for Universities and Science, John Denham, told the House of Commons it was: 'the most profound change in university funding since the University Grants Committee was set up in the 1920s' (HC Deb (2010–12) 520 col. 550).[2] Paul Temple of the UCL Institute of Education claimed it was the biggest change ever: 'Higher education in England has changed between 2010 and 2015 to a greater extent than in any other comparable time period' (Temple, 2015).

In Whitehall, it often felt as if this were so. The civil servants who worked on the Coalition's reforms felt like they were working from a blank slate. As a result of New Labour's repeated redrawing of departmental boundaries, higher education had bounced around Whitehall before the Coalition came to office—from the Department for Education and Skills to the short-lived Department for Innovation, Universities and Skills in 2007 and then in 2009 to the Department for Business, Innovation and Skills (BIS). After the 2010 election, the boundaries remained fixed but the turnover of civil servants working on higher education was accelerated by austerity-related re-organisations and reductions in staff (Hillman, 2014d). In the crucial three months between August 2010 and October 2010—during which the Independent Review of Higher Education Funding and Student Finance (the Browne review) completed its work, submitted its report to Government and published its findings—BIS had three different people filling the Permanent Secretary role.[3] In short, there was no institutional memory on which to rely.

Five surprises

This instability had a direct impact on the making of policy and the way it was presented. Vince Cable, the Liberal Democrat Secretary of State for Business, Innovation and Skills (2010–15), and David Willetts, the Conservative Minister of State for Universities and Science (2010–14), claimed that fees of £9,000 would be out of the ordinary: 'In exceptional cases, universities will be able to charge higher contributions [than £6,000], up to a limit of £9,000, subject to meeting much tougher conditions on widening participation and fair access' (Department for Business, Innovation and Skills, 2010a).

They should instead have been advised, on the basis of the 'variable fees' capped at £3,000 introduced in 2006, that the maximum would swiftly become the norm. It was not only a lack of contemporary history that infected Whitehall but also a poor understanding of OFFA's legal powers, which were more limited in scope than had been realised (Attwood, 2011).

If these were the first two surprises, a third occurred over the likely write-off cost of the new higher loans, known as the resource accounting and budgeting (RAB) charge, which the Government put at around 32% before gradually increasing their estimate to around 45% (Willetts, 2015). In the pithy words of David Willetts in the House of Commons soon after standing down as the Universities and Science Minister: 'There was an error' (HC Deb (2014–15) 590 col. 431).[4]

Fourthly, there was incomplete recognition that the extension of tuition fee loans to cover the increased fees of part-time students, which was portrayed as bold and progressive, was a modest policy in practice. Only one-third of part-time students were eligible, due to restrictions associated with earlier periods of study and course intensity, and an even smaller proportion would come to take the loans out (Hillman, 2015a).

Fifthly, it took the Department for Business, Innovation and Skills far longer than anyone outside realised to determine the precise parliamentary procedure for the new fees, which was neither—as many people before and since have erroneously assumed (see, for example, Dean, 2015)—via a new Bill nor through a single vote. Instead, two separate votes were needed in each of the House of Commons and the House of Lords, one to raise the maximum fee to £9,000 and one to raise the threshold for coming within the OFFA regime to £6,000.

Parliamentary process

The difficulty for the civil servants was that politics drove the timetable in key ways which hampered forensic and detailed policymaking. There was an appetite to keep tuition fees off the agenda of the political party conferences in autumn 2010 but, once the Browne report was published immediately afterwards on 12 October, all the pressures were for a speedy resolution. Quick parliamentary votes were necessary in order to limit the peeling away of Liberal Democrat Members of Parliament, who were under pressure from their constituents and other sources of public opinion not to support the proposals. Moreover, the Treasury was demanding the Business Department deliver up its portion of deficit-reduction savings in the quickest possible time, which meant real-world considerations came into play. Year 12 pupils typically read prospectuses and attend open days around 18 months before entering higher education, so they need to know then what fees they will face. In addition, the ageing computers at the Student Loans Company (SLC) were neither easy nor quick to change. So rapid parliamentary decisions were necessary if the new system was to be in place in time to operate smoothly.

Liberal Democrats fought successfully for some amendments to the package to shore up their MPs prior to the key votes. These included a £150 million National Scholarship Programme for less well-off students, annual uprating of the new £21,000 student loan repayment threshold in line with earnings to ease the financial burden on graduates and a consultation on fines for well-off graduates who wanted to pay their loans off early (Department for Business, Innovation and Skills, 2010b; HC Deb (2010–12) 520 cols 19WS-20WS).[5]

Despite the fraught political atmosphere, particularly within the Liberal Democrat half of the Coalition, the likely breakdown of votes in the House of Commons was more predictable and never as close as it had been for Tony Blair, whose £3,000 fees squeaked through with a majority of just five in the House of Commons in January 2004. Blair's overall majority (161) was more than twice that of the Coalition (76). Yet the majority was over four times larger in 2010 than in 2004, for both votes on the Coalition's new fees regime passed with a majority of 21 in the House of Commons. The breakdown in the House of Lords a week later was less predictable, partly because leading Conservative peers were concerned that exerting pressure to vote with the Government might look heavy-handed and turn out to be counterproductive. In the end, the Lords gave the reforms a bigger majority of around 70, which was encouraged behind the scenes by higher education institutions making use of their many links to peers.

Evolution not revolution

Despite the unprecedented environment of a Conservative and Liberal Democrat Coalition, the rushed policymaking and the common perception that £9,000 fees represented a radical new approach, the argument that 2010 represented a break with the past is deeply ahistorical. The principle that people should contribute materially and directly to the cost of their own higher education is an old one in the United Kingdom. The brief period when all regular full-time undergraduates had both the cost of their tuition and some or all of their maintenance costs covered by public grants lasted a mere eight years: from 1977, when undergraduates from the richest households became entitled to free tuition and a small maintenance grant, until 1985, when maintenance grants ceased to be universal (Hillman, 2013).

In 1990, maintenance loans appeared. In 1998, tuition fees were reintroduced at £1,000. In 2006, they were increased to £3,000. So Conservative and Labour Governments had shifted to the principle that graduates should contribute long before the Coalition came to office. Indeed, that is precisely why new primary legislation was not needed to implement the £9,000 system. The Higher Education Act (2004) that Tony Blair left behind not only facilitated the fee increase in procedural terms; it also provided the very mechanism that made the intellectual case for higher fees. When the legislation went through Parliament, tuition fee opponents had forced the Government to commit to a future review of fees, which in time became the Browne review that proposed higher fees and the removal of a fixed fee cap (Independent Review of Higher Education Funding and Student Finance, 2010).

The shift in funding that took place under the Coalition was the next step in a gradual process of evolution. While the shift to £9,000 fees was a big jump, the public subsidies for higher education remained substantial even after the new system had taken root. In 2015/16, the maintenance grant bill was £1.6 billion. The write-off value of new student loans taken out—the RAB charge—was calculated at nearly half of the £12 billion paid out.[6] In addition, £1.5 billion of public money was paid via institutional grants for the extra costs associated with students who had additional barriers to learning, were studying high-cost subjects or were attending institutions with specialised teaching methods. Indeed, the remaining subsidies remained so large that many observers claimed the changes would not save any money (Thompson & Bekhradnia, 2010).

There had been dire predictions of the impact higher fees would have on participation. A survey by the National Union of Students (NUS) and HSBC published in 2010 claimed, 'If university fees were increased, students are significantly more likely to be deterred from going to university; if fees were raised to £5,000 per annum over half (53%) state it would have deterred them from going to university. This proportion rises to 70% at £7,000 per annum and 78% at £10,000 per annum' (National Union of Students, 2010). Such warnings turned out to be wrong. In 2014, Mary Curnock Cook, Chief Executive of the University and College Admissions System (UCAS), reported on 'a stunning account of social change, with the most disadvantaged young people over 10 per cent more likely to enter higher education than last year and a third more likely than just five years ago—40 per cent more likely for higher tariff institutions' (UCAS, 2014). Even opponents of the fee regime had to eat their words: 'demand for university places from school leavers has shown a reversion to historical patterns with the application rate for English 18 year olds reaching a new high' (Independent Commission on Fees, 2015).

At least, that was the position for school and college leavers. There was an adverse and often overlooked impact on part-time and mature student numbers. The fall began before the rise in fees and is thought to have had various causes linked to both supply and demand (Universities UK, 2013). But other parts of the UK, which retained lower or no fees, did not face such a dramatic decline in part-time numbers and so higher fees do seem to have been a major contributory factor (Hillman, 2015a).

Student funding changes were the most well known but far from the only important higher education reform undertaken by the Coalition. For example, the reduction in the number of students necessary to become a university from 4,000 to 1,000 led to around a dozen institutions acquiring university title for the first time. By the end of the Coalition's time in office, Ministers had also promised to introduce postgraduate loans for both taught Masters students (announced in December 2014) and doctoral students (announced in March 2015). This neutralised potential attacks from the higher education sector as the 2015 election approached. So too did the commitment announced in June 2014 to protect research capital spending in real terms at £1.1 billion a year from 2015/16 until 2020/21, which came on top of the freeze in the £4.6 billion annual science and research budget between 2010 and 2015.

There were, however, reasons beyond the evolution of student support as to why higher education was not changed as profoundly by the Coalition as is often claimed. In particular, the refusal of Ministers to introduce new primary legislation to implement their own 2011 White Paper, *Students at the Heart of the System*, meant the make-do-and-mend nature of higher education regulation was maintained. This was sustainable in the short term but not in the longer term, as the legal framework governing higher education failed to reflect the new funding environment. In particular, with the majority of funding for teaching coming from student fees, there was rapid expansion of higher education providers where the students could claim financial support but which were not directly overseen by HEFCE.

These 'alternative providers' found a new business model as the maximum tuition fee loans their students were entitled to claim rose from £3,000 to £6,000 in autumn 2012, thereby making life outside the HEFCE-subsidised sector more sustainable. The education many of these providers delivered broadened access and provided a useful competitive challenge to the traditional higher education sector, but at others it was poor (National Audit Office, 2014). Without legislation, it was both too easy for lower-quality alternative providers to thrive and too challenging for higher-quality ones to grow. Innovative providers, such as the New College of the Humanities, found they had entered a lengthy obstacle course with ever-changing rules and no clear finish line. The gap between the Conservatives' rhetoric on supply-side reform and reality was big. The challenges were compounded by the absence of a lobby group for alternative providers, which was a problem they failed to remedy properly before the 2015 election.

The Coalition also shied away from altering some other critical elements of the higher education landscape. For example, the dual support system for funding research, in which some research funds are distributed by the UK funding bodies (such as HEFCE) on the basis of the Research Excellence Framework and more comes as project-based finance via the seven discipline-based Research Councils, was left alone.

Disrupting such arrangements, which largely worked well, seemed pointless, especially when it could have risked a row about politicians meddling in institutional autonomy, disturbing the true priorities of researchers and even overturning the sacred Haldane Principle.[7] UK academia is, in general, to the left of society as a whole and initiatives from centre-right governments are particularly prone to being misinterpreted. In the early months of the Coalition, a synthetic row stoked by *The Observer* over politicians supposedly telling the Arts and Humanities Research Council to look at 'the Big Society', a slogan of the Conservative Party's 2010 election campaign, showed what was at stake (Boffey, 2011).

This absence of activity over research funding streams is worth noting in part because the Conservative-majority Government elected in May 2015 rapidly began to reassess the research funding environment. Indeed, there had been signs of shifting sands even before the end of the Coalition's tenure, as Sir Paul Nurse, President of the Royal Society, was asked in late 2014 'to look at overall questions relating to UK research funding' (Department for Business, Innovation and Skills, 2015c). His report was received, and almost immediately accepted by, the subsequent Government (Nurse, 2015).

The Cabinet Office's desire to reduce the number of arms-length bodies had made little progress in higher education by the time of the 2015 election. Organisations such as HEFCE, the SLC, OFFA the Quality Assurance Agency (QAA) and the Research Councils continued with only limited changes. As the Browne review had recommended that HEFCE, the QAA, OFFA and the Office of the Independent Adjudicator should be replaced by a single Higher Education Council, this was one important area, along with the retention of a firm tuition fee cap, where the recommendations of the Browne review were ignored by Coalition Ministers (Independent Review of Higher Education Funding and Student Finance, 2010).

The Liberal Democrats' six mistakes

Before the 2010 election, all 57 Liberal Democrat candidates who went on to win put their name to the Vote for Students' promise of the NUS. This read: 'I pledge to vote against any increase in fees in the next parliament and to pressure the government to introduce a fairer alternative.' Associating themselves so closely with anti-fees campaigners won the Liberal Democrats a large proportion of the student vote (Fisher & Hillman, 2014). However, after the election, Clegg expressed regret at signing the pledge and it was a clear failure of leadership. Indeed, making opposition to fees a key plank of their 2010 election platform was the first of many mistakes the Liberal Democrats made in relation to the increase in tuition fees.

This is because the leaders of the party were known not to support their own policy. Less than two years before the election, in September 2008, *Times Higher Education* had reported:

The leaders of the Liberal Democrats plan to abandon the party's opposition to student tuition fees. Stephen Williams, Lib Dem Shadow Secretary of State for Innovation, Universities and Skills, said that the policy was not sustainable. In an interview with Times Higher Education, as his party gathered for its annual conference in Bournemouth this week, Mr Williams said that Nick Clegg, the leader of the party, had come to this conclusion after 'long internal discussions'. (Newman, 2008)

In the run-up to the election, the Liberal Democrats adopted a slower timetable for abolishing fees but the leadership failed in their attempt to unlatch the party from principled opposition to them. So, unwisely, they made the abolition of fees a central part of their election strategy instead. According to Michael White of the *Guardian*, 'Given that Clegg had spent two years ineffectually manoeuvring to ditch his own policy in favour of something more realistic, the puzzle is why he let himself be cornered into endorsing the anti-fees pledge in the election, complete with "read my lips" photos' (White, 2010).

The party's leaders did not undergo a Damascene conversion and become true opponents of fees. The Liberal Democrat team responsible for negotiating with the other parties in the event of a hung parliament agreed before the election that abolishing fees was a disposable policy:

> the group concluded that the party should not use valuable political capital pushing for the abolition of tuition fees. One of the Lib Dems' flagship policies would be ruthlessly sacrificed in any coalition negotiations: 'On tuition fees we should seek agreement on part time students and leave the rest. We will have clear yellow water with the other [parties] on raising the tuition fee cap, so let us not cause ourselves more headaches.' (Wilson, 2010)

In the event, the policy of opposing fee increases was thrown out immediately after the election. The Coalition Programme said: 'If the response of the Government to Lord Browne's report is one that Liberal Democrats cannot accept, then arrangements will be made to enable Liberal Democrat MPs to abstain in any vote' (Her Majesty's Government, 2010). Agreeing to a possible abstention was the second big mistake because it left Liberal Democrats MPs in a Catch-22 position where no course of action could satisfy both the NUS pledge and the Coalition Programme. The former held them to vote against fees and the latter held them to abstaining or voting in favour. Any of the three options—voting for, voting against or abstaining—broke one or other of their pledges.

It would have been distinctly odd if Vince Cable had not backed the policy of his own Department in raising fees, but a third big mistake was nonetheless the Liberal Democrats' decision not to deploy the right to abstain once they had secured it. This would have provided them with some respite even though it would not have satisfied all those who had supported them in the election.

In the run up to the crucial parliamentary votes, there were fraught conversations among the Liberal Democrat parliamentary party aimed at securing a coherent single position. But these failed and, instead, the party split three ways: around one-half of Liberal Democrat MPs supported the new fee levels but more than one-third voted against while the rest either abstained or were abroad on official business. This division was the fourth big mistake because the lack of a single position blocked them from being able to portray a clear stance in favour of or opposed to the new fee cap. The division was not merely among lesser-known or newly-elected Liberal Democrats, as a website for the party's activists made clear at the time: 'Leader Nick Clegg voted for; Deputy Leader Simon Hughes abstained while Party President-elect Tim Farron voted against' (Duffett, 2010). The confusion this engendered probably helped ensure there was little difference in the performance of Liberal Democrats standing for re-election at the 2015 general election. They did poorly whether they had rebelled, abstained or supported the tuition fee changes (Hillman, 2015b).

The fifth mistake was to insist on initiatives like the National Scholarship Programme, which lacked an evidence base, turned out to be an inefficient use of taxpayers' money and was swiftly wound up (Hillman, 2014c). After the scheme had ended, one academic assessment concluded: 'So the "National Scholarship Programme" was, in fact, not national; neither did it offer scholarships, nor a coherent programme' (Carasso & Gunn, 2015).

Many people, Liberal Democrats and independent observers alike, have claimed that various other elements of the final package—such as the fixed £9,000 tuition fees cap (rather than the abolition of a fee cap, as recommended by Browne) and the £21,000 repayment threshold—were secured by the Liberal Democrats. Such claims lack supporting evidence because they are incorrect: for example, the £9,000 cap was initially chosen by the Conservative Universities and Science Minister, David Willetts, and the Liberal Democrats' tortuous internal debates over accepting higher fees meant they paid relatively little attention to the precise level at which it was set. Similarly, the £21,000 repayment threshold was recommended by Lord Browne. The Liberal Democrats did win a few minor changes other than the National Scholarship Programme, most notably a promise to increase the £21,000 threshold in line with earnings each year. But, as the Conservative-majority Government elected in May 2015 reversed this commitment before it took effect, it was of little value (Department for Business, Innovation and Skills, 2015a).

In terms of good public policy, the sixth mistake was to remain so obsessed with fees that it undermined other important higher education reforms. Senior Liberal Democrats were so eager to keep higher education off the political agenda that they blocked the 2011 White Paper, *Students at the heart of the system*, from becoming law, thereby stopping the best mechanism for enabling the Coalition to build a new narrative. Liberal Democrats clearly wanted higher tuition fees to disappear as a topical issue yet, like a bullied child returning to the scene of their torture, they continuously reminded people of them, as when Nick Clegg infamously won headlines in 2012 with an apology for pledging to oppose fees before the election. Meanwhile, they blocked the one route that might have helped them out of a quagmire of their own making.

Their one possible line of defence is that parliamentary debates over new higher education legislation could have reopened the tuition fee issue by enabling an amendment on reducing or abolishing them. But, as a consequence of the lack of new legislation, the regulation of higher education did not catch up with the change in financing, the issue of how to deal with 'alternative providers' was not dealt with properly and measures to raise the student interest, such as making HEFCE a 'consumer champion', were not enacted.

By the time of the 2015 election, Liberal Democrats seem to have recognised this mistake because their manifesto, unlike those of the Conservative and Labour parties, promised new higher education legislation: 'We will legislate to reform regulation of the higher education sector, improving student protection' (Liberal Democrats, 2015). At the 2010 election, they had made a promise they went on to break. At the 2015 election, they made a promise they had already had every opportunity to keep but had failed to implement.

Whatever the wider success of the Liberal Democrats in taming and shaping the Coalition Government, they made numerous mistakes on higher education. Between 2008 and 2012, Nick Clegg went from opposing his party's no-fee policy to making it the centrepiece of his election campaign to distancing his party from it in the Coalition Programme to voting against it in Parliament and then apologising for the mess. He was at the mercy of many forces but he did less than he might have done to resist being buffeted by them.

In one sense, this mattered less than is sometimes supposed. It is often said that the decision to sign the NUS pledge but then to reject it led to a collapse in Liberal Democrat support. In fact, their poll rating declined sharply soon after entering office with the Conservatives, when their left-leaning voters peeled away, and months before the Browne report was even published. The broken pledge did, however, make the road to recovery more challenging. Research conducted in Nick Clegg's constituency of Sheffield Hallam during the run up to the 2015 election found:

> many could still not excuse the deal with the Conservatives, or the reversal on tuition fees: 'He [Clegg] traded that for a ministerial car.' The argument that a junior coalition party inevitably has to take what it can get (and had indeed scored a number of successes that they themselves recognised) was not enough for them because the promise to vote against the fee rise had been so public and unequivocal. What would he let them down on next time? (Ashcroft & Culwick, 2015)

Opposition

There were numerous critics of the Coalition's higher education reforms among academics, commentators and students. In 2012, for example, some current and retired academics launched a Council for the Defence of British Universities (CDBU) to oppose policymakers whose reforms were supposedly changing higher education 'fundamentally, permanently, and virtually overnight.' They claimed the changes lacked a mandate: 'Although opposed by student protests, devastated by scholarly criticism, and unsupported by even the most elementary analysis of the empirical evidence, these changes are being driven forward relentlessly without benefit of Parliamentary debate or public scrutiny.'[8] The verdict did not improve by the end of the Parliament, when one academic study claimed: 'Coalition policy in higher education was a colossal failure in both its own terms and in the terms of its critics' (Finn, 2015).

There was considerable opposition among commentators too, although it was not a simple split along left-wing and right-wing lines. The *Guardian* columnist and former Editor of the *New Statesman*, Peter Wilby, criticised the Opposition for kowtowing to the middle class: 'Labour has been seduced into sentimental, sloppy thinking that defends the interests of the affluent, not the poor' (Wilby, 2010). In contrast, the former Editor of the *Daily Telegraph*, Charles Moore, complained: 'loans are being presented as a tax on the rich to pay for social mobility. Everyone, whatever their politics, can see that this is not a good way of achieving the desired effects. So absolutely everyone is cross' (Moore, 2011).

The reforms encouraged the most fervent street protests of the Coalition's period in office, which were organised by the NUS and the University and College Union. These came to be remembered mainly for an invasion of Conservative Campaign Headquarters, for a Cambridge student (and son of a pop star) swinging off a Union Flag at the Cenotaph and for Prince Charles's car being attacked in the West End. Once Parliament agreed to higher fees, the protests lost their force. Low-level disruption continued on campus but it typically petered out around the end of each term as students drifted off home.

There is scant evidence to suggest any of this opposition had much effect and it is not hard to understand why.

First, the primary goal of the increase in tuition fees was to ensure the Business, Innovation and Skills Department, which had an unprotected budget, contributed sufficiently to the planned reduction in the deficit to which all the major political parties had committed prior to the 2010 election. Every penny of savings from reducing the HEFCE teaching grant helped reduce the nation's deficit while not one penny of the higher student loans contributed to it, according to standard accounting conventions (McGettigan, 2015). For Conservative Ministers, the fact that higher fees could make higher education more like a regulated market, with students coming to resemble consumers, was a bonus but it was not the primary purpose. The need to save money made the Coalition relatively impervious to criticism not least because a u-turn would have necessitated a search for alternative savings. These may have had to come from the same Department, which could have meant drastic cuts to other educational priorities, such as research or apprenticeships.

Secondly, the opponents lacked workable alternatives. Critiques by serving academics typically ended after the easy bit of saying what was wrong and before reaching the difficult part of saying what should be done instead. Perhaps the most trenchant criticism came in a report from the Higher Education Commission, which said:

> the Government is investing, but not getting any credit for it, damaging the perception of the public value associated with higher education. Students feel like they are paying substantially more for their higher education, but are set to have a large proportion of their debt written off by the Government. Universities are perceived to be 'rolling in money' in the eyes of students, as their income from tuition fees has tripled, yet the cuts to the teaching grant are not well understood by students and a fixed fee cap means an annual erosion of real terms income. We have created a system where everybody feels like they are getting a bad deal. This is not sustainable. (Higher Education Commission, 2014)

It is telling that, despite joining the chorus of voices opposing the high fees and loans, nowhere in their 86-page report were the Commission able to agree on a better approach. Fierce critics of student loans were so short of alternative ideas that they typically proposed helping postgraduates by extending the very income-contingent loans they opposed for undergraduate students (Hillman, 2014b).

As the 2015 election approached, the Director of Education at the Organisation of Economic Co-operation and Development, Andreas Schleicher, gave the Government a useful third-party endorsement to use against those who said that the funding model was unsustainable due to the large debt write-off costs: 'Keep in mind that the added tax income of those graduates who end up in employment, on average over £80,000 in the UK, is many times larger than any conceivable bad debt' (Schleicher, 2015).

Thirdly, the Official Opposition were little better. In autumn 2010, the Labour Party voted against higher fees but their position seemed inauthentic because, in office, they had reintroduced tuition fees in 1998, tripled them in 2006 and promised a review of fees which eventually became the Browne review in 2009. The paperback edition of Lord Mandelson's memoirs claimed in early 2011 that Labour would have doubled tuition fees had they stayed in office (Mandelson, 2011). During his successful campaign to become Labour Party Leader in the summer of 2010, Ed Miliband had set out a different course by promising, 'I will in coming months produce a plan for replacing tuition fees with a new graduate tax' (Miliband, 2010). However, that plan never appeared and, at the 2011 Labour Party Conference, he backed a tuition fee cap of £6,000 instead. A party spokesperson told the *Observer* they might go further by the time of the general election: 'This is what we would do now. But in three and a half years' time we might be able to do even more' (Helm, Rawnsley & Boffey, 2010). After a great deal of uncertainty and mixed messaging, Miliband reannounced the £6,000 fee cap in February 2015 alongside a commitment to deliver a modest increase in maintenance grants (Wintour, 2015). This cleared the fog but could not satisfy principled opponents of fees. Overall, Labour's policy on higher education funding between 2010 and 2015 had all the disadvantages of inconsistency while remaining remarkably consistent.

Fourthly, the academic community was not united: vice-chancellors and other leaders, who needed to know there would be sufficient income to continue running their institutions successfully, tended to support the reforms (Smith et al., 2010). It was often lukewarm support based on the fact that other options were less palatable, such as a cut to the number of student places, or politically unfeasible, such as a big increase in direct support from taxpayers. But many sector leaders recalled that the amount of funding per student had halved during the period of Conservative rule between 1979 and 1997, with a dire impact on the quality of education, and they wanted above all to avoid a repeat (Greenaway & Haynes, 2003). Whatever the cause, over half of institutional leaders backed the changes, which proved the academy was far from the single entity that some university staff liked to imply.[9]

Fifthly, as Channel 4 neatly captured in a 2011 episode of the comedy *Fresh Meat*, the academic and student demonstrators often came across as middle-class protestors supporting a public subsidy for better-off people on their way to well-paid careers. This thought was captured by the Secretary of State for Education, Michael Gove, when he told the BBC, 'Someone who is working as a postman should not subsidise those who go on to become millionaires' (Shepherd & Stratton, 2010). Visits to higher education institutions by the Minister for Universities and Science, David Willetts, were more likely to be disrupted at relatively wealthy institutions with large numbers of middle-class students than at those with more diverse student bodies, and at institutions based in London somewhat more than those in the regions. So it was at the University of Cambridge where he was shouted down and unable to deliver a prepared speech and it was at Birkbeck, which specialises in evening courses for people already in work, where a prestigious lecture he had been asked to deliver was cancelled in advance due to evidence of organised troublemaking.[10]

Sixthly, the Coalition claimed their method of funding undergraduates enabled an improvement in social mobility by making it affordable to remove the restrictions on recruitment at individual higher education institutions and across the sector as a whole: 'This expansion is affordable within a reducing level of public sector net borrowing as a result of the reforms to higher education finance the government has enacted' (Her Majesty's Treasury, 2013). There was too little due diligence undertaken on the removal of student number controls before it was announced but it gave the Conservative Party something forward-looking to talk about in the run up to the 2015 election (Hillman, 2014a). The Labour Party's supply-side response of new earn-as-you-learn degrees appeared opaque and bureaucratic alongside the Coalition's demand-driven approach (Byrne, 2014).

Those who opposed the Government's higher education reforms were not only ineffectual; they were also counter-productive. The focus on the increase in the tuition fee cap came at the expense of other important issues. Ministers were not going to reverse the increase in fees given the political capital that had been spent on the policy and the contribution the cut in direct funding made to reducing the deficit, not to mention the absence of workable alternatives and the likelihood that student issues would not be decisive at the 2015 general election. Yet by focusing on fees to the exclusion of other issues, opponents were unable to pin problems such as the drastic reduction in part-time students on the Coalition.

Conclusion

If it lasts, the Coalition's decision to remove the student numbers cap may turn out to be a more dramatic policy change than their decision on fees. The history of UK higher education shows the best way to widen participation is to have more places: otherwise well-heeled people do all they can to ensure they obtain the rationed places. Yet the significance of removing student number controls was all but ignored, particularly by those who wished to paint the Coalition's reforms in a negative light (see, for example, Temple, 2015). Only by ignoring the policy altogether was Konstanze Spohrer able to argue that 'the measures in relation to widening participation adopted by the Coalition mean a move away from a general concern with opening up higher education to a wider share of the population towards "creaming off" academically high-performing individuals' (Spohrer, 2015). As well as aiding social mobility, removing student number controls was likely to produce a sharper element of marketisation than loading the costs of higher education on to graduates in the form of income-contingent loans. It also seemed likely to encourage shifts in the shape of the higher education sector, with institutions facing more competition for students and more new entrants.

On the other hand, the Coalition's refusal to implement a new legal framework ensured they ended their time in power having made some significant changes to higher education but without ever placing them within a new permanent backdrop. It was a sticking-plaster approach to higher education. The vacuum it created was partially filled by other regulatory forces, some of which lacked an intimate knowledge of higher education, such as the Home Office and the Competition and Markets Authority.

Moreover, despite improvements in the information available for potential students, there was no serious challenge to the hierarchical nature of British higher education, which was reinforced by the 2014 Research Excellence Framework and the continuing importance of university league tables. This mattered because employers and others continued to use problematic proxies for teaching quality, such as the age of institutions, which blunted the incentives for both younger and older institutions to improve.

The Coalition also left office without ever reconciling itself fully to the internationalisation of higher education. While BIS pressed for more educational exports, including more international students, the Home Office sought repeatedly to reduce the numbers coming to study in the UK as part of its wider policy to cut net inward migration (Department for Business, Innovation and Skills, 2013). Foreign students continued to arrive in large numbers, but the UK lost market share compared to other countries (British Council, 2015).

This inability to reflect wider trends within higher education had a parallel in the discussions on greater devolution of power from Westminster. It was feared some parts of the UK were acting increasingly like local providers of higher education just as it was becoming a truly global endeavour (Hunter Blackburn, 2015). One example of this was the decision by the ruling Scottish National Party to establish a formal but inward-looking review of university governance arrangements in Scotland.

So England continued to enjoy the benefits of a world-class higher education system without setting it into either a new legal framework or a world-class context, while also witnessing the watering down of the concept of a single university sector across the four corners of the UK. Once it was clear England's high-fees regime could prove sustainable, the other parts of the UK began deeper debates about the consequences for their own jurisdictions. For example, a review of higher education funding and student finance was established in Wales in 2013 and a 'Higher Education Big Conversation' consultation process occurred in Northern Ireland in late 2015. But there was little reason to think such initiatives would lead to a strengthening of the concept of a single UK higher education system. The leaders of

Scottish higher education institutions proved very reluctant to defend the concept of a single system fully in public in the run-up to the 2014 referendum on Scottish independence.

As the Coalition left office, the issue of the UK's place in the European Union rose up the political agenda, with the higher education sector's leaders apparently united in fearing the consequences of disengagement. The argument that it could be regarded as inappropriate for sector leaders to play a role in such important questions on the UK's future, which had been common during the Scottish referendum, was quickly forgotten. A few weeks after the 2015 general election, Universities UK launched Universities for Europe, which aimed to be a strong voice on the 'stay' side of the European question.

In its first few months, the Conservative Government which replaced the Coalition proposed a Teaching Excellence Framework, a new emphasis on widening participation, a clearer entry and exit regime for higher education providers, more efficient distribution of research spending, the abolition of student maintenance grants, a freeze to the £21,000 student loan repayment threshold, a review of the RAB charge calculation, a major revamp of higher education regulation and new primary legislation (Department for Business, Innovation and Skills, 2015b). So they clearly saw plenty of 'unfinished business', in the words of David Willetts (Gill, 2015).

Those who had criticised the Coalition's approach to higher education found the need to reach for even more excessive hyperbole than they had used between 2010 and 2015, but it was further proof that the centre-right Coalition's higher education policies were more evolutionary than revolutionary. Given that the administration fell between Labour's period in office and the first majority Conservative Government for a generation, perhaps that should not seem so surprising.

Notes

1. Figures from the 2012 and the two 2015 grant letters sent by the Department for Business, Innovation and Skills to the Higher Education Funding Council for England.
2. http://www.publications.parliament.uk/pa/cm201011/cmhansrd/cm101209/debtext/101209-0002.htm#10120946000003
3. Simon Fraser, Philip Rutman and Martin Donnelly.
4. http://www.publications.parliament.uk/pa/cm201415/cmhansrd/cm150108/debtext/150108-0002.htm#15010857000902
5. http://www.publications.parliament.uk/pa/cm201011/cmhansrd/cm101208/wmstext/101208m0001.htm#10120858000009
6. In late 2015, the Government reduced the discount rate applied to student loans and froze the repayment threshold, which reduced the official calculation of the RAB charge to 30%.
7. The Haldane Principle states the precise use of research funds should be determined by the research community rather than politicians.
8. http://cdbu.org.uk/about/a-world-class-system/
9. As the special adviser to the Minister for Universities and Science, the author was tasked with compiling the list of vice-chancellors who supported the policy.
10. http://www.bbc.co.uk/news/uk-england-cambridgeshire-15855838; http://www.bbk.ac.uk/downloads/BernalLecture2012_DavidWilletts.pdf.

Disclosure statement

No potential conflict of interest was reported by the author.

References

Ashcroft, M., & Culwick, K. (2015). *Pay me forty quid and I'll tell you: The 2015 election campaign through the eyes of the voters who largely ignored it*. London: Biteback Publishing.

Attwood, R. (2011, February 24). You mean Offa is toothless? The reason for policy chaos. *Times Higher Education*.

Boffey, D. (2011, March 27). Academic fury over order to study the big society. *The Observer*.

British Council (2015). *UK competitiveness slips again. But all is not lost*. London: British Council.

Byrne, L. (2014). *Robbins rebooted: How we earn our way in the second machine age*. London: Social Market Foundation.

Carasso, H., & Gunn, A. (2015). Fees, fairness and the National Scholarship Programme: Higher education policy in England and the Coalition Government. *London Review of Education, 13*, 70–83.

Dean, J. (2015). 'Angelic spirits of '68': Memories of 60s' radicalism in responses to the 2010–11 UK student protests. *Contemporary British History*.

Department for Business, Innovation and Skills. (2010a). *Changes to tuition fees and higher education*. 15 December.

Department for Business, Innovation and Skills. (2010b). *Progressive plans for higher education*. 3 November.

Department for Business, Innovation and Skills. (2013). *International education: Global growth and prosperity*. London: Department for Business, Innovation and Skills.

Department for Business, Innovation and Skills. (2015a). *Consultation on freezing the student loan repayment threshold*. London: Department for Business, Innovation and Skills.

Department for Business, Innovation and Skills. (2015b). *Fulfilling our potential: Teaching excellence, social mobility and student choice*. London: Department for Business, Innovation and Skills.

Department for Business, Innovation and Skills (2015c). *Nurse Review of research councils: Call for evidence*. London: Department for Business, Innovation and Skills.

Duffett, H. (2010). Tuition fees: How Liberal Democrat MPs voted. Blogpost. Retrieved from http://www.libdemvoice.org/tuition-fees-how-liberal-democrat-mps-voted-22346.html

Finn, M. (2015). Education beyond the Gove Legacy: The case of higher education (2)—ideology in action. In M. Finn (Ed.), *The Gove legacy: Education in Britain after the Coalition* (pp. 87–100). Basingstoke: Palgrave Macmillan.

Fisher, S. D., & Hillman, N. (2014). *Do students swing elections? Registration, turnout and voting behaviour among full-time students*. Oxford: Higher Education Policy Institute.

Gill, J. (2015, June18). David Willetts interview: 'What I did was in the interests of young people'. *Times Higher Education*.

Greenaway, D., & Haynes, M. (2003). Funding higher education in the UK: The role of fees and loans. *The Economic Journal, 113*, 150–166.

Helm T., Rawnsley, A., & Boffey, D. (2010, September 25). Labour would cut top university fees to £6,000, says Ed Miliband. *The Observer*.

Her Majesty's Government (2010). *The Coalition: our programme for government*. London: Cabinet Office.

Her Majesty's Treasury (2013). *Autumn statement*. London: Her Majesty's Treasury.

Higher Education Commission (2014). *Too good to fail—The financial sustainability of higher education in England*. London: Higher Education Commission.

Hillman, N. (2013). From grants for all to loans for all: Undergraduate finance from the implementation of the Anderson Report (1962) to the implementation of the Browne Report (2012). *Contemporary British History, 27,* 249–270.

Hillman, N. (2014a). *A guide to the removal of student number controls*. Oxford: Higher Education Policy Institute.

Hillman, N. (2014b, October 23). Are postgraduate loans on the horizon? *Times Higher Education.*

Hillman, N. (2014c). The parallels between admissions to independent boarding schools and admissions to selective universities. *Higher Education Review, 46,* 5–19.

Hillman, N. (2014d). *In defence of special advisers—Lessons from personal experience*. London: Institute for Government.

Hillman, N. (Ed.). (2015a). *It's the finance, stupid! The decline of part-time study and what to do about it*. Oxford: Higher Education Policy Institute.

Hillman, N. (2015b). *Students and the 2015 general election: Did they make a difference?*. Oxford: Higher Education Policy Institute.

Hunter Blackburn, L. (2015). *Whose to lose? Citizens, institutions and the ownership of higher education funding in a devolved UK*. Oxford: Higher Education Policy Institute.

Independent Commission on Fees (2015). *Final report*. London: Independent Commission on Fees.

Independent Review of Higher Education Funding and Student Finance (2010). *Securing a sustainable future for higher education*. London: Independent Review of Higher Education Funding and Student Finance.

Liberal Democrats. (2015). *Manifesto 2015: Stronger economy*. Liberal Democrats: Fairer society. Opportunity for everyone. London.

Mandelson, P. (2011). *The third man*. London: HarperCollins.

McGettigan, A. (2015). *The accounting and budgeting of student loans*. Oxford: Higher Education Policy Institute.

Miliband, E. (2010, June 25). Why I'd bin tuition fees. *Guardian.*

Moore, C. (2011, May 14). University tuition fees: What started as a better way to pay for universities is now a mess. *Daily Telegraph.*

National Audit Office. (2014). *Investigation into financial support for students at alternative higher education providers*. London: National Audit Office.

National Union of Students/HSBC. (2010). *Student experience report: Finance and debt*. London: National Union of Students.

Newman, M. (2008, September 18). Leaders of Lib Dems to ditch fees policy. *Times Higher Education.*

Nurse, P. (2015). *Ensuring a successful UK research endeavour: A review of the UK Research Councils*. London: Nurse Review.

Schleicher, A. (2015). The sustainability of the UK's higher education system. Blogpost. Retrieved from http://oecdeducationtoday.blogspot.co.uk/2015/01/the-sustainability-of-uks-higher.html

Shepherd, J., & Stratton, A. (2010, November 3). Tuition fees rise 'won't put off poor students'. *Guardian.*

Smith, S. et al. (2010, December 8). If MPs fail to support higher tuition fees, student numbers are likely to be cut, putting social mobility at risk. *Daily Telegraph.*

Spohrer, K. (2015). Opening doors or narrowing opportunities? The Coalition's approach to widening participation, social mobility and social justice. In M. Finn (Ed.), *The Gove legacy: Education in Britain after the Coalition* (pp. 101–115). Basingstoke: Palgrave Macmillan.

Temple, P. (2015). What has the Coalition Government done for higher education? *London Review of Education, 13,* 174–178.

Thompson, J., & Bekhradnia, B. (2010). *The government's proposals for higher education funding and student finance—An analysis*. Oxford: Higher Education Policy Institute.

Universities UK. (2013). *The power of part-time: Review of part-time and mature higher education*. London: Universities UK.

White, M. (2010, December 7). Nick Clegg could be left with a four-way split when MPs vote on tuition fee rise. *Guardian.*

Wilby, P. (2010, December 7). Ed Miliband is wrong. Tuition fees gave poorer students hope. *Guardian.*

Willetts, D. (2015). *Issues and ideas on higher education: Who benefits? Who pays?*. London: The Policy Institute at King's College London.

Wilson, R. (2010). *5 days to power: The journey to Coalition Britain*. London: Biteback Publishing.

Wintour, P. (2015, February 27). Ed Miliband promises to slash tuition fees and boost maintenance grant. *Guardian*.

Education in Northern Ireland since the Good Friday Agreement: Kabuki theatre meets *danse macabre*

John Gardner

ABSTRACT

The Good Friday Agreement (1998) between the UK and Irish governments, and most of the political parties in Northern Ireland, heralded a significant step forward in securing peace and stability for this troubled region of the British Isles. From the new-found stability, the previous fits and starts of education reform were replaced by a determination for modernisation and innovation, infused with a new energy and momentum. This sense of purpose embraced a complex weave of ideas and ideals; all designed variously to smooth, celebrate and harness community differences for the collective good. Much progress has been made in the intervening years since 1998, particularly in political structures and relationships. However, the euphoria of the new dawn of the Agreement had barely begun to shape the future before entrenched 'tribal' tensions reproduced the same political and legislative impasses of former years and visited their all-too-familiar blight on the economic, cultural and educational landscapes. This paper focuses on two signature dimensions of education that have been sustained by this partisanship: segregation by religion and segregation by academic selection.

Introduction

Northern Ireland society may be characterised as a spectrum of political aspirations bookended by violent extremists pursuing either continued union with Great Britain (loyalist paramilitaries) or reunification of Ireland (republican paramilitaries). The large majority in between may have unionist or nationalist sympathies but their overarching desire for a peaceful resolution of their differences was given voice with their 71% 'Yes' vote in the referendum on the Good Friday Agreement. Also known as the Belfast Agreement, it was signed by the British and Irish governments and most of the political parties in Northern Ireland on Good Friday, 10 April 1998 (NIO, 1998). Prior to this, there had been 26 years of direct rule in which the UK government-of-the-day appointed a secretary of state to run the country because, to put it bluntly, the local politicians could not be trusted to do it themselves. In 1972, direct rule by Westminster had finally brought the unionist-controlled Northern Ireland parliament to book for its 50 years of partiality and self-aggrandisement since the state was established in 1921. With a tenacious civil rights movement seeking equality of opportunity for the Catholic community, in employment, housing, education and a host of other social contexts, a London appointed secretary of state was viewed in many quarters as having the potential to be objective and fair, and most importantly a force for reform. Regrettably, the genie of vicious community and paramilitary violence had already been released from the bottle and for many years the London appointees, and their portfolio ministers and civil servants, were as much under siege as the communities they were serving.

The Good Friday Agreement returned a semblance of self-determination to these communities and was indisputably one of the most positive and momentous events in Northern Ireland's troubled history. It had a profound effect on how Northern Ireland politics work and the relative stability that Northern Ireland now enjoys, with its own devolved assembly established in December 1998, can be directly linked to the Agreement's founding principle of power sharing. Although one of the largest parties, the Democratic Unionist Party (DUP), had categorically rejected the Agreement (and arguably accounted for most of the 29% 'No' vote in the referendum), it breathed new life into Northern Ireland society. A generation was waking up to the novel prospect, for them, of self-government in many key areas of devolved responsibility; and the wave of optimism that accompanied the Agreement gave a strong fillip to those who saw a need for reform in the education system. For too long a variety of problematic issues had had insufficient scrutiny in terms of their fit to a changing world. Some of these still obtain today, for example the statutory requirement for children as young as 4-years 2-months to enter formal schooling, but the focus of this paper will be on the two signature dimensions of the Northern Ireland education system that make it stand out as unusual in the UK and indeed in comparison to most modern developed societies. These are the segregation of schoolchildren on the basis of religion and segregated access to secondary-level education based on controversial assessments of children's ability to benefit from a grammar school education. The one is variously blamed for the lack of social cohesion that fuels inter-community strife whilst the other is similarly tarred with the brush of condemning thousands of young people each year to lowered aspirations and life-chances.

There are many commentators on the strengths and weaknesses of schooling in Northern Ireland; some of them explicitly political, leaning left or right. Informing the various debates down through the years are the reports of specially commissioned review bodies, research evidence from academics and educational organisations including charities, and the data captured and processed by statutory curriculum and governance bodies, including the school inspectorate. Inevitably, much of this evidence gives rise to demands for intervention and to proposals for system change, designed to correct the perceived imbalances and weaknesses. These in turn sponsor various attempts at change, for example in how the school system is organised or how teacher training is provided. However, experience has it that Newton's Third Law invariably holds: forces for change generate equally energetic counter forces seeking to maintain the status quo.

Given the complexity outlined above, there was a temptation in writing this paper to explore the layers of Bourdieusian 'doxa' and 'habitus', the entrenched beliefs and practices underlying the invariant positions and intransigence of many of the actors in the Northern Ireland political system. When powerful opposing groups seem deliberately to eschew the reflexivity that might modify their centuries-old dispositions, and instead attempt to browbeat or simply coerce the 'opposition' to their own unchanged way of thinking, the impact on social constructs such as education is massive. Innovation is smothered, and 'moving with the times' is more a stuttering journey, stopped and interrogated at every decision point, than a seamless process informed by international norms and tailored for local needs. There is a sense in which academics have always viewed Northern Ireland education as a type of sociological experiment existing within, and sometimes attempting to change, a society of polar opposites and multiple antagonists. However, instead of trying to unravel the deep-down psyches or the fundamental belief systems that govern the main actors' contributions, this paper seeks to chart developments in relation to education segregated by religion and academic selection since the time of the Agreement. Any such overview, however, must be prefaced with the acknowledgement that the matters being considered go to the very heart of Northern Ireland's riven society and it is therefore important to offer a brief history for each dimension.

Religious segregation of schools

Schooling in Ireland was first formalised In 1812 wlth government grants for those proposing to create schools that 'banished even the suspicion of proselytism' (Stanley, 1831, p. vii). However, by 1831 the Chief Secretary for Ireland, E. G. Stanley, was noting in a letter to the Duke of Leinster that the existing scheme's intention of creating national schools, which taught the 'Holy Scriptures without Note or Comment … must be particularly obnoxious to a church which denies, even to adults, the right of unaided private interpretation' (Stanley, 1831, p. viii). Stanley's famous letter recognised the Catholic Church's by then long-established opposition to the basis on which schools were being founded and sought to 'unite in one system children of different creeds' (Stanley, 1831, p. x). The intention was to create an integrated system in which government aid for schools would only be available if joint applications were made by representatives of both denominations. Over time, however, any semblance of integration was lost and most of these national schools took on the complexion and ethos of their majority community.

Universal education, introduced in England by the Elementary Education Act (1870), proved particularly tricky in Ireland and was not enacted until 1892. The delay was primarily due to opposition from all of the churches to the basic premise of the 1870 Act, which compelled 'every parent and guardian of a child to have it taught, at least, the rudiments of education, and that without reference to any religious creed or persuasion'. How could this be done unless the schools were non-denominational? A non-starter for the churches.

The Northern Ireland state came formally into being in 1921, under the Government of Ireland Act (1920) which partitioned Ireland into two territories: the unionist, Protestant-majority north and the nationalist, Catholic-majority south. Brewer and Higgins (1998) describe how Northern Ireland had been established amidst grievous and violent antagonism between the two states. As a consequence, it was formed on the basis of a deliberate anti-Catholic and anti-nationalist rationale to counter the perceived threat of encroachment from the neighbouring Irish Free State that had emerged from the civil war between nationalist factions; a state that just as forcefully espoused a Catholic and anti-British nationhood. The effect in the north was to ensure that the processes of government were already deeply tinged with the divisions that would persist in the future. The Catholic Church hierarchy and nationalist politicians in the north felt very much under siege and actively promoted a boycott of the Northern Ireland government. The result was that the members of the new parliament at Stormont were almost exclusively from the unionist tradition. Sectarian sentiment in the parliament on all issues, including education and employment, was largely unrestrained in its early days as elected Catholic nationalist members stayed away from the proceedings. In sectarian terms it was not a forum for the fainthearted and even some 10 years into its life, when a nationalist politician challenged the perceived discrimination against Catholics in government appointments, James Craig, the then prime minister, asserted that seeking appointees with 'unimpeachable loyalty to the King and Constitution … [was his] … whole object in carrying on a Protestant Government for a Protestant People' (Craig, 1934, p. 73).

However, not all thinking in the new parliament was entrenched in diehard positions and in the early days there was some cause for hope. For example, a vigorous attempt to intro-duce integrated education was made by the parliament's first Minister of Education, Lord Londonderry. He commissioned the Lynn Committee to bring forward proposals for the re-organisation of Northern Ireland schools, which he then took forward in the Education (Northern Ireland) Act 1923. However, his final proposals, including his rejection of the Lynn Committee's recommendation to introduce common scripture study into all schools, were attacked by both denominations primarily because the new school system would be secular and would wrest control of the schools from the churches. One unionist MP detected Londonderry's fading resolve in the face of this church opposition and expressed his regret that he did not 'take courage into his hand and give us secular schools … but not godless by any means' (McGuffin, 1923, p. 139). Londonderry finally tried to get buy-in from the churches with an impassioned appeal for them not to be 'the stumbling block in the way of an ideal system owing to a determination to segregate their flocks from birth and create a division' (Londonderry, 1923, p. 125). In retrospect, they were more than mere stumbling blocks and the opportunity to disband segregated schooling in the new Northern Ireland state was lost.

School structure today

In 1923, the Lynn Committee proposed three types of school for Northern Ireland education: county schools controlled by the Ministry of Education; so-called '4 and 2' schools in which the management committees had two ministry nominees with four nominated by the rel-evant church (mostly aimed at Catholic schools); and independently managed voluntary schools mostly aimed at the existing grammar school bloc. The Protestant churches resisted at first and then transferred their schools to government control ('controlled' schools of today) in return for the financial stability on offer. However, such was the resistance of the Catholic Church to any encroachment on their control of schools that it was not until 1968 that a form of the '4 and 2' management model (Catholic 'maintained' schools of today) was finally agreed with them. To this day, 'voluntary' Catholic and Protestant grammar schools are independent of government control, albeit within the boundaries of financial depend-ency and curricular and related compliance.

Table 1 sets out the main types of primary and secondary-level schools that exist in Northern Ireland in 2014/15 (for expedience, the table does not list preparatory departments of grammar schools (14), nurseries (96), special schools (39), independent schools (14) and one hospital school). 'Controlled' schools are often described as non-denominational and the figures bear out their much greater diversity in comparison to Catholic 'maintained' schools, albeit still with 68.3% and 81.4% designated Protestant majorities in the primary and non-selective secondary schools respectively. The Total Enrolment column also includes

Table 1. Numbers of schools (2014/15 and 1998/99) and their enrolments.

School Types	98/99 N	14/15 N	%	Total Enrolment 14/15 N	Enrolments Recorded as Protestant* 14/15 N	%	Enrolments Recorded as Catholic 14/15 N	%
Primary								
Controlled		370	45.0	75688	51708	68.3	5051	6.7
Catholic Maintained		381	46.4	75771	579	0.8	73197	96.6
Other Maintained		29	3.5	2872	276	9.6	2369	82.5
Controlled Integrated		19	2.3	3733	1518	40.7	1118	29.9
Grant Maintained Integrated		23	2.8	5671	1800	31.7	2443	43.1
Totals	916	822	100	163735	55881	34.1	84178	51.4
Secondary Non-Grammar								
Controlled		51	36.4	27918	22714	81.4	860	3.1
Catholic Maintained		68	48.6	39347	467	1.2	38189	97.1
Other Maintained		1	0.7	581	0.0	0.0	542	93.3
Controlled Integrated		5	3.6	2502	1634	65.3	402	16.1
Grant Maintained Integrated		15	10.7	9492	4026	42.4	3867	40.7
Totals	165	140	100	79840	28841	36.1	43860	54.9
Secondary Grammar								
Controlled		18	26.5	15787	11959	75.8	1335	8.5
Voluntary (Catholic)		29	42.6	27391	260	0.9	26658	97.3
Voluntary (Other)		21	30.9	19535	12701	65.0	2381	12.2
Totals	72	68	100	62713	24920	39.7	30374	48.4
Grand Totals	1153	1030	100	306288	109642	35.8	158412	51.7

*Excludes pupils recorded as 'Catholic', 'Other Christian', 'Non-Christian' or 'No Religion/Not Recorded'
Sources: DENI, 2012; DENI, 2015a.

pupils designated as 'Other Christian', 'Non-Christian' or 'No Religion/Not Recorded' in 2014/15 and of these the very large majority (80.0%) attend controlled schools, 8.4% attend Catholic schools and 10.7% attend grant maintained integrated schools. Designated Catholic pupils make up 6.7% and 3.1% of controlled primary and non-selective secondary schools respectively whilst non-Catholic pupils represent 3.4% and 2.9% respectively in the mirror image Catholic maintained schools. Controlled and non-Catholic voluntary grammar schools have 8.5% and 12.2% designated Catholic enrolments respectively but Catholic grammar schools are almost exclusively Catholic (97.3%). The 62 integrated schools together host 7.0% (21,398) of all primary and secondary-level pupils, of whom 36.6% are Catholic.

Integrated education has been a feature of the education landscape since the opening of the first school, Lagan College, in 1981. For some time the prospects for a radical alternative to the bipartite system looked bright, bolstered by the 1989 Education Reform Order, which placed a statutory onus on the Department of Education to 'encourage and support integrated education' (ERO, 1989, Art 64 (1)). However, the sector has faced many difficulties including open opposition from the Catholic Church, which for many years refused to minister to the spiritual needs of Catholic children in integrated schools, and antagonism from some sections of communities when the creation of a new integrated school threatened the sustainability of existing local schools. The granting of controlled integrated status to schools with little or no prospect of meeting integrated criteria (which require 10% enrolment from the minority community in year 1 and the potential to reach 30% in the longer term) has for some schools been a safety net against closure in the face of falling rolls. It is an open question as to whether this type of faux-integration has undermined the development of integrated education. Despite consistently strong public endorsement (e.g. 68% reported in the *Belfast Telegraph*, 2013) and the high profile support of such dignitaries as President Obama (during his January 2013 visit) this form of shared education has grown very slowly to its present 7% proportion of the national enrolment (for a thorough overview of integrated education see Hansson, O'Connor-Bones & McCord, 2013; Montgomery, Fraser, McGlynn, Smith & Gallagher, 2003).

Hughes (2011) argues that 'integrated schools for all children are not a realistic option. Nor is it conceivable that education will ever become secularized' (2011, p. 847). She makes three observations: that the separateness of schools and their pupils is based on their strong interconnectedness with their local community (borne out empirically by Graham & Nash, 2006, and Roulston & Young, 2013); that teachers are reluctant to challenge strong in-group identities; and that school status is identity. With this latter observation she argues that a Catholic school has a clear Catholic identity, whilst however much some might promote a 'non-denominational' ethos for controlled schools they are much more accurately identified as Protestant. The non-denominational approach 'could be construed as subordinating Protestant identity distinctiveness, thereby denying Protestant pupils a basis on which to engage with their Catholic peers' (Hughes, 2011, p. 846). Her argument continues by asserting that sustained collaboration between schools, i.e. shared education, is one pathway to better inter-group relations but is contingent on controlled schools 'taking ownership of their distinctly Protestant identity' (p. 847).

As a concept, 'shared education' was first formally enshrined in government-speak during the term of office of the direct rule Secretary of State, Paul Murphy. Entitled *A shared future: Policy and strategic framework for good relations in Northern Ireland* (OFMDFM, 2005), the framework envisaged a shared society at all levels and in all spheres including the community, the workplace and education. Shared education was one of the main themes of the seminal Burns Report (2001, see below) and since 2007 it has also been the subject of a major continuing project, the Sharing Education Programme (Gallagher, Stewart, Walker, Baker & Lockhart, 2010) sponsored by Atlantic Philanthropies and the International Fund for Ireland. The concept is complex and involves schools of various types working together to promote efficient use of resources, equality of opportunity and identity, and respect for diversity and community cohesion (Gallagher's paper, in this issue, addresses shared education developments in detail). The most recent development, a Shared Education Bill, is currently being drafted by the Minister of Education for approval in early 2016 (DENI, 2015b) based on an all-encompassing vision for: 'Vibrant, self-improving Shared Education partnerships delivering educational benefits to learners, encouraging the efficient and effective use of resources, and promoting equality of opportunity, good relations, equality of identity, respect for diversity and community cohesion' (p. 4).

Implications of segregated schooling

Segregated schooling in Northern Ireland is considered by some sections of the public to be a good thing for protecting culture, promoting faith-based values and, close to many people's concerns, providing safety for children in what at times can be a volatile environment. None of these considerations can be seriously faulted but many might agree with the Democratic Unionist First Minister, Peter Robinson, that the Northern Ireland education system is a 'benign form of apartheid' and that 'we cannot hope to move beyond our present community divisions while our young people are educated separately' (*Belfast Telegraph*,

2010). However, his solution—that the government should stop funding Catholic schools—was unlikely to find favour with many people beyond his party faithful.

The duplication of schools, or indeed triplication in instances where an integrated school competes with local controlled and Catholic schools, underpins an economic argument against such national-scale segregation, and the figures are startling. In 2006, the Bain Review, which focused on the wasteful inappropriateness of the system, estimated that 53,000 places (15% of the total capacity) in existing schools were unfilled. The report strongly endorsed the need for the school estate to be rationalised and for schools to share resources. The Northern Ireland Audit Office (NIAO) now estimates that there are 71,000 surplus places in schools (NIAO, 2015). This represents approximately 20% of capacity and crosses both sectors: 45% in non-denominational schools and 49% in Catholic schools. The NIAO (2015) suggests that 70% of the surplus places are in primary schools and that 271 of these have enrolments of less than 100 pupils.

Table 1 shows that at the time of the Agreement In 1998 there were 916 primary schools (DENI, 2012) and every minister of education since then, faced with dwindling budgets, has struggled with the problem of school duplication and small schools. The closure of schools for budgetary or operational reasons in any part of the UK, and in many developed countries, often faces considerable community opposition but in Northern Ireland it is invariably more contentious. As parents face the choice of enrolling their children in a school that mainly serves the 'other' community or sending them on much longer journeys to an alternative school serving their own community, it is not unknown for unsavoury elements to mount a more menacing opposition to closure proposals. Although the number of primary schools has fallen to 822 (DENI, 2015a), a reduction of 94 in 17 years, the NIAO note that the 2014/15 cost to sustain small schools (some with as few as 19 pupils) remains very high at £36 million in additional grants; and they pull no punches in pressing the Department of Education to do more to plan and manage the surpluses and school sustainability.

Another implication of segregated education is the need for teachers to be trained in the ethos appropriate to the schools in which they teach, i.e. segregated teacher education. Most tertiary education in Northern Ireland, comprising the large further education colleges and the two universities, is integrated; i.e. students of all cultural backgrounds routinely study together. The two teacher education colleges, however, largely reflect the primary school communities they serve: the one non-denominational (Stranmillis), the other Catholic (St Mary's).

Over time, this segregation of teacher education has been challenged politically and academically, especially as the two universities have been training teachers successfully in an integrated fashion for many years. In 1982, for example, the Chilver Committee's review of Northern Ireland higher education precipitated a furore by proposing a merger of the colleges (Chilver, 1982). The Catholic Church's reaction involved rallying opposition in its schools and parishes and ultimately the proposals were shelved. It was not until the early 2000s, on foot of the Agreement, that a new impetus began to form around the pursuit of integrated teacher education. Under the devolved government structure, the Department for Employment and Learning (DEL) had responsibility for funding higher education, including teacher education, and in consort with the Department of Education (with responsibility for schools) it renewed efforts to unify teacher education. Consultations and workshops involving all stakeholders teased out different models of integration, federation and collaboration. There were mixed reactions from the Protestant churches and Stranmillis University

College but resolute intransigence from the Catholic authorities and St Mary's University College. Interpreting the various proposals as attempts to undermine Catholic education, all arguments relating to such benefits as improved social cohesion, community integration and financial efficiencies were met with at best silence and at worst vociferous rejection. Chastened by the aggressive tone of the various negotiations, DEL repositioned itself and in 2013 commissioned an international team to review the teacher education arrangements.

The ensuing *Report of the International Review Panel on the structure of initial teacher education in Northern Ireland* (DEL, 2014) was particularly hard-hitting, with the panel asserting that the teacher education system has a number of serious weaknesses and unsustainable characteristics relating to:

- A small and deeply fragmented system with only 1400 students between the institutions;
- Inappropriate policy making that aims to keep the university colleges financially viable rather than addressing the skill base needed for an advanced economy;
- The quality of provision in relation to international trends;
- Unemployment among new graduating teachers of almost 82%;
- Significantly higher costs compared to UK norms for teacher education in the two small and largely mono-technic institutions: 38% higher costs in Stranmillis and 31% in St Mary's;
- Inequitable treatment of Stranmillis students who must complete a Glasgow University programme if they wish to teach in Catholic primary or nursery schools;
- The anomalous system of accepting applicants who have not registered with the UK Universities and Colleges Admissions Service, UCAS.

It is clear that teacher education in Northern Ireland has a considerable distance to travel if it is to present itself as a modern system fit for the needs of today's society.

Segregation by academic selection

The second key focus of this paper is Northern Ireland's almost unique system of state-endorsed academic segregation in secondary education. Children leaving primary education may transfer directly to non-selective secondary schools or they may compete for a place in a grammar school, with entry dependent on their performance in academic transfer tests. However, many of the children who wish to transfer to a grammar school are turned away because of their grades and may face the stigma of having 'failed' the transfer tests well into their adult life. The reforming mood inspired by the Agreement initiated a raft of studies, policy reviews and attempts at changing this system but also faced the same conservative and partisan reactions as attempts at addressing religiously segregated education had faced for decades before (and since). The irony, however, is that the threat to academic selection found common ground across the segregated systems with Catholic and Protestant grammar schools united in defending middle-class interests under their umbrella group, the Governing Bodies Association (GBA). These class-based motivations for academic selection are tellingly underlined by its socially segregating effect on Northern Ireland's children. In 2012/13, for example, 56 of the 68 grammar schools had less than 10% of pupils who were entitled to free school meals, and of these at least ten schools had less than 4% (Nolan, 2014).

The selective system had its origins in the Education Act (Northern Ireland) 1947 as a follow-on to the UK Conservative government's 1944 introduction of free entry to all English and Welsh schools. The Education Act (1944) enabled admission to grammar schools on the basis of performance in academic '11+' tests, so-called as they were administered in the child's last year at primary school, normally at 11 years of age. According to Walker (2010), the GBA had opposed the Order because it wished to continue to admit students on a fee-paying basis (the main income stream for grammar schools at that time) regardless of their performance on any academic selection test. The privileging of fee-payers was ultimately conceded by the Northern Ireland government, though subject to capped numbers, and the Order passed through parliament. Inequalities remained, however, and according to Walker pupils attending non-grammar schools were not permitted to take public examinations right up to the 1970s (Walker, 2010, p. 12).

Whilst controversy around religion-based segregation has flared and smouldered over the decades, academic selection has been a constant feature of educational concern and debate. Successive government reports from the 1960s onward had expressed concerns about it. In 1964, for example, the Northern Ireland Minister of Education noted that the most serious educational problem of the time was the 11+ examination for grammar school entry; and posed the question as to 'whether the existing system of secondary education should be continued or replaced by a new system based on some form of comprehensive school' (HMSO, 1964, p. 8). In 1971, the Advisory Council for Education in Northern Ireland specifically examined the selection procedure and in an almost hidden caveat to their conclusions they felt the Council 'would be in danger of conveying a false impression ... if it did not express grave disquiet regarding the principle of selection' (ACENI, 1971, p. 27). In 1973, the Council returned more resolutely to the issue when they recommended that the Minister of Education should declare the intention to eliminate selection at 11+ as soon as possible (ACENI, 1973).

Public attention waxed and waned during the 1980s and early 1990s until in 1996 the Department of Education released a report, *Free school meals and low achievement*, which powerfully illustrated the inequalities in the system (DENI, 1996). Children who were entitled to free school meals were much less likely to stay at school after the compulsory age (16 years) or to proceed to further or higher education. The focus fell on grammar schools again and the advantages/disadvantages that academic segregation creates for pupils. Time after time over the period since the Agreement, significant bodies have criticised the Northern Ireland education system for the inequalities in opportunities and outcomes of the type and extent that were illustrated in the DENI Free School Meals bulletin above. In the review of 1992–99, for example, the Chief Inspector of Schools observed that many young people left compulsory education with low standards of literacy and numeracy (ETI, 2001).

Right up to the present day, the Education and Training Inspectorate has unequivocally identified the weaknesses of the system in relation to disadvantaged pupils. In the 2010–12 Chief Inspector's Report (ETI, 2012) it was expressed as the need to improve outcomes in English and mathematics for those entitled to free school meals ('only 32% of all school leavers entitled to free school meals achieved five GCSE A*–C grades including English and mathematics' p. 6). In the 2012–14 report (ETI, 2014) a slight improvement to 34% is registered (p. 3) with the rider that 'The outcomes for our most vulnerable learners are not good enough' (p. 7). The report highlights the diminishing performance gap between grammar and non-selective schools, with only 30% difference in the proportions of all pupils achieving at least five GCSEs at A*–C grades—compared to the 53% gap in 2005/6. Perhaps more tellingly the report registers the need to 'reduce the variability in the life chances of children and young people' (p. 3).

One of the most repeated arguments from proponents wishing to maintain academic selection is that Northern Ireland's education system is the envy of Britain if not the world. Pupils taking A-levels often accumulate more high grades than their counterparts in England and Wales, and the observation is often made that a system designed to deliver such high quality outcomes would be very expensive in England (via private fee-paying school places) but in Northern Ireland it is free, i.e. grammar schools focus on attaining high grades and attendance at them is at a cost to the taxpayer not the pupil or parents. Non-grammar schools are also fully funded by the taxpayer but their outcomes are lower despite the attenuating difference mentioned above. The factors contributing to the difference can be at least partly ascribed to pupil-based characteristics such as commitment to education, family back-ground, level of aspiration and disadvantage through poverty. Poverty is a major dimension of disadvantage in Northern Ireland with estimates ranging from 95,000 (Nolan, 2014) to 149,000 Northern Ireland children (Hillyard, Kelly, McLaughlin, Patsios & Tomlinson, 2003) living in designated 'poor' households. Indeed, the socio-economic differences between the two parts of the state-funded system are often commented upon by international observers, the most recent being the Organisation for Economic Cooperation and Development (OECD): 'The concentration of less socio-economically advantaged students in some schools is a recognized challenge in Northern Ireland' (Shewbridge, Hulshof, Nusche & Staehr, 2014, p. 28).

The performance of grammar schools, in light of the decreasing difference above, is wor-thy of some scrutiny. With 44% of all secondary-level admissions, grammar schools cannot justify the segregation of children on the basis of an arbitrary potential to benefit from a grammar school education. The question is begged: in what sense would the other 56% not benefit from this? Additionally, their much vaunted performance is not as universally good as the GBA might propose. In a recent analysis of their performance, (Belfast Telegraph, 2015) ten of the 68 grammar schools had pupils with three good A-level passes at proportions less than the 65% average for the whole secondary sector. This compares unfavourably to five non-selective schools with 64+ percentage success (Nolan, 2014, p. 96).

The two main unionist parties and the GBA have consistently blocked any attempt to abolish academic selection despite widespread concern about its impact on the sizeable group of pupils who each year fail to get a place in a grammar school. In 2006, the Westminster Public Accounts Committee (Belfast Telegraph, 2006) expressed its concern about outcomes for some pupils from the non-selective secondary sector and especially the outcomes for disadvantaged Protestant children in controlled schools. They described the statistic for pupils obtaining A*–C grades in GCSE mathematics as 'appalling' (4.4%) with better but still very poor figures for GCSE English (17%). The proportion of Northern Ireland Protestant boys, who are entitled to free school meals, achieving five GCSEs at A*–C grades (including maths and English) is 19.7%, the third lowest performing grouping in the UK and a long way below the 62% average for all Northern Ireland pupils (Nolan, 2014, p. 98). Nevertheless, the unionist parties and the GBA continue to defend the system, prompting Kelly (2011, p. 94) to observe that the unionists appear to treat Protestant working-class children as mere 'education fodder in this middle-class system' when it comes to educational achievement.

The debate about inequalities, which some consider to be caused or at least perpetuated by the selective system, took on renewed vigour when a Labour government was returned in the UK in 1997. However, the direct rule minister did not seek to remove selection and called instead for more research. In the year of the Agreement, the Department of Education duly commissioned a 27-member team of academics from four institutions to examine a wide variety of effects of the selective system. The project reported in September 2000 (Gallagher & Smith, 2000) and was a tour de force of objective analysis of the effects of selection on Northern Ireland society. In parallel research into the 11+ transfer tests themselves, Gardner and Cowan (2000, 2005) used three versions of the tests with 52 primary schools and over 2,000 pupils to demonstrate unequivocally that the tests were technically unreliable and could only be trusted to differentiate the cohort into the top 12% and lowest 18% performing pupils. To add salt to the wounds, the data showed that only 18 marks (out of 150) separated the top A grading band from the lowest D band—and in the year in question this would have scaled up to affect over 12,000 children. The conceit of discriminating fairly between so many children over an 18 mark range was comprehensively exposed.

Academic selection since the Good Friday Agreement

The selection debate began to gather momentum almost as soon as the devolved assembly was inaugurated in 2000. The first Minister of Education, Martin McGuinness, came from Sinn Fein, a party which was on record as being opposed to selection. Following on the Gallagher and Smith reports, he commissioned a major review of Northern Ireland education, the Burns Review.

The Burns Report (Burns, 2001), officially published as the *Report of the Review Body on Post-Primary Education*, caught the reformist mood of the educational community but not the wider public and their political representatives. Strong forces railed against the proposals to abolish academic criteria for transfer to secondary education (the report proposed criteria ranging from having siblings at a school to distance from the child's home) and to create 20 'collegiate' networks of secondary-level schools, with each collegiate comprising Catholic, controlled, integrated and Irish-medium schools. The grammar school bloc was particularly outraged that their academic ethos could be lost and unionist politicians baulked at the idea of a Sinn Fein minister telling them what to do with Northern Ireland's schools.

The Burns Report galvanised the reformers and provoked the naysayers with its innovative and far-reaching proposals. However, during 2002 the strains of shared government were precipitating a constitutional crisis, which quickly led to the suspension of the Northern Ireland Assembly and a new period of direct rule, which was to last until 2007. The Sinn Fein Minister of Education's parting shot, dramatically close to midnight on the eve of suspension (13 October 2002), was to abolish the transfer tests with effect from 2004. His action initiated several years of turmoil born of uncertainty fuelled by a political vacuum. What would replace the transfer tests? What would happen to grammar schools?

The 'objective' actors in this escalating situation were the direct rule ministers of education. Although at times they must have felt they were trying to bring order to a room full of precocious and squabbling children, they tried earnestly to move matters forward. The first in a series of four, Jane Kennedy, commissioned the Costello Working Group in early 2003 to review the Burns proposals. The Costello Report (2004) broadly endorsed the direction of travel of Burns but proposed looser confederations of schools, instead of fixed collegiate networks, to share resources and engage in cross-community activities. The group also endorsed the abolition of academic selection for entry to secondary level schools. In accepting all of the Costello recommendations, Kennedy (BBC, 2004) confirmed that the last tests would now be in 2008 (four years after the McGuinness target of 2004). In 2005, the then secretary of state, Angela Smith, drew up proposals for a new Education (Northern Ireland) Order, which inter alia would confirm in statute that selection on academic grounds was abolished.

In an attempt to appease opposition from unionist politicians and the grammar schools, Smith's proposals (DENI, 2005) signalled categorically that the Order would not abolish grammar schools and would not impose a system of all-ability comprehensive schools. Nevertheless, the analysis of the consultation responses (DENI, 2006) illustrates how a campaign-style opposition was marshalled. Of 10,118 written responses, 8,900 were on a common form distributed by a group, Concerned Parents for Education, strongly opposed to the abolition of academic selection. In contrast, a wide range of bodies supported the proposal to prohibit the use of academic selection as an admissions criterion. These included three of the five education and library boards (the authorities for controlled, non-denominational schools), the Catholic Maintained Schools Commission, the Catholic Trustees group, the Northern Ireland Council for Integrated Education, Sinn Fein, the Social Democratic and Labour Party and the main teacher unions. More qualified support, tempered for example by concerns about putting the criteria into operation, was expressed by the Transferor Representatives Council, the General Teaching Council and others. Ultimately, the range and combination of the more thoughtful responses, though much smaller in number, was considered to be more valid than the monopolising potential of the multiple response campaign groups.

However, bigger prizes were at stake. Prime Minister Tony Blair had designs on getting agreement for a return to a devolved government and one of the key elements prompting the DUP's very public intransigence in negotiations with him was the threat surrounding grammar schools arising from the abolition of academic selection. He subsequently had the draft order amended, in June 2006, to make the abolition of academic selection subject to the decision of Northern Ireland Assembly if the parties agreed to a new model of devolved government by November 23 of that year (DENI, 2006). The decision horrified those in favour of desegregating the two-tier, non-selective and grammar school system and delighted those who wished the status quo to be maintained. In due course, however, the intervention helped Blair to achieve a last gasp deal at the negotiations in St Andrews, Scotland. If Blair's tactics might be considered cynical, in seeking agreement at any cost for another breakthrough feather in his diplomacy cap, Sinn Fein's agreement to a de facto veto for the unionist bloc on matters of academic selection was an extraordinary volte-face, sacrificing their avowed social justice principles for the prize of shared power. Eventually, a devolved assembly was restored and as expected the unionist bloc did exercise their right not to allow the abolition of academic selection.

During a long drawn out battle in the Assembly chamber and the media, in which the future life-chances of thousands of children played second fiddle to party politics and middle-class pressure, the unionists and GBA rejected a series of proposed compromises from the new Sinn Fein Minister of Education, Catriona Ruane. Finally all she could do was ensure that state involvement in academic selection would end whilst permitting grammar schools to organise their own, unregulated entrance tests. This they duly did. However, having won the battle to save academic selection as a unified opposition, they quickly retreated to their tribal comfort zones and opted to replace the fundamentally flawed state system with their own independent systems. Northern Ireland children now have the unenviable choice of separate 'Protestant' and 'Catholic' test systems for grammar schools; test systems with serious ethical questions to answer (see Elwood, 2013), of uncertain technical reliability and validity, no comparability of outcomes between them and no significant government oversight.

Concluding remarks

The Good Friday Agreement prompted considerable optimism for a brighter future for Northern Ireland and in many respects it has delivered, albeit with a few false-starts. In education, however, the wider Northern Ireland society remains unreconciled on a system segregated by religion and by academic selection. Much innovative work has been carried out on the former, most recently and intensely in exploring shared education; though without any sizable impact on the segregated system as yet. However, attempts at resolution of the latter have foundered on deeply entrenched views that Northern Ireland's children should be systematically separated at 11 years of age into grammar and non-grammar schools. Grammar schools are perceived as offering a direct line to university and employment; and this avenue to opportunity is jealously guarded by the middle classes in both communities who benefit most from it.

Successful change in these crucial matters might reasonably have been guaranteed by common cause between the two communities. Alas, this has been a rare commodity, often usurped or eclipsed by horse-trading between the main political parties. Nothing exemplifies the continuing unedifying lack of leadership and integrity in the country's governance better than the seven years and £17 million expended on attempts to create a unitary Education and Skills Authority (see BBC, 2014). Designed to bring under one management system the employing authorities of all schools (education and library boards, the Staff Commission, Catholic Council for Maintained Schools and the Youth Council) it had the endorsement of Sinn Fein but predictably, therefore, the opposition of the DUP. Ultimately it was brought down by a combination of unionist politicians concerned about the management of controlled (Protestant) schools and the GBA, who feared the erosion of grammar school autonomy. A watered down version, the Education Authority, is now in operation.

In the context of academic selection at 11, the various actors have retreated to their traditional positions. The Catholic Church continues to swither between not wishing to promote the immorality of state-sponsored disadvantage and the cynical protection of some of its top grammar schools; the GBA maintains their 'not an inch' stance on what it sees as the cream of UK education under attack, the DUP remain callously indifferent to the effects of a system that condemns children in their heartland working-class constituencies to poorer outcomes than their Catholic peers, and Sinn Fein continue to make their social justice agenda expedient to their power hungry pragmatism.

In the years since the Good Friday Agreement, the various protagonists have repeatedly taken up counter positions on these important matters, ostentatiously scoring points off each other in an education sub-plot of the Kabuki-esque theatre that is Northern Ireland politics. The centuries old scripts rarely change as entrenched views provoke predictable behaviours, replete with their customary posturing and bluster and the colourful but often menacing mix of symbolic masks, emblems, costumes and regalia. Unlike Kabuki, however, there is little of entertainment value as cynical politicians and some education leaders pursue their unmoderated sectional interests in a ritual of tit-for-tat obstruction and manipulation. The ultimate casualties of this relentless '*danse macabre*' are not the main participants; they are the children of Northern Ireland and their life-chances.

Disclosure statement

No potential conflict of interest was reported by the author.

References

ACENI. (1971). *The existing selection procedure for secondary education in Northern Ireland* (Advisory Council on Education for Northern Ireland Cmd 551). Belfast: Her Majesty's Stationery Office.

ACENI. (1973). *Reorganisation of secondary education in Northern Ireland* (Advisory Council on Education for Northern Ireland Cmd 574). Belfast: Her Majesty's Stationery Office.

Bain, G. (2006). *Schools for the future: Funding, strategy and sharing. Report of the Independent Strategic Review of Education*. Retrieved from http://dera.ioe.ac.uk/9777/1/review_of_education.pdf

BBC. (2004). *11+ to be abolished*. Retrieved from http://news.bbc.co.uk/1/hi/northern_ireland/3429541.stm

BBC. (2014). *ESA: John O'Dowd scraps Education and Skills Authority plan*. Retrieved from http://www.bbc.co.uk/news/uk-northern-ireland-27627932

Belfast Telegraph. (2006). How the school system is failing Protestant children in deprived areas. Retrieved from http://www.belfasttelegraph.co.uk/news/how-the-school-system-is-failing-protestant-kids-in-deprived-areas-28116864.html

Belfast Telegraph. (2010). Peter Robinson calls for the end to school segregation. Retrieved from http://www.belfasttelegraph.co.uk/news/education/peter-robinson-calls-for-end-to-school-segregation-28565048.html

Belfast Telegraph. (2013). Public mood in Northern Ireland is for an end to segregation in schools. Retrieved from http://www.belfasttelegraph.co.uk/opinion/debateni/public-mood-in-northern-ireland-is-for-an-end-to-segregation-in-schools-29372424.html

Belfast Telegraph. (2015). Northern Ireland schools league tables—Catholic grammars lead the way at GCSE but top schools failing at A-level. Retrieved from http://www.belfasttelegraph.co.uk/news/education/exclusive-northern-ireland-schools-league-tables-catholic-grammars-lead-the-way-at-gcse-but-top-schools-failing-at-alevel-31089536.html

Brewer, J. D., with Higgins, G. I. (1998). *Northern Ireland: 1921–1998*. Retrieved from http://cain.ulst.ac.uk/issues/sectarian/brewer.htm

Burns, G. (2001). *Report of the review body on post-primary education*. Retrieved from https://www.deni.gov.uk/publications/report-review-body-post-primary-education-burns-report

Chilver, H. (1982). *The future of higher education in Northern Ireland. Report of the Higher Education Review Group for Northern Ireland*. Belfast: HMSO.

Costello, S. (2004). *Report of the post-primary review working group*. Retrieved from https://www.deni.gov.uk/publications/costello-report-full

Craig, J. (1934, 21 November). *The Stormont Papers, 35*, 73. Retrieved from http://stormontpapers.ahds.ac.uk/stormontpapers/pageview.html?volumeno=17&pageno=73

DEL. (2014). Final Report of the international review panel on the structure of initial teacher education in Northern Ireland. Retrieved from https://www.delni.gov.uk/sites/default/files/publications/del/Structure%20of%20Initial%20Teacher%20Education%20in%20Northern%20Ireland%20Final%20Report.pdf

DENI. (1996). *Free school meals and low achievement. Statistical bulletin SB2*. Bangor, ME: Department of Education for Northern Ireland

DENI. (2005). *New post-primary arrangements: A statement by Angela Smith, MP, Minister for Education*. Bangor, ME: Department of Education for Northern Ireland.

DENI. (2006). *Proposal for a draft Education (Northern Ireland) Order: Summary of the responses to the consultation on the proposal for a draft education order*. Bangor, ME: Department of Education for Northern Ireland.

DENI. (2012). *Compendium of Northern Ireland education statistics, 1998/99 to 2010/11*. Bangor, ME: Department of Education for Northern Ireland. Retrieved from https://www.deni.gov.uk/sites/default/files/publications/de/compendium-9899-to-1011.pdf

DENI. (2015a). *Enrolments at schools and in funded pre-school education in Northern Ireland, 2014/15*. Bangor, ME: Department of Education for Northern Ireland. Retrieved from https://www.deni.gov.uk/sites/default/files/publications/de/Statistical%20bulletin%20-%20February%202015%20FINAL%20%2824.06.15%29.pdf

DENI. (2015b). *Sharing works: A policy for shared education* (Education Act (1944)). Bangor, ME: Department of Education for Northern Ireland. Retrieved from https://www.deni.gov.uk/sites/default/files/publications/de/shared-education-policy.pdf

Education Act (Northern Ireland). (1947). Retrieved from http://www.educationengland.org.uk/documents/acts/1947-education-act-ni.html

Elwood, J. (2013). Educational assessment policy and practice: A matter of ethics. *Assessment in Education: Principles, Policy and Practice, 20*, 205–220.

ETI. (2001). *Chief inspector's review, 1992–99*. Bangor, ME: Education and Training Inspectorate. Retrieved from http://www.etini.gov.uk/report_detail.asp?id=239

ETI. (2012). *Chief inspector's report, 2010–12*. Bangor, ME: Education and Training Inspectorate. Retrieved from http://www.etini.gov.uk/index/inspection-reports/the-chief-inspectors-report/ci-report-2012.pdf

ETI. (2014). *Chief inspector's report, 2012–14*. Bangor, ME: Education and Training Inspectorate. Retrieved from http://www.etini.gov.uk/index/inspection-reports/the-chief-inspectors-report/ci-report-2012-2014.pdf

Gallagher, A. M., & Smith, A. (2000). *The effects of the selective system of secondary education in Northern Ireland, Main Report and Research Papers volumes 1 and 2*. Retrieved from http://www.education.gg/CHttpHandler.ashx?id=97491&p=0

Gallagher, T., Stewart, A., Walker, R., Baker, M., & Lockhart, J. (2010). Sharing education through schools working together. *Shared Space, 10*, 65–74.

Gardner, J., & Cowan, P. (2000). *Testing the test: A study of the reliability and validity of the Northern Ireland transfer procedure test in enabling the selection of pupils for grammar school places*. Retrieved from http://core.ac.uk/download/pdf/309206.pdf

Gardner, J., & Cowan, P. (2005). The fallibility of high stakes '11-plus' testing in Northern Ireland. *Assessment in Education: Principles, Policy and Practice, 12*, 145–165.

Graham, B., & Nash, C. (2006). A shared future: Territoriality, pluralism and public policy in Northern Ireland. *Political Geography, 25*, 253–278.

Guardian (2012). *The religious divide in Northern Ireland's schools*. Retrieved from http://www.theguardian.com/news/datablog/2012/nov/24/religious-divide-northern-ireland-schools

Hansson, U., O'Connor-Bones, U., & McCord, J. (2013). *Integrated education: A review of policy and research evidence 1999–2012*. Retrieved from http://www.unescocentre.ulster.ac.uk/pdfs/pdfs_unesco_centre_publications/2013_02_21_int_ed-a_review_of_the_evidence_1999_to_2012-review_of_policy_and_research_evidence-full_report_jan_2013.pdf

Hillyard, P., Kelly, G., McLaughlin, E., Patsios, D., & Tomlinson, M. (2003). *Bare necessities: Poverty and social exclusion in Northern Ireland. Key findings*. Retrieved from http://www.ofmdfmni.gov.uk/bare-necessities.pdf

HMSO. (1964). *Educational development in Northern Ireland 1964 (Cmd 470)*. Belfast: Her Majesty's Stationery Office.

Hughes, J. (2011). Are separate schools divisive? A case study from Northern Ireland. *British Educational Research Journal, 37*, 829–950.

Kelly, A. (2011). Educational effectiveness and school improvement in Northern Ireland: Opportunities, challenges and ironies. In C. P. Chapman, P. Armstrong, A. Harris, D. Muijs, D. Reynolds, & P. Sammons (Eds.), *School effectiveness and improvement research, policy and practice: Challenging the orthodoxy?* (pp. 81–96). Abingdon: Routledge.

Londonderry, Lord (1923, 14 March). *The Stormont Papers, 3*, 125. Retrieved from http://stormontpapers.ahds.ac.uk/stormontpapers/pageview.html?volumeno=3&pageno=125

McGuffin, S. (1923, 23 February). *The Stormont Papers, 3*, 139. Retrieved from http://stormontpapers.ahds.ac.uk/stormontpapers/pageview.html?volumeno=3&pageno=139

Montgomery, A., Fraser, G., McGlynn, C., Smith, A., & Gallagher, T. (2003). *Integrated education in Northern Ireland: Integration in practice*. Retrieved from http://www.unescocentre.ulster.ac.uk/pdfs/pdfs_alan/2003_Integrated_Education_in_NI_Integration_in_Practice.pdf

NIAO. (2015). *Department of Education: Sustainability of schools. Report by the Comptroller and Auditor General*. Belfast: Northern Ireland Audit Office. Retrieved from http://www.niauditoffice.gov.uk/135119_niao_sustnblty_in_schls_for_web_v6.pdf

NIO. (1998). *The Belfast Agreement*. Belfast: Northern Ireland Office. Retrieved from https://www.gov.uk/government/publications/the-belfast-agreement

Nolan, P. (2014). *Northern Ireland peace monitoring report no. 3*. Retrieved from http://www.community-relations.org.uk/wp-content/uploads/2013/11/Peace-Monitoring-Report-2014.pdf

Roulston, S., & Young, O. (2013). GPS tracking of some Northern Ireland students—patterns of shared and separated space: Divided we stand? *International Research in Geographical and Environmental Education, 22*, 241–258.

Shewbridge, C., Hulshof, M., Nusche, D., & Staehr, L. S. (2014). *Northern Ireland, United Kingdom*. OECD Reviews of Evaluation and Assessment in Education. Retrieved from http://www.oecd.org/edu/school/Reviews%20of%20Evaluation%20and%20Assessment%20in%20Education%20Northern%20Ireland.pdf

Stanley, E. G. (1831). Letter. In *Reports of the Commissioners of National Education in Ireland for the Years 1834, 1835 and 1836*. Retrieved from http://tinyurl.com/otrjq2q

Walker, A. (2010). *Selection challenged: The case against selection for 11+*. Newtownards: Colourpoint.

Shared education in Northern Ireland: school collaboration in divided societies

Tony Gallagher

ABSTRACT

During the years of political violence in Northern Ireland many looked to schools to contribute to reconciliation. A variety of interventions were attempted throughout those years, but there was little evidence that any had produced systemic change. The peace process provided an opportunity for renewed efforts. This paper outlines the experience of a series of projects on 'shared education', or the establishment of collaborative networks of Protestant, Catholic and integrated schools in which teachers and pupils moved between schools to take classes and share experiences. The paper outlines the genesis of the idea and the research which helped inform the shape of the shared education project. The paper also outlines the corpus of research which has examined various aspects of shared education practice and lays out the emergent model which is helping to inform current government practice in Northern Ireland, and is being adopted in other jurisdictions. The paper concludes by looking at the prospects for real transformation of education in Northern Ireland.

Introduction

Northern Ireland is a society in which national, political and religious identity coalesce. It is also a society which recently experienced a quarter century of political violence, the legacy of which continues to influence political life. Despite the fact that schools in Northern Ireland have always been denominational, with parallel systems for Protestants and Catholics, people looked to the school system to help young people deal more positively with diversity and promote reconciliation. This paper will outline the range of interventions that were implemented during the years of violence and assess their impact, before going on to consider a new approach which has developed over the past decade. This new approach is termed 'shared education' and involves the establishment of collaborative networks of schools in local areas, with pupils and teachers moving between schools to take classes and share experience. The paper will look at the genesis of this model and the effects of its implementation, before going on to consider ways in which it is being mainstreamed within the education system in Northern Ireland, and being taken up as an approach in other divided societies. The paper will argue that the shared education model offers a novel way of addressing diversity through education by reframing the way we understand school systems to operate. Before doing this we will outline briefly the context for schools and politics in Northern Ireland.

Schools in Northern Ireland

For centuries the island of Ireland lay within the United Kingdom, but the rise of Irish nationalism in the 19th century lead to a movement for independence that was successful in the 1920s. Support for nationalism came from the majority Catholic community on the island, but in the north eastern part of the island a local Protestant majority preferred to retain the link with the UK for cultural, religious, political and economic reasons. In consequence, the island of Ireland was partitioned in 1922/23: the largest part of the island became the Irish Free State, later the Irish Republic, while the area to the north became Northern Ireland, a self-governing region within the UK. Unlike the Irish Free State, where the vast majority of the population was Catholic and nationalist, in Northern Ireland there was a significant Catholic minority who clung to the possibility of the two parts of the island being re-united in an independent Ireland. The fractious relationship between the Protestant, unionist majority and the Catholic, nationalist minority in Northern Ireland continues to shape politics to this day (Darby, 1997).

At two key moments in the history of schools on the island there was an official preference that they would be open to children from all denominations: when the National School system was established in the 1830s it was declared that preference would be given to joint applications from Catholic and Protestant clergy to establish new schools (Akenson, 1970); in a similar vein, when the new Northern Ireland government set about reorganising its schools in 1923, the official preference was that the Churches would hand control of their schools to the new local authorities, and that schools would be open to pupils from all denominations (Akenson, 1973). At both moments the official aspiration was thwarted by the combined efforts of the Churches, all of which preferred to run their own schools, for their own communities. In Northern Ireland the effect was slightly nuanced: the Catholic Church would not entertain the idea of handing control of its schools over, even at a financial cost to the community, but it emerged that the Protestant Churches were not prepared to hand over their schools either, unless they received guarantees that gave them effective control over the schools anyway, without the burden of ownership. In the post-war expansion of free secondary education the parallel denominational arrangements were maintained by treating new 'state' secondary schools as if they had once belonged to the Protestant Churches, and giving them similar rights as they had maintained for schools they had once owned (Farren, 1995).

When Northern Ireland descended into political turmoil and violence in the latter part of the 1960s many commentators assumed this was linked to, perhaps even a consequence of, separate denominational schools for Protestants and Catholics (Heskin, 1980). There was an alternative analysis which suggested that the problems in Northern Ireland were rooted in social injustice and inequality (Conway, 1970). This perspective also argued that separate schools for the Catholic minority provided some of the only public space in which their cultural and national identity could be expressed (O'Boyle, 1993) and formed an important source of high quality employment in a society where Catholics otherwise faced job discrimination (Aunger, 1983).

There was no consensus on the effects, or otherwise, of separate schools. Two major interventions were put in place over the next 30 years to address issues related to educational and societal divisions and reconciliation. The first focused on the promotion of reconciliation and tolerance and included curriculum interventions, contact programmes, and the development of new religiously integrated schools. This last option included the facility for parents to vote to transform an existing Protestant or Catholic school into an integrated school. The second strand focused on equality, and the link between differential funding levels for Protestant and Catholic schools, and the consequences for educational outcomes and labour market opportunity. We will briefly examine the evidence on each of these areas of intervention and assess their impact, before going on to outline the conditions of the peace process which allowed for a new approach based on collaboration, or shared education, to emerge.

Promoting reconciliation

Curriculum interventions have included projects on pedagogy (Malone, 1973), the teaching of History (Smith, 2005), Religious Education (Francis & Greer, 1999), early years programmes (Connolly, Fitzpatrick, Gallagher & Harris, 2006) and citizenship education (Arlow, 2004). Although there has been significant learning from these interventions the impact of these themes has been limited (Richardson & Gallagher, 2011). Schools were encouraged to run contact programmes, bringing young Protestants and Catholics together in joint projects; but here too the impact was limited as contact was generally not used to address issues related to conflict or division and often lacked any real ambition to promote change (O'Connor, Hartop & McCully, 2002). This led some to question the value of the contact hypothesis itself as a basis for addressing issues of division and equality (Connolly, 2000).

The other main approach within this strand was to establish new, religiously integrated schools, the first of which opened in 1981 (Moffat, 1993). Government committed itself to support further developments in integrated education in the 1989 Education Reform (NI) Order, and included a provision for parents to vote to transform an existing Protestant or Catholic school to Integrated status. Not surprisingly this initiative generated a lot of interest and a significant corpus of research on a range of issues. The schools do appear to be genuinely mixed (Irwin, 1993), and have shown evidence of developing innovative pedagogical and curriculum approaches (Gallagher, Osborne, Cormack, McKay & Peover, 1995). Studies which have compared outcomes for pupils in integrated, as opposed to Protestant or Catholic schools, have found them to have higher levels of contact, more moderate political views and more favourable views of the other community (Hayes, McAllister & Dowds, 2009; Stringer et al., 2010) and there is no evidence that Catholic pupils in integrated schools had weaker religious views than their peers in Catholic schools (Gallagher & Coombs, 2007)

The challenge facing the integrated schools is two-fold. First, after a period of rapid growth through the 1990s and early 2000s, the sector's expansion appears now to have stalled: currently about 7% of pupils in Northern Ireland attend integrated schools and it looks unlikely that this percentage will rise significantly in the foreseeable future. Second, the sector is facing a problem of participation: when schools vote to transform typically their minority enrolment is quite small, but the intention is that it will rise so that the Protestant and Catholic proportions of their enrolment will each be at least 30%. However, the 2014/15 school census revealed that 25 of the 42 integrated primary schools (59.5%) and 11 of the

20 post-primary schools (55%) did not meet this criterion (source: Department of Education). For both these reasons, therefore, the integrated school option has not led to the systemic transformation that some had wished, and the majority of young people in Northern Ireland continue to be educated in schools where the vast majority of their peers are drawn from the same community.

The overall assessment of these various initiatives is that they failed to make any systemic change in education, for four main reasons: first, while the ideas behind the programmes were generally quite good, the quality of their implementation was mixed, with a focus often on short term activities, rather than medium or longer-term outcomes, and there was a significant lack of thinking given to the sustainability of any activity. Second, too many projects were dependent on individual, committed teachers: there were many such teachers and the work they did was often inspirational, but they were too isolated from the mainstream culture of schools to effect systemic change. Third, while the education system, and education leaders, often identified the goal of reconciliation as a priority for schools in Northern Ireland, it was clear that it was only one among many priorities, many of which were clearly more important. And finally, the education system in Northern Ireland often demonstrates a risk-averse culture and often encourages, implicitly or explicitly, the avoidance of controversial or difficult issues.

Promoting equality

The 1960s Civil rights campaign in Northern Ireland highlighted allegations of discrimination against the Catholic minority and a series of reform measures to address the most egregious examples was implemented up to 1976. The equity issue returned to the agenda in the mid-1980s when evidence emerged about differential outcomes from schools, to the disadvantage of those leaving Catholic schools (Gallagher, Cormack & Osborne, 1994) and the link to lower levels of public funding for Catholic schools. In consequence the government, in a demonstration of its commitment to equality, agreed that Catholic schools should have access to full public funding. Since then performance patterns have changed so that now leavers from Catholic schools achieve, on average, higher performance in comparison with leavers from Protestant schools. Despite this, some criticised this policy change on funding on the grounds that it further entrenched separate schools.

Education, the peace process and shared education

Following peace talks the paramilitary organisations in Northern Ireland declared ceasefires in 1994, followed by formal political talks and referendum support for the Good Friday Agreement (GFA) in 1998. The Northern Ireland Assembly was established in 2000, and although it was suspended in 2002 it was restored in 2007 and has continued through two further election cycles. In this new context there was an extensive debate on community relations policy and the extent to which government should or should not pro-actively build connections between the divided communities. Where did work in education fit within this emerging context, especially since the research considered above suggested that the impact of most of the previous interventions aimed at promoting reconciliation had been limited?

In framing an alternative intervention a number of considerations seemed to be important: there is an undeniable right to separate schools (Minority Rights Group, 1994), but they are likely to incur social and financial costs. As we have seen, past attempts to address these issues had produced little discernible systemic change in education, but there was evidence which suggested that connections which cut across social cleavages could have beneficial effects (Varshney, 2002), and the idea of porous boundaries and bridging between communities had been a feature of work on effective communities of learning (Lave & Wenger, 1991; Wenger, 1998, 2000). Granovetter (1973) had demonstrated the strength of weak ties, that is, that we learn more from people with whom we have weak links, as compared with people with whom we have strong ties, because we are more likely to access new information. Meanwhile, Flecha (1999) criticised postmodernist notions which cast identity as immutable and fixed, in favour of a conceptualisation which saw identity as fluid, and encouraged dialogic processes aimed at the evolution of identity and hybridity.

Gallagher (2004, 2005) developed some of these ideas through a comparative analysis of the role of education in divided societies and concluded that no single structural arrangement 'solved' the challenges of diversity. He went on to suggest that mechanisms to support participative dialogue, perhaps through school collaboration, might offer a way forward. School collaboration had been used in other jurisdictions, largely as a mechanism to support school improvement, but there was little evidence of its use to promote social cohesion (Atkinson, Springate, Johnson & Halsey, 2007). A report on the effects of the selective system of secondary education in Northern Ireland (Burns Report, 2001; Gallagher & Smith, 2000) had recommended the establishment of Collegiates containing diverse schools to encourage cooperative interdependence, as compared with the competitive interdependence that was characteristic of a market system of open enrolment (Sherif, 1958). This recommendation was not implemented, but the idea of school collaboration as a way of mitigating the negative consequences of separate schools was one of a series of options put to a funding body, Atlantic Philanthropies, in unpublished briefing papers by the present author seeking to identify ways of underpinning the peace process through education. A series of studies were carried out to explore aspects of collaboration and 'joined-up' practice. This included a literature review on school collaboration in other contexts (Atkinson et al., 2007) and a survey of extant collaboration between post primary schools in Northern Ireland (Donnelly & Gallagher, 2008).

O'Sullivan, Flynn & Russell (2008) explored examples of shared practice in a number of contexts, including the co-location of denominational and local authority schools in Scotland, and joint-faith schools in England. They also explored the views of local communities in Northern Ireland on school collaboration. Their evidence suggested that, despite their different goals, the Scottish and English initiatives had been largely successful in leading to educational and social benefits, and protecting denominational ethos. In Northern Ireland O'Sullivan et al. (2008) found parents and educators willing to support collaborative initiatives, as long as these were not forced and the ethos of schools was protected. Their overall conclusion was that these initiatives would, most probably, attract support, but careful consultation and engagement with parents and teachers would be important.

Public attitudes to school collaboration had been explored in another way through the use of a 'deliberative poll' in a medium-sized market town in Northern Ireland (Fishkin et al., 2007). This study found a willingness to support school collaboration in which pupils took some of their classes in other schools and for the sharing of facilities. Parents, it seemed, were less wedded to a plethora of school types, and more concerned with the quality of education they might reasonably expect their children to receive from the schools they attended.

A study of multiagency working in Northern Ireland, based on social activity theory and including a network of five collaborating schools as one of its research sites, concluded that while trust among school leaders was crucial to their cooperation, challenges remained in mainstreaming collaboration throughout the schools (Daniels, Edwards, Engeström, Gallagher & Ludvigsen, 2009; Edwards, Daniels, Gallagher, Leadbetter & Warmington, 2009; Gallagher & Carlisle, 2009). This study also highlighted issues on the potential role of external agencies, which could act as a constraint or a support for collaboration: this role even extended to researchers as they foregrounded issues that had, up to then, been shrouded in the silence that has been used as a coping mechanism in Northern Ireland (Gallagher, 2004).

All of this work suggested that school collaboration might have value as a means of promoting greater social cohesion in Northern Ireland because it side-stepped the issue of whether there should be separate or common schools by allowing for both: collaboration between separate schools in which pupils and teachers moved between schools to take classes on a regular basis would allow for a degree of mixing and contact, while at the same time protecting the ethos and existence of separate schools. There was evidence of public support for such an initiative, as long as there was effective consultation, but it also suggested that reconciliation goals alone were unlikely to produce support for these initiatives unless they also provided access to a wider range of facilities and contributed to school improvement. All of this also implied an important role for contact, even though, as noted above, this approach had been significantly discredited. An important difference, however, was that collaboration could involve contact that was sustained, whereas one of the main problems with previous contact initiatives was that they were short-term and lacked a developmental aspect. Furthermore, significant development on work on the contact hypothesis was underway in Northern Ireland. Most of the work emanating from Allport (1954) had focused on the conditions required to produce 'effective' contact, although we have already noted the criticism that it reified group identities (Connolly, 2000). Working with Northern Ireland samples, Hewstone, Tausch, Hughes & Cairns (2008) highlighted the value of sustained, regular contact; the potential benefit of indirect contact; the role of non-contentious super-ordinate goals in contact encounters; and the facilitation of opportunities to develop 'intimate', as opposed to superficial contact. They recommended the use of long-term contact initiatives, initially addressing anxieties over contact and then seeking to build enduring relationships of trust.

Thus, the emergent corpus of research pointed to the idea of school collaboration as a means for promoting reconciliation at a systemic level without requiring a radical restructuring of the schools. It did require rethinking the way we understood school systems: schools are often seen as autonomous units, each largely in charge of its own destiny. In the new model schools were seen as part of an interdependent network within which changes in one part of the system will have consequences for other schools in the system. Building on the idea of Collegiates, which had emerged in the debate over academic selection, the new model sought to use network effects to promote positive interdependencies, directly encouraging sustained connections across the denominational divide by having students take classes in each other's schools, and teachers teaching in each other's schools.

Atlantic Philanthropies agreed to fund a project on school collaboration, involving Protestant, Catholic and Integrated schools working together, and matched funding was provided by the International Fund for Ireland (IFI). The term 'shared education' was adopted to distinguish this approach from previous interventions, and the first project was called the Sharing Education Project (SEP). Previous educational interventions in Northern Ireland had foregrounded reconciliation as the key goal, but the SEP strategy was based on a four-stage delivery model:

(1)   establish a school partnership;
(2)   establish collaborative links between the schools;
(3)   run shared classes;
(4)   promote economic, educational and reconciliation outcomes.

Funding from Atlantic Philanthropies and the International Fund for Ireland meant that it was possible to offer schools participating in the programme development and logistical support, and access to funding for staffing, equipment and programmatic running costs. There were two main SEP cohorts run from Queen's University:

SEP1 operated between 2007 and 2010 and involved 65 schools in 12 collaborative partnerships;

SEP2 operated between 2010 and 2013 and involved 80 schools in an additional 11 partnerships and one carry-over partnership.

Follow-on activities continued with some of the SEP partnerships up to 2014 at which point the Shared Education Signature Project (SESP) was established by the Education Authority (further details below). Between 2011 and 2014 the project was funded by the Office of the First Minister and Deputy First Minister (OFMDFM) of the NI Assembly to run a shared education project as part of a programme of work in interface areas. This project involved collaborative work between three post-primary and five primary schools in a disadvantaged urban area, and included links with a range of statutory agencies (see Duffy & Gallagher, 2015, for further details). In addition Atlantic Philanthropies and the International Fund for Ireland funded two parallel shared education projects, one run by a voluntary organisation and the other by a local authority.

From the start of the work there was an explicit commitment to seek to change the school system in Northern Ireland, so that if collaboration could be shown to provide economic, educational and social benefits, then all or most schools would engage in collaborative activities as a matter of course. For this reason it was important that the strategic approach to SEP should complement or accelerate existing policy directions. For SEP1 the first 12 specialist schools in Northern Ireland were invited to act as the anchors for collaborative networks. The request to the schools was that they work with the SEP support team to develop and test collaborative initiatives, allow the support team to review and evaluate what worked best, and prepare teachers to engage with diversity issues. Each school was invited to submit proposals for specific collaborative activities and was supported in trying to make these work as effectively as possible.

An independent governing body was established to oversee SEP: representatives from all the education interest groups in Northern Ireland were invited to join. The first chair was Sir George Bain, former Vice Chancellor of Queen's University, and when he stood down he was replaced by Sir Tim Brighouse. The collaborative partnerships received annual funding to support activities and could apply each year for additional funds for new developments.

Day-to-day oversight was provided by the SEP support team in Queen's University. An annual residential conference was held for teachers and CPD support was provided to individual partnerships on request. Regular seminars were held to provide evidence on the ongoing work of the partnerships and to hear presentations on relevant research and practice. In addition, a Masters programme in Collaborative leadership was established in the School of Education and bursaries were made available to teachers from SEP schools to undertake this course. A small number of bursaries were also available for teachers from SEP schools to undertake doctoral level study.

For SEP2 all schools in Northern Ireland were invited to submit proposals for collaborative networks. Of the 40 or so proposals that were submitted, 24 were shortlisted and given seed-corn funding to cover the opportunity costs of developing a more elaborate proposal. The development teams from all 24 shortlisted partnerships had an opportunity to meet and engage with the SEP1 school partnerships during a transition day between the final SEP1 residential conference and the inaugural SEP2 residential conference. A total of 12 partnerships were funded for SEP2.

Tables 1 and 2 show basic activity indicators for the SEP1 and SEP2 cohorts and include the number of pupils involved in shared classes across all the partnerships and the number of shared classes run by the schools. Overall these data point to a rising level of participation in shared education across the partnerships in each of the three years of both cohorts. Most notable, however, is the rising number of shared education classes run by the partnerships over time.

Table 3 shows the denominational patterns of participation in the SEP schools. A relative balance of participation was maintained between pupils from Protestant and Catholic schools across the SEP programme, and while this varied a little year by year the variation did not indicate any problems in participation levels. Since Integrated schools comprise about 7% of total enrolment in NI schools, Table 3 shows that these pupils were under-represented in SEP1, but over-represented in SEP2.

Table 1. Number of pupils in shared classes and the number of shared classes run by all SEP1 school partnerships by year and term (number).

All SEP1 Partnerships	Year 1 Term 1	Year 1 Term 2	Year 1 Term 3	Year 2 Term 1	Year 2 Term 2	Year 2 Term 3	Year 3 Term 1	Year 3 Term 2	Year 3 Term 3
Pupils in shared classes	1,749	2,155	2,118	3,755	3,658	3,585	2,803	3,158	3,321
Shared classes	469	469	495	736	684	648	901	1,032	1,025

Table 2. Number of pupils in shared classes and the number of shared classes run by all SEP2 school partnerships by year and term (number).

All SEP2 Partnerships	Year 1 Term 1	Year 1 Term 2	Year 1 Term 3	Year 2 Term 1	Year 2 Term 2	Year 2 Term 3	Year 3 Term 1	Year 3 Term 2	Year 3 Term 3
Pupils in shared classes	4,582	5,448	3,303	5,070	4,986	4,710	4,360	4,108	2,992
Shared classes	1,268	1,337	424	1,894	1,753	829	2,098	1,592	1,183

Table 3. School type of pupils participating in shared education classes, SEP1 and SEP2 by year (percentages).

	SEP1 Year 1	SEP1 Year 2	SEP1 Year 3	SEP2 Year 1	SEP2 Year 2	SEP2 Year 3
Protestant schools	47	50	49	40	44	41
Catholic schools	50	47	46	47	44	45
Integrated schools	3	4	5	13	13	14
All pupils	100	100	100	100	100	100

When the SEP1 partnerships began their work the project leaders did not have a template to give the schools in order to guide their collaborative activity: this was very much a context where project leaders had to trust the professional judgement of the teachers to identify the opportunities for collaboration and the potential barriers that might be faced. The SEP support team were able to help the teachers as they identified and tested potential solutions to barriers. This approach required a willingness to accept that not all attempted solutions would work, but that when they failed it was possible to learn from the experience: this is, in fact, the only way to develop innovative solutions to novel problems (Hannon, 2008). It also meant that each of the 12 partnerships in SEP1 were very different in approach and, to some extent, scale. What we learned from their experience was, first, that partnership activity was more likely to affect school culture if it was curricular, rather than extra-curricular, focused; second, small-scale initiatives would benefit the pupils directly involved, but were much less likely to have an impact across the schools in the partnership; third, partnerships were more likely to be effective in providing sustained, regular engagement if they were relatively close to one another; and finally, since the challenge facing communities varies across different parts of Northern Ireland, the scale and pace of partnership work that is possible will vary across schools as well.

On the basis of our experience of SEP1, the parameters for SEP2 schools were set a little more narrowly. Schools were encouraged to focus largely on curricular work in their pro-posals, and significant scale was encouraged. In addition, schools were encouraged to build in additional professional development support for teachers in their bids. By the time the SEP2 cohorts had completed their work, significant developments in mainstreaming collab-oration across the system had already begun, and this is considered below.

When the SEP work began there were some who felt the initiative was taking unnecessary risks and that sectarian incidents would occur when pupils moved between schools. Some also felt that the barriers to collaboration were so extensive that they would prove insuper-able. In fact there were very few incidents where sectarian issues emerged, and in the few cases that did occur, the schools normally dealt with this in an open and explicit way—the over-arching, and public, framework provided by SEP seemed to provide a context when these issues could be dealt with openly, whereas in the past the more usual response would have been to hush things up and suspend activity until things 'quietened down'. In fact the most significant challenges faced by the schools were largely logistical ones: how did the schools reorganise their timetables to ensure they were matched? How did teachers in dif-ferent schools find time to plan and maintain effective communications? How did they deal with transportation of pupils and not have time spent on buses rather than in classrooms? How did teachers taking classes with pupils from two or more schools deal with their parents? And how did teachers use technology as an aide to supporting collaborative work, between themselves or between pupils? These very practical issues were the ones which largely exercised teachers' attention: two of these, on timetabling and the use of technology, provided the basis for additional residential activities to allow schools to share practice and experience with each other.

Conclusions

A significant corpus of research has emerged on different aspects of shared education, including evaluation of the implementation of shared education through SEP (Booroah & Knox, 2013; ETINI, 2012, 2013; FGS McClure Watters, 2009, 2010; Gallagher, Stewart, Walker, Baker & Lockhart, 2010; Knox, 2010), examination of the impact of contact (Blaylock & Hughes, 2013; Hughes, 2014; Hughes, Campbell, Lolliot, Hewstone & Gallagher, 2013; Hughes, Lolliot, Hewstone, Schmid & Carlisle, 2012; Tausch et al., 2010), a consideration of its role in improving standards (Booroah & Knox, 2014, 2015a, 2015b) and in-depth analyses of the dynamics of specific partnerships (Duffy & Gallagher, 2015; Hughes & Loader, 2015; Loader, 2015; Nelson, 2013). In addition, some work has examined the sustainability of partnerships (Duffy & Gallagher, 2014), or sought to draw out a broader theoretical framework for the future of shared education and its role in promoting tolerance or reconciliation in divided societies (Gallagher, 2013; Gallagher & Duffy, 2016). There has also been a growing international interest in the shared education model with related work being undertaken in Macedonia (Leitch, 2011), Israel (Payes, 2013, 2015) and the United States (Gallagher, Duffy & Baker, 2015; Kindel, 2015), while Gallagher (2013) has tried to locate this approach within the wider conspectus of structural and curricular initiatives in divided or diverse societies.

The shared education model which developed from the SEP cohorts contains five core elements:

- First, they need to be based on bottom-up, locally tailored solutions, as each school partnership needs to address local circumstances, challenges and opportunities.
- Second, partnerships are unlikely to be successful unless they involve teacher empowerment. In SEP1 and SEP2 there was a commitment to work with the expertise of teachers, as they were best placed to understand the challenges of their own context, and identify potential solutions to overcome barriers to collaboration. We also recognised the need to encourage innovative solutions using a 'next practice' approach (Hannon, 2008, 2009) and allow for some tolerance of failure. This encouraged teachers to be creative and imaginative, and it raised their sense of ambition on what was possible.
- Third, the importance of regular, sustained contact was confirmed. In the SEP partnerships the original intention had been to create contexts where pupils with different uniforms might be seen in the corridors of schools on a routine basis to create a 'new normality' of diversity whereas previously the 'uniformity of uniforms' had highlighted the separateness of schools.
- Fourth, the importance of combining economic, education and social goals was also confirmed. Partnerships should seek to enhance social, educational and efficiency gains for the participating schools: pupils will have access to a wider range of curriculum choice and facilities; teachers will have access to a wider repertoire of practice; all members of the school community, including parents, will have opportunities to engage across the traditional religious divides in Northern Ireland.

- Fifth, our experience was that connections between people were crucial to cultural change and sustainability. Co-location of schools helps provide enhanced opportunities for partnership work, but schools need to be encouraged and supported to take advantage of these opportunities.

One of the original goals of SEP had been to mainstream shared education within the school system in Northern Ireland and considerable gains have been made. The 2011–2015 Programme for Government contained specific shared education commitments. A Ministerial Advisory Group (Connolly, Purvis & O'Grady, 2013) recommended further extension of the shared education approach. The NI Assembly has held debates on shared and integrated education, while between 2011 and 2015 the Education Committee commissioned three reports on aspects of shared education and published the results of its enquiry into shared and integrated education in 2015. The Shared Education Signature Programme (SESP) was established in 2014 with £25m to support school partnerships; £500m has been allocated over a ten-year period to support capital developments in shared education campuses; and the next phase of European Peace Funding (Peace IV) will allocate £26m to support partnership work in schools. A Shared Education Bill has been laid before the NI Assembly and it was expected to become law before the end of the current mandate in May, 2016. In a relatively short period of time shared education seems to have transformed the educational landscape in Northern Ireland.

Acknowledgements

The research upon which significant parts of this paper are based was funded from a number of sources, including Atlantic Philanthropies, International Fund for Ireland, Economic and Social Research Council, and the NI Community Relations Council. Members of the SEP team in Queen's University who worked with the many schools and teachers involved in the projects included Alistair Stewart, Mark Baker, Gavin Duffy, Richard Walker, Niki Moat, Jacqueline Lockhart and Gareth Amos.

Disclosure statement

No potential conflict of interest was reported by the author.

Funding

This work was supported by Office of the First Minister and Deputy First Minister [grant number 003/112/08044]; International Fund for Ireland [grant number 16510, 110815]; The Atlantic Philanthropies [grant number 16510, 18590, 110815, 21722].

References

Akenson, D. H. (1970). *The Irish education experiment: The national system of education in the nineteenth century*. London: Routledge & Kegan Paul.

Akenson, D. H. (1973). *Education and enmity: The control of schooling in Northern Ireland 1920–1950*. London: David & Charles.

Allport, G. W. (1954). *The nature of prejudice*. Reading, MA/London: Addison-Wesley.

Arlow, M. (2004). Citizenship education in a divided society: The case of Northern Ireland. In S. Tawil & A. Harley (Eds.), *Education, conflict and social cohesion*. Geneva: International Bureau of Education.

Atkinson, M., Springate, I., Johnson, F., & Halsey, K. (2007). *Inter-school collaboration: A literature review*. Slough: NFER.

Aunger, E. A. (1983). Religion and class: An analysis of 1971 census data. In R. J. Cormack & R. D. Osborne (Eds.), *Religion, education and employment*. Belfast: Appletree Press.

Blaylock, D., & Hughes, J. (2013). Shared education initiatives in Northern Ireland: A model for effective intergroup contact in divided jurisdictions. *Studies in Ethnicity and Nationalism, 13*, 477–487.

Borooah, V., & Knox, C. (2013). The contribution to Catholic-Protestant reconciliation in Northern Ireland: A third way? *British Educational Research Journal, 39*, 925–946.

Borooah, V., & Knox, C. (2014). Access and performance inequalities: Post primary education in Northern Ireland. *Journal of Poverty and Social Justice, 22*, 111–135.

Borooah, V., & Knox, C. (2015a). Segregation, inequality and educational performance in Northern Ireland: Problems and solutions. *International Journal of Educational Development, 40*, 196–206.

Borooah, V., & Knox, C. (2015b). *The economics of schooling in a divided society: The case for shared education*. London: Palgrave Macmillan.

Burns Report (2001). *Education for the 21st century: Report of the post primary review body*. Bangor: Department of Education (Northern Ireland).

Connolly, P. (2000). What now for the contact hypothesis? Towards a new research agenda. *Race Ethnicity and Education, 3*, 169–193.

Connolly, P., Fitzpatrick, S., Gallagher, T., & Harris, P. (2006). Addressing diversity and inclusion in the early years in conflict-affected societies: A case study of the Media Initiative for Children—Northern Ireland. *International Journal of Early Years Education, 14*, 263–278.

Connolly, P., Purvis, D., & O'Grady, P. J. (2013). *Advancing shared education: Report of the Ministerial Advisory Group*. Bangor: Department of Education (Northern Ireland).

Conway, W. (1970). *Catholic schools*. Dublin: Catholic Communications Institute.

Daniels, H., Edwards, A., Engeström, Y., Gallagher, T., & Ludvigsen, S. R. (Eds.). (2009). *Activity theory in practice: Promoting learning across boundaries and agencies*. London: Routledge.

Darby, J. (1997). *Scorpions in a bottle: Conflicting cultures in Northern Ireland*. London: Minority Rights Group.

Donnelly, C., & Gallagher, T. (2008). *School collaboration in Northern Ireland: Opportunities for reconciliation?*. Belfast: Queen's University.

Duffy, G., & Gallagher, T. (2014). Sustaining school partnerships: The context of cross-sectoral collaboration between schools in a separate education system in Northern Ireland. *Review of Education, 2*, 189–210.

Duffy, G., & Gallagher, T. (2015). Collaborative evolution: The context surrounding the formation and the effectiveness of a school partnership in a divided community in Northern Ireland. *Research Papers in Education, 30*, 1–24.

Edwards, A., Daniels, H., Gallagher, T., Leadbetter, J., & Warmington, P. (2009). *Improving inter-professional collaborations: Multi-agency working for children's wellbeing*. London: Routledge.

ETNI (2012). *The Education and Training Inspectorate first interim evaluation on the International Fund for Ireland's Sharing in Education programme*. Belfast: Education and Training Inspectorate Northern Ireland.

ETINI (2013). *A final evaluation of the International Fund for Ireland's Sharing in Education programme*. Belfast: Education and Training Inspectorate Northern Ireland.

Farren, S., & Queen's University of Belfast (1995). *The politics of Irish education 1920–65*. Belfast: Institute of Irish Studies, The Queen's University of Belfast.

FGS McClure Watters (2009). *The Sharing Education Programme consultancy report*. Belfast: FGS.

FGS McClure Watters (2010). *The Sharing Education Programme attitudinal research results*. Belfast: FGS McClure Watters.

Fishkin, J., Gallagher, T., Luskin, R., O'Grady, J., O'Flynn, I., & Russell, D. (2007). *A Deliberative Poll on education: What provision do informed parents in Northern Ireland want?*. Newcastle/Belfast/Stanford: Newcastle University/Queen's University/Stanford University.

Flecha, R. (1999). Modern and postmodern racism in Europe: Dialogic approach and anti-racist pedagogies. *Harvard Educational Review, 69*, 150–171.

Francis, L. J., & Greer, J. E. (1999). Religious experience and attitude toward Christianity among Protestant and Catholic adolescents in Northern Ireland. *Research in Education, 61*, 1–7.

Gallagher, A. M., Cormack, R. J., & Osborne, R. D. (1994). Religion, equity and education in Northern Ireland. *British Educational Research Journal, 20*, 507–518.

Gallagher, A. M., Osborne, R. D., Cormack, R. J., McKay, I., & Peover, S. (1995). Hazelwood Integrated College. In National Commission for Education (ed.) *Success against the odds: Effective schools in disadvantaged areas*. London: Routledge.

Gallagher, T. (2004). *Education in divided societies*. Basingstoke: Palgrave Macmillan.

Gallagher, T. (2005). Balancing difference and the common good: Lessons from a post-conflict society. *Compare, 35*, 429–442.

Gallagher, T. (2013). Education for shared societies. In M. Fitzduff (Ed.), *Public policies in shared societies: A comparative approach* (pp. 129–148). London: Palgrave.

Gallagher, T., & Carlisle, K. (2009). Breaking through silence: Tackling controversial barriers through inter-professional engagement. In H. Daniels, et al. (Eds.), *Activity theory in practice: Promoting learning across boundaries and agencies*. London: Routledge.

Gallagher, T., & Coombs, A. (2007). The impact of integrated education on religious beliefs. In F. Leach, & M. Dunne (eds.), *Education. Conflict and reconciliation: International perspectives*. Berne: Peter Lang.

Gallagher, T., & Duffy, G. (2016). Recognising difference while promoting cohesion: The role of collaborative networks in education. In I. Honohan & N. Rougier (Eds.), *Tolerance and diversity in Ireland, North and South*. Manchester, NH: Manchester University Press.

Gallagher, T., Duffy, G., & Baker, M. (2015). *The Sharing Education programme in Northern Ireland*. Paper presented at the AERA 2015 Annual Meeting in a paper session entitled: Collaboration as an antidote to contested spaces in education: the cases of Northern Ireland, Israel and Los Angeles. AERA Annual Conference, Chicago.

Gallagher, T., & Smith, A. (2000). *The effects of the selective system of secondary education in Northern Ireland, Main Report*. Bangor: Department of Education (Northern Ireland).

Gallagher, T., Stewart, A., Walker, R., Baker, M., & Lockhart, J. (2010). Sharing education through schools working together. *Shared Space, 10*, 65–74.

Granovetter, M. S. (1973). The strength of weak ties. *American Journal of Sociology, 78*, 1360–1380.

Hannon, V. (2008). *'Next Practice' in education: A disciplined approach to innovation*. London: The Innovation Unit.

Hannon, V. (2009). The search for next practice: A UK approach to innovation in schools. *Education Canada, 49*, 24–27.

Hayes, B. C., McAllister, I., & Dowds, L. (2009). Integrated education, intergroup relations, and political identities in Northern Ireland. *Social Problems, 54*, 454–482.

Heskin, K. (1980). *Northern Ireland: A psychological analysis*. Dublin: Gill & Macmillan.

Hewstone, M., Tausch, N., Hughes, J., & Cairns, E. (2008). *Can contact promote better relations? Evidence from mixed and segregated areas of Belfast*. Belfast: OFMDFM.

Hughes, J. (2014). Contact and context: Sharing education and building relationships in a divided society. *Research Papers in Education, 29*, 1–18.

Hughes, J., Campbell, A., Lolliot, S., Hewstone, M., & Gallagher, T. (2013). Inter-group contact at school and social attitudes: Evidence from Northern Ireland. *Oxford Review of Education, 39*, 761–779.

Hughes, J., & Loader, R. M. (2015). 'Plugging the gap': Shared education and the promotion of community relations through schools in Northern Ireland. *British Educational Research Journal*,. doi: http://dx.doi.org/10.1002/berj.3206.

Hughes, J., Lolliot, S., Hewstone, M., Schmid, K., & Carlisle, K. (2012). Sharing classes between separate schools: A mechanism for improving inter-group relations in Northern Ireland? *Policy Futures in Education, 10*, 528–539.

Irwin, C. (1993). Making integrated education work for pupils. In C. Moffatt (Ed.), *Education together for a change*. Belfast: Fortnight Educational Trust.

Kindel, M. (2015). *Convening in contested spaces: The education success project*. Paper presented in a session entitled: Collaboration as an antidote to contested spaces in education: the cases of Northern Ireland, Israel and Los Angeles. AERA Annual Conference, Chicago.

Knox, C. (2010). *Sharing education programme: Views from the White Board*. Jordanstown: Social and Research Policy Institute, University of Ulster.

Lave, J., & Wenger, E. (1991). *Situated learning: Legitimate peripheral participation*. Cambridge/New York: Cambridge University Press.

Leitch, R. (2011). *Sharing education: Lessons from Northern Ireland*. Paper presented at a conference at the Centre for Human Rights and Conflict Resolution Conference, Skopje, Former Yugoslav Republic of Macedonia.

Loader, R. M. (2015). *Shared education in Northern Ireland: A qualitative study of intergroup contact (Unpublished PhD dissertation)*. Belfast: Queen's University Belfast.

Malone, J. (1973). Schools and community relations. *The Northern Teacher, 11*, 19–30.

Minority Rights Group (1994). *Education rights and minorities*. London: Minority Rights Group.

Moffat, C. (Ed.). (1993). *Education together for a change, integrated education and community relations in Northern Ireland*. Belfast: Fortnight Educational Trust.

Nelson, J. (2013). *Common education and separate schools: A study of sharing education in Northern Ireland using a grounded theory methodology (Unpublished PhD dissertation)*. Belfast: Queen's University Belfast.

O'Boyle, M. (1993). Rhetoric and reality in Northern Ireland's Catholic secondary schools. In R. D. Osborne, R. J. Cormack, & A. M. Gallagher (Eds.), *After the reforms: Education and policy in Northern Ireland*. Aldershot: Avebury.

O'Connor, U., Hartop, B., & McCully, A. (2002). *A review of the schools community relations programme*. Northern Ireland: Department of Education.

Osborne, R. D., Gallagher, A. M., & Cormack, R. J. (1993). The funding of Northern Ireland's segregated education system. *Administration [Dublin], 40*, 316–332.

O'Sullivan, P., Flynn, I., & Russell, D. (2008). *Education and a shared future: Options for sharing and collaboration in Northern Ireland schools*. Belfast: Queen's University/Community Relations Council.

Payes, S. (2013). Separate education and hegemonic domination: Civil society challenges in the Arab-Jewish city of Jaffa. *Intercultural Education, 24*, 544–558.

Payes, S. (2015). *Shared education between Jewish and Palestinian Arab citizens in Israel*. Paper presented in a paper session entitled: Collaboration as an antidote to contested spaces in education: the cases of Northern Ireland, Israel and Los Angeles. AERA Annual Conference, Chicago.

Richardson, N., & Gallagher, T. (Eds.). (2011). *Education for diversity and mutual understanding*. Oxford, Bern, Berlin, Bruxelles, Frankfurt am Main, New York, Wien: Peter Lang.

Sherif, M. (1958). Superordinate goals in the reduction of intergroup conflict. *American Journal of Sociology, 63*, 349–356.

Smith, M. (2005). *Reckoning with the past: Teaching history in Northern Ireland*. USA: Lexington Books.

Stringer, M., Irwing, P., Giles, M., McClenahan, C., Wilson, R., & Hunter, J. (2010). Parental and school effects on children's political attitudes in Northern Ireland. *British Journal of Educational Psychology, 80*, 223–240.

Tausch, N., Hewstone, M., Kenworthy, J. B., Psaltis, C., Schmid, K., Popan, J. R., Cairns, E., & Hughes, J. (2010). Secondary transfer effects of intergroup contact: Alternative accounts and underlying processes. *Journal of Personality and Social Psychology, 99*, 282–302.

Varshney, A. (2002). *Ethnic conflict and civic life: Hindus and Muslims in India* (2nd ed.). New Haven: Yale University Press.

Wenger, E. (1998). *Communities of practice: Learning, meaning, and identity*. Cambridge: Cambridge University Press.

Wenger, E. (2000). Communities of practice and social learning systems. *Organization, 7*, 225–246.

Index